Textile and Garments : Fashion Design and Technology

ASHA AWASTHI, KANIKA SINGH

AMIGA PRESS INC.

DELHI (INDIA)

AMIGA PRESS INC.
H.O.: 28-A, Indra Park, Chander Nagar
Delhi-110051 (India)
Tel.: 011-22504028, +91-90706 57000
E-mail: amigapub@gmail.com
Website : www.amigapress.co.in

This edition is published by Amiga Press Inc.

ISBN: 978-93- 87295-05- 6

First Published 2019

Printed and bound by Amiga Press Inc. New Delhi-India

Preface

A textile is anything that is made up of fibers, yarns, or fabrics. The basic building blocks of textile products are fibers. Fibers are usually long thin materials that have a length at least one hundred times their diameter. To be useful in textiles fibers must have some desirable properties such as strength, abrasion resistance, flexibility, or moisture absorption.

Textile Industries all over the world are taking the support of Information technology to ensure smooth production operations. The IT department in a Textile house helps in managing the supply chain. Today, textile companies employ many information technology solutions, including supply chain management (SCM), material requirements planning (MRP), data warehousing, e-commerce and e-tailing. The goal is to make information processing, order processing and product distribution more efficient.

IT helps to maximize the value of the textile industry through the integration of supply chain operations inside and outside the organization and collaborate acts of suppliers and customers based on forecasts shared. Internet adds IT contribution to the management of the supply chain by automating coordination, integration and also of critical business processes. New game system supply chain emerges as a result of business innovation powered by the Internet.

Textile design is the process of creating designs for knitted, woven or printed fabrics. Designs for both woven and printed textiles often begin with a drawing or watercolour sketch of the finished design. Technology levels in the garment industry are on the whole relatively low. Most Thai and Indonesian firms still use standard industrial sewing machines, and only the large Thai establishments producing high-quality clothing have introduced computers for design, special sewing operations and inventory control. Garment production in Bangladesh uses simple operator-guided electric machines, although some firms in Export Processing Zones (EPZs) are beginning to use computerized attachments. Local establishments make extensive use of second- hand machinery. Students, scholars and teachers in the field will find this book most useful and informative.

– Author

Contents

1. **Information Technology in Textile Industry** 1
Technological Capabilities in the Garments Industry; Technical Or Industrial Textiles; Operating at the Boundaries of Textiles; Development of Technical Textiles; Developments in Fibre Materials - Natural Fibres; Technological Change in the Textile Industry; Technological Change in the Garment Industry; Empirical Evidence from Country Case Studies; Technological Capabilities in Textiles; Technology Industry of Textile; Textile and Apparel Industry Production; Interaction of Information Technology with Textile Supply Chain; Future of the Technical Textiles Industry;

2. **The Principles and Elements of Textile Design** 31
Design Principles; The Principle of Digital Printing; Drop-Spraying Techniques; The Process Printing Technique; Spot Printing Technique; Design Principles and Elements; Design Elements; Graphic or Multimedia Design; Industrial or Product Design; Fashion Design; Textile Design; Jute; Jute Diversification; Diversification is not Necessarily Commercialization; Design Council (Uk); Inspiration for Textile Designs; The Activities of a Textile Designer; How Design Work is Done; Range Planning; The Diversity of Textile Design and Textile Designers; Timing in the Textile and Clothing Industries; Printed and Constructed Textiles.

3. Digital Textile Printing and Dyeing Process 67

Digital Textile Printing; Methods of Printing; Origins; Printing Technique; Production of Textile Industry Pollution; Textile Dyeing Waste Water Risk; Biochemical and Physicochemical Combination Processes; Cutting-Edge Treatment Process; Aspects of Robotic Materials Handling in Textiles; Dyes Applied to Fibre Classes; Application Methods and Factors Affecting Dyeing; Disperse Dyeing; Basic Principle; The Effects of Variations in Disperse Dyeing; Recent Requirements in Disperse Dyeing Technology; Main Methods of Disperse Dyeing; Carrier Dyeing; High Temperature Dyeing.

4. Textile Fabric Computing 134

Textile Fabrics; Features of Fibres; Fibre Classification; Fibre Properties; Fibre Length to Width Ratio; Fibre Uniformity; Fibre Strength and Flexibility; Fibre Extensibility and Elasticity; Fibre Cohesiveness; Moisture Absorption and Desorption; Fibre Resiliency and Abrasion Resistance; Resistance to Chemicals in The Environment; Thermal and Flammability Characteristics; Primary Fibre Properties From An Engineering Perspective; Fibre Formation and Morphology; Polymer Formation; Fibre Spinning; Fibre Drawing and Morphology; Cross-Section; Bulking, Texturising, and Staple Formation; Staple Formation; Fabrics of Plain Weave Nature; Variation of Plain Weave; Treating Fabrics With Chemical Reagents; Manufacture of The Individual Fibers; Location Theory and The Synthetic-Fiber Industry.

5. Modernisation and Automation of Textile Industry 187

Dyeing and Finishing; Textile Industry; Clothing Manufacturing; Structures of Textile Markets; Basic Clothing; Characteristics of Textile Market; World's Total Textile Demand and Production Base Distribution; The Global Textile and Clothing Industries; Textile Materials, Processes and Products; Recent Trends in Textile Manufacture; Hat Felt; Rugs and Carpets; Flat-Surfaced Weaves; Knotted-Pile Weaves; Materials.

Index 215

1

Information Technology in Textile Industry

Today, Information technology (IT) plays a vital role in the field of textile industry. Any manufacturing unit employs four Ms that is, Men, Material, Machine and of course Money. To get organizational success, managers need to focus on synchronizing all these factors and developing synergies with in and outside organizational operations. With the increased competition, companies are taking support of IT to enhance its Supply Chain Management (SCM) and using it as a competitive edge. In short, many textile companies are leveraging the technological power to adding value to their business.

Supply Chain Management includes: sourcing, procuring, converting, and all the logistic activities. It seeks to increase the transaction speed by exchanging data in real-time, reduce inventory, and increased sales volume by fulfilling customer requirements more efficiently and effectively.

TECHNOLOGICAL CAPABILITIES IN THE GARMENTS INDUSTRY

Technology levels in the garment industry are on the whole relatively low. Most Thai and Indonesian firms still use standard industrial sewing machines, and only the large Thai establishments producing high-quality clothing have introduced computers for design, special sewing operations and inventory control. Garment production in Bangladesh uses simple operator- guided electric machines, although some firms in Export Processing Zones (EPZs) are beginning to use computerized attachments. Local establishments make extensive use of second-hand machinery.

Female employment in the garments industry has grown rapidly, with the demand motivated by the presence of an untapped pool of cheap labour, particularly suited to the nature of production and the low-skill technology. This has in some instances, especially in Bangladesh, been enhanced by a 'supply push', with economic necessity forcing women to sell their labour well below the rate acceptable to men. Widespread subcontracting has facilitated the growth of female employment in Thailand and Indonesia. Since unsophisticated mass production still predominates in the textile and garment industry, it is not surprising that the issue of human resource development receives relatively little attention in the three countries (although Indonesia does have a textile technology institute and a modest textile/garments training programme).

The situation is also slightly better in transnational firms, which are more aware of the increasing importance of skills improvement. In-plant training is generally confined to simple on-the-job training for new employees by more experienced machine operators.

Where more structured training programmes are available, they tend to concentrate on the middle and high level technical and managerial staff. Women tend to be seriously under-represented at these levels, although in Indonesia a relatively large number of women occupy middle or high-level positions in the garments industry. This is primarily explained by their well- established role in traditional garment making.

The trend towards diversification and higher value-added products which is associated with technology improvements results in skill polarization. This tends to marginalize women in quantitative and qualitative terms: they are in danger not only of losing jobs, but also of being excluded from operations requiring new skills. These tendencies are not so strongly apparent as in the newly industrializing economies (NIEs), but they can be observed in the garment EPZ of Bangladesh, in the textile and garment industries in Thailand, and in the textile industry in Indonesia. No statistical documentation is available as yet, as these trends have been masked by the increase in the absolute number of employees, both men and women.

Policies in Textiles

Import substitution policies formed the basis of the modern textile industry in all three countries. After Bangladesh became independent in 1972, there was a policy shift away from promoting large mills to traditional handloom production, in an attempt to cope with the serious unemployment problem. Also in Indonesia, conscious labour market policies favoured labour- intensive technologies to create much needed employment opportunities.

By the end of the 1970s, export promotion became a major focus of government policies for the industry in all three countries. The background for these policies was the need to increase foreign exchange earnings and to capitalize on opportunities arising from the textile industry relocation strategies of producers in the developed countries and the NIEs. Foreign investors have been attracted by favourable legislation and/or the provision of special facilities (such as the Bangladesh EPZ). Serious attempts to let domestic industries benefit from technology transfer connected to private foreign investment seem to have been made only in Indonesia. The export promotion drive in all three countries stimulated the demand for cheap female labour, and the supply was increased by the decline of rural job opportunities.

The result is a heavy predominance of women in the textile industry in Thailand and Indonesia. In Bangladesh, the number of women in the industry has not grown as rapidly. Men have retained their traditionally predominant role, partly because backward technologies require considerable physical strength and also because of lack of alternative employment opportunities.

In addition, labour regulations allowing women to do only work which is 'appropriate to women' leave considerable scope for discrimination in hiring practices, which are still heavily influenced by traditional sociocultural values. The adherence to values which confine women to traditional roles and sanction the gender division of labour affect not only the employers' attitudes but also women's perception of themselves. This is also the case in Indonesia.

Policies in Garment Manufacturing

Policies for garment manufacturing in Bangladesh have been linked to the export promotion drive from the start, whereas in Indonesia and to some extent Thailand, import substitution provided the original impetus for the industry. In stimulating garment (and textile) manufacturing, the governments have exploited the international relocation and restructuring trends which resulted from technological change and increasing wage levels in the industrialized countries.

The Multi-Fibre Arrangement (MFA) and Generalised System of Preferences (GSP) have facilitated an easier access to markets in developed countries for all three countries. In addition, a trade agreement with the USA in 1971 provided Thai garment manufacturers with very favourable export conditions.

It is clear that export promotion of the garment industry has created new possibilities for female industrial employment, which has grown much faster than in the textile industry, especially in Bangladesh. There is also little doubt that the growth of the industry has been built upon the dexterity, easy subordination and low wages of the female labour force.

Although the governments in all three countries recognize the present and still untapped potential role of women in industry there are few signs of any significant measures to improve the qualitative aspects of the female labour force. The literacy rates and education levels of women are still well below those of men, and so is women's access to relevant technical and managerial training. Also, special rules covering working conditions for women are neither observed nor endorsed. They are often used not for the benefit of women workers, but to their disadvantage.

The Experience of Japan and the Asian NIEs

The industries of the Asian NIEs have clearly left the low-wage, labour- intensive phase behind and are moving to technology-intensive manufacturing, with the attendant need for highly skilled human resources. Japan is already one step further, at the 'brain intensive' stage of development, marked by the predominance of activities based on knowledge and information taking place outside the manufacturing sector. The trend away from manufacturing towards services is already visible in the NIEs, with increasing employment in the service sector, including activities previously classified within the manufacturing sector. These activities represent highly productive inputs into the production system and have very little, if anything, in common with the traditional notion of services as low-skill, low-production activities.

The textile industry is rapidly becoming marginalized in the process, although a 'hard core' of highly sophisticated textile firms will no doubt remain. The declining share of female labour in the textile industry is indicative of changes in skill requirements, for which women seem to be less prepared than men. The textile branch is thus becoming of relatively small importance as a supplier of female jobs. Skill upgrading or diversification of the female workforce is needed if their share in the textile labour force is to be maintained.

In the garment industry, slower progress in automation has been compensated for by organizational changes and the introduction of computerized management systems. These changes have had little impact on the composition of the garment labour force, which remains overwhelmingly female. While this situation is unlikely to change in the near future, there is a longer-term need for skill improvement and diversification, in view of the industry's need to respond to changes in demand and to anticipated changes in technology.

Women can be seen to be moving into services or into the growth industries. Services would generally be the domain of those with better educational levels, which are definitely rising. In the new growth sectors and branches, women are still predominantly found at the lower occupational levels. An increase can be detected among the higher ranks of professionals, but the numbers involved remain small. A new group of generally better- skilled marginal workers also seems to be emerging: home workers and subcontractors who are dependent on information-intensive activities. The most vulnerable group is older married women doing unskilled work: their skill/education levels being too low to be of much use in the rapidly-changing economy.

The educational and training systems are responding with varying means and degrees of success in the individual economies. But women are still a minority of the students in the subjects that matter, particularly with regard to the skills and knowledge needed in manufacturing.

Women appear to be better represented in education and training for services. Seen in the broader perspective of a shift towards service-dominated economies, the situation is therefore not altogether unfavourable for women, even if they have to cope with other obstacles, such as biased hiring practices, which have not been discussed here. However, there is a need to further increase the participation of women in the relevant types of education and training, while paying particular attention to those female workers in low-skill positions who are likely to be marginalized in the process.

TECHNICAL OR INDUSTRIAL TEXTILES

For many years, the term 'industrial textiles' was widely used to encompass all textile products other than those intended for apparel, household and furnishing end-uses. It is a description still more widely favoured in the USA than in Europe and elsewhere.

Technical Textiles Market

This usage has seemed increasingly inappropriate in the face of developing applications of textiles for medical, hygiene, sporting, transportation, construction, agricultural and many other clearly non-industrial purposes. Industrial textiles are now more often viewed as a subgroup of a wider category of technical textiles, referring specifically to those textile products used in the course of manufacturing operations (such as filters, machine clothing, conveyor belts, abrasive substrates etc.) or which are incorporated into other industrial products (such as electrical components and cables, flexible seals and diaphragms, or acoustic and thermal insulation for domestic and industrial appliances).

If this revised definition of industrial textiles is still far from satisfactory, then the problems of finding a coherent and universally acceptable description and classification of the scope of technical textiles are even greater. Several schemes have been proposed. For example, the leading international trade exhibition for technical textiles, Techtextil (organised biennially since the late 1980s by Messe Frankfurt in Germany and also in Osaka, Japan), defines 12 main application areas (of which textiles for industrial applications represent only one group):

- *Agrotech:* Agriculture, aquaculture, horticulture and forestry
- *Buildtech:* Building and construction
- *Clothtech:* Technical components of footwear and clothing
- *Geotech:* Geotextiles and civil engineering
- *Hometech:* Technical components of furniture, household textiles and floorcoverings
- *Mobiltech:* Automobiles, shipping, railways and aerospace
- *Oekotech:* Environmental protection
- *Packtech:* Packaging
- *Protech:* Personal and property protection
- *Sporttech:* Sport and leisure.

The search for an all embracing term to describe these textiles is not confined to the words 'technical' and 'industrial'. Terms such as performance textiles, functional textiles, engineered textiles and high-tech textiles are also all used in various contexts, sometimes with a relatively specific meaning (performance textiles are frequently used to describe the fabrics used in activity clothing), but more often with little or no precise significance.

Inconsistent Statistical Reporting

To add to this complexity, different geographical regions and countries tend to adopt rather different viewpoints and definitions with regard to all of the above. A widely quoted misconception that technical textiles in Japan account for over 40% of all textile output or nearly twice the level in Western Europe can largely be put down to the different statistical bases employed. In Europe, the most authoritative source of fibre consumption (and therefore textile output) data is CIRFS (Comité International de la Rayonne et des Fibres Synthétiques), the European artificial fibre producers association.

However, CIRFS' reported statistics (at least until recently) have specifically excluded tape and film yarns (a significant proportion of all polyolefin textiles), coarser monofilaments and all glass products (as well as natural fibres such as jute, flax, sisal, etc.). The merger of CIRFS and EATP, the European Polyolefin Textiles Association, should go some way towards resolving this anomaly.

The Japanese 'Chemical' Fibres Manufacturers Association, JCFA, at the other extreme, includes all these products, including natural fibres, within its definition of technical/industrial textiles while the Fiber Statistics Bureau in the USA includes polyolefin tape and monofilament yarns but excludes glass. The relative usage of the main technical fibres and yarns on a more consistent basis.

In this new light, Japan still retains a leading position worldwide in terms of the proportion of its total textile manufacturing output devoted to technical textiles. However, this is largely a reflection of the importance of its automotive manufacturing industry (a key user of technical textiles) combined with the relatively smaller size of its apparel and furnishing textile sectors (especially floor coverings). The USA apparently accounts for the lowest proportion of technical textile output of the three major industrial regions but still produces and consumes the largest quantity per capita, especially when all glass textile and technical fibre uses are included.

OPERATING AT THE BOUNDARIES OF TEXTILES

If the adjective 'technical' is difficult to define with any precision, then so too is the scope of the term textiles. The principal materials, processes and products which are commonly regarded as falling within the scope of technical textiles manufacturing. However, there remain many grey areas. For example, the manufacture and processing of metallic wires into products such as cables, woven or knitted screens and meshes, and reinforcing carcasses for tyres are not generally regarded as lying within the scope of the textile industry. This is despite the fact that many of the techniques employed and the final products obtained are closely related to conventional textile fibre equivalents.

Within the composites industry, woven, knitted, braided, nonwoven and wound yarn reinforcements made from glass, carbon fibre and organic polymer materials such as aramids are all now widely accepted as being technical textile products. On the other hand, more loosely structured reinforcing materials such as chopped strand mat, milled glass and pulped organic fibres are often excluded.

The nonwovens industry has developed from several different technology directions, including paper manufacturing. The current definition of a nonwoven promulgated, for example, under the International Standards Organization standard ISO 9092 acknowledges a number of borderline areas, including wet-laid products and extruded meshes and nets. Likewise, distinctions between textile fibres and filaments, slit or fibrillated films, monofilaments and extruded plastics inevitably boil down to some fairly arbitrary and artificial criteria.

Diameter or width is often used as the defining characteristic, irrespective of the technologies used or the end-uses served. Many of the definitions and categories embodied within existing industry statistics reflect historical divisions of the main manufacturing sectors rather than a functional or market- based view of the products involved.

Polymer membranes, composite materials and extruded grids and nets are other products which challenge traditional notions of the scope of technical textile materials, processes and products. Increasingly, technical textiles are likely to find their place within a broader industry and market for 'flexible engineering materials'. A number of companies and groups have already adopted this outlook and operate across the boundaries of traditional industry sectors, focusing a range of materials, process technologies and product capabilities upon specific functions and markets such as filtration and health care.

DEVELOPMENT OF TECHNICAL TEXTILES

Although the development of technical and industrial applications for textiles can be traced back many years, a number of more recent milestones have marked the emergence of technical textiles as we know them today. Very largely, these have centred upon new materials, new processes and new applications.

Viscose Rayon

The first commercially available synthetic fibre, viscose rayon, was developed around 1910 and by the 1920s had made its mark as reinforcement material for tyres and, subsequently, other mechanical rubber goods such as drive belts, conveyors and hoses. Its relatively high uniformity, tenacity and modulus (at least when kept dry within a rubber casing), combined with good temperature resistance, proved ideal for the fast emerging automotive and industrial equipment markets. At a much later stage of its lifecycle, other properties of viscose such as its good absorbency and suitability for processing by paper industry-type wet laying techniques contributed to its role as one of the earliest and most successful fibres used for nonwoven processing, especially in disposable cleaning and hygiene end-uses.

Polyamide and Polyester

Polyamide (nylon) fibre, first introduced in 1939, provided high strength and abrasion resistance, good elasticity and uniformity as well as resistance to moisture. Its excellent energy absorbing properties proved invaluable in a range of end-uses from climbing ropes to parachute fabrics and spinnaker sails. Polyamide-reinforced tyres are still used much more extensively in developing countries where the quality of road surfaces has traditionally been poor as well as in the emerging market for off-road vehicles worldwide. This contrasts to Western Europe where average road speeds are much greater and the heat-resistant properties of viscose are still valued.

From the 1950s onwards, the huge growth in world production of polyester, initially for apparel and household textile applications, provided the incentive and economies of scale needed to develop and engineer this fibre as a lower cost alternative to both viscose and polyamide in an increasing range of technical applications.

Nowhere is this more true than Japan and the developing industrial economies of Asia, including China, where production capacities for both polyester staple and filament yarn are extremely high and there is an urgent search for new applications. Some high volume applications for technical textiles which would typically use poly-olefins in western Europe and North America such as geotextiles, carpet backing and coverstock are more likely to use polyester in Asia largely because of the greater availability and better economics of fibre supplies in those regions. At a slightly less obvious level, differences in the polyamide supply situation -Western Europe and North America are more strongly oriented towards nylon 66 while Asia and Eastern Europe produce predominantly nylon 6 - are reflected in different manufacturing practices, product types and technical applications for this fibre.

Yet another example is the production and use of Vinylon (PVA, polyvinyl alcohol) fibres in Japan, where they were developed for a variety of industrial and technical applications at a time when that country lacked other raw materials and fibre production capabilities. Use of this fibre for technical textiles is almost non-existent in the West.

Polyolefins

The development of polyolefin (mostly polypropylene but also some polyethylene) fibres as well as tape and film yarns in the 1960s was another milestone in the development of technical textiles. The low cost and easy processability of this fibre, combined with its low density and good abrasion and moisture-resistant properties, have allowed its rapid introduction into a range of applications such as sacks, bags and packaging, carpet backings and furniture linings as well as ropes and netting. Many of these markets were directly taken over from jute and similar fibres but newer end-uses have also been developed, including artificial sports surfaces.

Properties of the polyolefins such as their poor temperature resistance and complete hydrophobicity have been turned to advantage in nonwovens. Initially used in conjunction with viscose to permit thermal bonding, polypropylene has now benefited from a growing appreciation of the important role that moisture wicking (as opposed to absorption) can play in hygiene applications such as coverstock for diapers (nappies). Finally, the relatively low extrusion temperatures of the polyolefins have proved ideally suited to the fast developing technologies of spin laying (spun bonding and melt blowing).

The development of the polypropylene industry was initially focused on European and North American markets. However, it is undergoing a major expansion worldwide as new investment in polymer capacity offers more favourable economics to new geographical markets.

High Performance Fibres

The above 'conventional' fibre types, both chemical and natural, still account for over 95% of all organic fibre technical textiles in use (i.e. excluding glass, mineral and metal fibres). Many of them have been modified and tailored to highly specific end-uses by adjustment of their tenacity, length, decitex, surface profile, finish and even by their combination into hybrid and bicomponent products. However, it is the emergence of the so-called high performance fibres since the early 1980s that has provided some of the most significant and dramatic impulses to the evolution of technical textiles. First and foremost of these are the aramids, both the highly temperature-resistant meta-aramids (widely used in protective clothing and similar applications) and the high strength and modulus para-aramids (used in a host of applications ranging from bulletproof vests to reinforcement of tyres, hoses, friction materials, ropes and advanced composites).

From their commercial introduction in the 1970s, world demand for p-aramids is expected to reach almost 40000 tonnes per annum by 2000 while for m-aramids, consumption will be around 17-18000 tonnes. While not huge in overall terms (representing less than 0.5% of total world technical fibre and yarn usage in volume terms but closer to 3-4% in value), the aramids represent a particularly important milestone in the development of the technical textiles industry.

Partly practical and partly symbolic, the introduction of the aramids not only led to the injection of large amounts of technical and market support into the industry and for users by leading fibre manufacturers such as DuPont and Akzo, but also concentrated the minds of many developers of new products upon the possibilities (and practicalities) of using similar new generation materials. The early success of the aramids was a welcome contrast to the development of carbon fibres, which have been commercially available since the 1960s but largely constrained by their high material and processing costs to selected high value markets, particularly aerospace applications. Total world demand for carbon fibres was still only some 8-9000 tonnes per annum as recently as 1995. In fact, their market actually shrank in the early 1990s owing to cutbacks in military spending.

At long last, carbon fibres appear to be emerging from the doldrums, with the appearance not only of important new civil aerospace markets but also of high technology sporting goods and industrial applications such as wind generator turbine blades and reinforced fuel tanks. As new manufacturing methods and greater economies of scale start to bring prices down, the feasibility of even larger scale applications such as the reinforcement of buildings and structures in earthquake zones becomes more attractive. Currently, (2000), consumption is considered to be over 13 000 tonnes per annum, rising to almost 19 000 tonnes by the year 2005.

The introduction of other high performance fibres proliferated, particularly during the late 1980s, and in the wake of the aramids. These included a range of heat and flameproof materials suitable for protective clothing and similar applications (such as phenolic fibres and PBI, polybenzimidazole), ultra-strong high modulus polyethylene (HMPE) for ballistic protection and rope manufacture, and chemically stable polymers such as polytetrafluoroethylene (PTFE), polyphenylene sulphide (PPS) and polyethyletherketone (PEEK) for use in filtration and other chemically aggressive environments. Individually, none of these other fibres has yet achieved volume sales anywhere near those of the aramids (or even carbon fibres). Indeed, the output of some speciality fibres can still be measured in tens of tonnes per year rather than hundreds or thousands. The widespread industrial recession of the early 1990s caused many fibre manufacturers to review their development strategies and to focus upon narrower ranges of products and markets.

Glass and Ceramics

Glass has, for many years, been one of the most underrated technical fibres. Used for many years as a cheap insulating material as well as a reinforcement for relatively low performance plastics (fibre glass) and (especially in the USA) roofing materials, glass is increasingly being recognised as a sophisticated engineering material with excellent fire and heat-resistant properties. It is now widely used in a variety of higher performance composite applications, including sealing materials and rubber reinforcement, as well as filtration, protective clothing and packaging.

The potential adoption of high volume glass-reinforced composite manufacturing techniques by the automotive industry as a replacement for metal body parts and components, as well as by manufacturing industry in general for all sorts of industrial and domestic equipment, promises major new markets. Total world con- sumption of 'textile' glass in technical applications was some 2.3 million tonnes per annum in 1995 and is considered likely to be over 2.9 million tonnes at 2000, representing over 20% of all technical fibre consumption. Various higher performance ceramic fibres have been developed but are restricted to relatively specialised applications by their high cost and limited mechanical properties.

DEVELOPMENTS IN FIBRE MATERIALS - NATURAL FIBRES

Until early in the 20th century, the major fibres available for technical and industrial use were cotton and various coarser vegetable fibres such as flax, jute and sisal. They were typically used to manufacture heavy canvas-type products, ropes and twines, and were characterised by relatively heavy weight, limited resistance to water and microbial/fungal attack as well as poor flame retardancy.

Some of the present day regional patterns of technical textiles manufacturing were established even then, for example Dundee, on the east coast of Scotland and located at the centre (then) of an important flax growing area as well as being a whaling port. Following the discovery that whale oil could be used to lubricate the spinning of the relatively coarse jute fibres then becoming available from the Indian subcontinent, jute fabrics were widely used for sacking, furniture and carpet manufacturing, roofing felts, linoleum flooring, twine and a host of other applications.

Although its jute industry was to decline dramatically from a peak at around 1900 owing to competition from other materials as well as from cheaper imports, Dundee and the surrounding industry subsequently become a nucleus for development of the UK polypropylene industry in the 1960s. The then newly available polymer proved not only to be an ideal technical substitute for the natural product but was also much more consistent in terms of its supply and price.

Traditional end-uses for sisal were similarly rapidly substituted throughout the established rope, twine and net making centres of Europe and America. Wool proved far less versatile and economic for most industrial applications although it is still valued for its insulating and flame retardency properties and finds use in several high temperature and protective clothing applications.

Silk is an even more exotic fibre, rarely used in technical applications other than for highly specialised uses such as surgical suture thread. However, the traces of the early silk industry are still to be seen in the present day location of centres for technical filament weaving such as the Lyons area of France. The traditional silk industry has also contributed to the development of technical textiles in Asia, especially in Japan.

Textile Processes

The wide range of processes employed in the manufacture of technical textiles. Apart from the use of plaiting and knotting for the manufacture of ropes and nets, weaving was, for many years, the pre-eminent technology employed in the manufacture of 'industrial' textiles. In terms of the total weight of textiles produced, weaving still plays a leading role and developments such as three-dimensional and crimpless weaving have opened up many new product and end-use possibilities.

However, the historical progress of technical textiles has seen the advance of alternative textile forming technologies, most prominently the broad family of non-woven techniques but also warp and weft knitting, stitchbonding and modern braiding methods. The use of loose fibres with sophisticated cross- sectional profiles for insulation, protection and fibrefill applications is another important growth area. Fibres, yarns and textiles of all types also provide the starting point for a diverse and fast expanding range of composite reinforcement and forming technologies.

According to a major study of the world technical textiles industry and its markets projected to 2005, nonwovens are set to overtake weaving (in terms of the total weight of textiles produced) by around 2002/2003. In area terms, nonwovens already far exceed woven and other fabric forming methods because of their lower average weight per unit area. On the other hand, woven and other yarn-based fabrics will remain in the lead in value terms, at least for the foreseeable future. There is, therefore, something for every section of the textile industry in the future of technical textiles. Most product areas will see more rapid growth in value than in volume as technical textiles become increasingly sophisticated and employ more specialised and higher value raw materials. On the other hand, the total value of yarns and fibres and of all technical textile products will grow slightly less fast than their volume because of a changing mix of materials and technologies, especially reflecting the growth of nonwovens.

TECHNOLOGICAL CHANGE IN THE TEXTILE INDUSTRY

Technological changes in the textile industry during the last forty years can be broadly divided into three phases. High-speed spinning frames and looms, with reduced vibration levels, were developed in the 1950s and early 1960s. The most radical alterations in the core technology of spinning and weaving came in the late 1960s and during the 1970s, with the introduction of rotor spinning and shuttleless looms.

This was the period when new technology was sought to increase productivity and thereby to combat the cost-based competitiveness of lower wage producers from Asian countries. From the late 1970s onwards, the changes in the textile industry of the developed countries have been characterized by the introduction of microelectronics based technology and the automation of industrial processes.

The new technologies have allowed the various production stages to become one continuous process of interrelated activities, resulting in higher quality and flexibility and thus a faster response to changing market conditions. The full exploitation of these technological improvements is dependent on further complementary changes in organization and management. Du©ring the 1990s, rapid response to market conditions is likely to become an even more important force behind technological innovation and is likely to focus on increases in speed and flexibility rather than on cost-cutting.

Investment costs associated with technology improvements in the textile sector have risen considerably. About US $1 billion per year has been invested in the European Union, and twice as much in the USA, throughout the late 1980s and early 1990s. These levels could double in the coming years. The impact of automation on employment has also been significant. During the last 15 years, employment in the textile and clothing industry in the entire EU area has declined by 40 per cent, and the forecast for the 1990s is a loss of 700,000 to I million jobs in the textile sector alone. The occupational structure has also changed, with the proportion of operators and unskilled labourers decreasing while the share of technical and management staff increases. The new technologies require specialized skills in textile engineering, maintenance, design, computer science, and marketing.

TECHNOLOGICAL CHANGE IN THE GARMENT INDUSTRY

The pace of technological innovation in the garment industry was slow up to the beginning of the 1980s. The main innovations before 1980 were in sewing technology, with faster and more durable machines and the development of attachments for specialized tasks, which later resulted in the emergence of task-dedicated machines. In the pre-assembly phase the introduction of fast, automated cutters in the late 1970s replaced the operator- driven hydraulic die cutting machine. The major technological changes occurred in the 1980s, when microelectronics penetrated all stages of garment production to some degree. The most significant innovations took place in the pre-assembly stage, where computer-aided design (CAD), computer numerical control (CNC) cutting systems, and computer-aided manufacturing (CAM) led to material and labour savings. In the assembly stage, which accounts for 80 per cent of the manufacturing value added (MVA) and of the workforce in the industry, technological change has so far been relatively modest.

The main improvements have been microelectronic control units which are attached to the standard industrial sewing machine to handle the more complex tasks. These can either be used to speed up production on task dedicated machines or to increase the flexibility of multi-purpose machines. The major technological innovations of the 1990s are likely to build on these developments. The introduction of computer-based technology has increased the cost of clothing machinery enormously, yet nearly sixty advanced CAD systems are already in Hong Kong, the Republic of Korea and Thailand alone, with over 60 per cent of these having been installed in the last three years.

Organizational Changes in Textiles and Clothing

Organizational changes complement the technological drive towards greater market responsiveness. These changes affect not only production itself, but also the relationship between suppliers and buyers. The emphasis in the organization of production is shifting to a multi-skilled workforce, closer management-workforce cooperation, and increasing reliance on externally supplied industrial services.

There is also a tendency towards vertical integration within the textile and garment industry. In the field of buyer-supplier relations, textile producers, garment makers and retailers are working together in design teams. Price is no longer the only important determinant of sourcing: elements such as quality, timely delivery and technical cooperation between buyer and supplier play an increasingly important role. The buyer-supplier relationship is also intensified by the reduced lead time and shortened production runs. This means that close proximity to the markets and availability of efficient international telecommunication and transport networks have become an important competitive factor for the producer countries.

EMPIRICAL EVIDENCE FROM COUNTRY CASE STUDIES

The following characteristics of the textile and garment sector were identified in the case studies of Bangladesh, Thailand and Indonesia.

Resource Endowments - The Textile Industry

The presence of natural resources - mainly cotton, but in the case of Thailand also silk - was an important initial factor in the emergence of the textile industry in Bangladesh (when it was a part of India), Indonesia and Thailand. In all three countries the development of modern textile manufacturing, especially for export, was based on extensive use of abundant low-cost labour. This factor has made the industry an important source of employment and secured it a competitive advantage in export markets. Bangladesh and Indonesia have retained this relative advantage, but this is no longer the case for Thailand.

In Thailand, local raw material production has not grown sufficiently, and cotton yarn is now imported on a large scale, as well as man-made fibres. The quality of domestic raw silk is also hampering the modernization of handloom production, but joint R&D efforts are being undertaken by the Government and private business to introduce new varieties of raw silk suited to more advanced technology. In Indonesia, local production of man-made fibres has been facilitated by the local availability of oil and timber. While the production of man-made fibres has developed sufficiently to cover most of the textile industry's requirements, most of the raw cotton is imported.

The Garments Industry

The modem garments industry developed much later than the textile industry in all three countries. At the initial stage of the import substitution period, the industry benefited from upstream linkages with the textile sector in Thailand and Indonesia. In Bangladesh, with no substantial local demand for manufactured garments, the industry was export-driven from the start. Today, Bangladesh and Thailand rely increasingly on imported textiles, because local textile producers are no longer capable of providing the quantity, quality and variety of cloth required for export garments. In Indonesia, local fabric still satisfies almost 80 per cent of the industry's demand. In all three countries the competitive strength of the garment industry has been built upon a cheap labour force, predominantly women.

The Sub-sector's Role in Manufacturing

In Bangladesh, the textile branch accounts for some 35 per cent of MVA, down from over 50 per cent in the early 1970s. In Thailand and Indonesia (which are further along the path to a modern, diversified manufacturing sector) the textile sector accounted for 11 per cent and 10 per cent of MVA, respectively, at the end of the 1980s. The industry is still one of the largest employers of manufacturing labour in Bangladesh but has been surpassed by other industrial branches in Thailand and Indonesia. Its significance as an export earner has declined in all three countries. In Thailand and Indonesia this can largely be explained by the diversion of output to the local market.

In Bangladesh, textiles continue to be produced largely by traditional cottage industries (the handloom sector) although the pre-liberation period in the early 1960s saw a rapid expansion of integrated mills. Small-scale industries also play a very important role in Indonesia and Thailand (silk production).

Indonesian microenterprises have made more technical progress than those in Bangladesh and Thailand. In Thailand, however, improvements in the organization and management of subcontracting have increased the number of home-based silk producers and contributed to the growth of the silk industry. Public ownership of large-scale enterprises is more pronounced in Bangladesh than in Thailand and Indonesia, where local and foreign investment (private or joint ventures) dominate.

The MVA share of the garment industry is quite modest in all three countries: I per cent in Bangladesh, 7 per cent in Thailand, and 1.8 per cent in Indonesia. But the trend is still upwards, and the branch is one of the major contributors to foreign exchange earnings in spite of its low MVA share, especially in Bangladesh. Cheap, mass-produced clothes remain the main export item. In the Indonesian and particularly the Thai garment industries, there is now a trend towards quality products based on local design and diversification. In all three countries, small and medium-size enterprises predominate, often subcontracting for foreign firms which are responsible for high value added, industry-related, services such as design, distribution and marketing.

TECHNOLOGICAL CAPABILITIES IN TEXTILES

Overall, technology levels in the textile industry in the three countries have not changed much since the 1960s. Technological stagnation is most evident in Bangladesh. There is as yet no sign of automation in the large-scale mills, and traditional handloom weaving predominates in the informal sector, although semi-automatic Chittaranjan looms have been introduced on a modest scale.

In Thailand and Indonesia, advanced technologies are now being introduced, especially in foreign-owned mills producing synthetic textiles. But these technologies cover only isolated aspects of production, such as spinning. There are as yet no integrated modem mills. Thai producers have partly compensated for the lack of technological progress by better organization and maintenance. Efforts are also being made to modernize the traditional Thai silk industry. In Indonesia, power looms have become common in cottage industries. In all three countries, there is a traditional female presence in the textile industry, although in Bangladesh women were traditionally confined to yarn processing and excluded from weaving activities. This explains the unusually low share of women in the textile sector in Bangladesh, about 10 per cent compared to about 80 per cent in Thailand. No figures are available for Indonesia, but the rate can be estimated at between 40 and 60 per cent.

Small enterprises and subcontracting are important for female employment in all three countries. The introduction of a semi-automated loom in the traditional handloom sector, and the formation of female cooperatives, have created new employment for women weavers in Bangladesh. But in the 'modern' sector, outdated technology and a heavy reliance on physical strength are real obstacles to increasing female participation. The prevalence of traditional values and strong competition from men in the saturated labour market makes it even harder for women to increase their share.

In Thailand, it is too early to judge the effect of the recent modernization of the traditional silk industry on overall female employment in this sector. It is, however, possible that some of the newly-created opportunities for female factory employment, mostly for young and unmarried women, could be at the expense of women working as subcontractors from their homes. In Indonesia, the available information suggests a decrease in employment opportunities in the traditional weaving sector and in small enterprises as the result of modernization and competition from the modern, large-scale sector. The growth of the modern sector seems to have compensated for this loss so far, but this is unlikely to continue.

TECHNOLOGY INDUSTRY OF TEXTILE

A high technology industry will employ fewer employees, but these will be more highly educated. The postulation for management and technology trained people will increase, but clerical jobs will decrease. The causes for the decline in employment are: import penetration, higher productivity with new technology, and the death of appropriate marketing aggressiveness of the manufacturers. These factors influence the different industry segments in various degrees. In the aggregate, rising imports influence the growth of the industry but not employment.

TEXTILE AND APPAREL INDUSTRY PRODUCTION

The textile and apparel industry production growth is still at 2%. Saving jobs is not a useful argument to keep the textile and apparel industry going. Textile and apparel industry segments seen to have completely different structure and performance profiles.

For some industry segments, prospects are good, for others, prospects are bad. Employment, competitiveness, productivity and profitability are the critical variables. Prospects are good for weaving industries, non-woven industries, and the tufting industry.

Prospects are common for the throwing, winding, and thread industries and the knitted outerwear industry. Lastly, prospects are bad for the circular and warp knit industries, the hosiery and knit underwear industry, and the apparel industry, in general. The following are the reasons for good prospects of certain industries. The weaving industries invest heavily in new technology which increases productivity and profitability.

The technology is chiefly foreign development. The non-wovens industry is clearly in the early stages of the industry life cycle with heavy exports and increasing employment, whereas the tufting industry is fragmenting due to negative returns to scale. This implies that larger firms do not enjoy higher productivities due to their large size. This has, however, not led to decreases in employment. Exports are extensive.

Industries with average prospects are the knitted outerwear, throwing, winding, and thread industries. The knitted outerwear industry has high positive returns to scale in the productivity sense. This reasons consolidation, but with no effect on employment. The throwing, winding and thread industries substitute lower cost capital for high cost labour with increasing automation. There will be further investments in new technology in chiefly large scale plants. The industry is competitive.

One can expect decreasing employment due to technologies. Mainly bad prospects face the apparel and knitting-related industries. The hosiery and knitted outerwear industries are disinvesting due to imports and not technology. In the circular and warp knit industries, both technology and imports reduce employment.

For instance, highly flexible and innovative marketing of sweaters by foreign firms has gained a large share of the sweater market, but the foreign firms have no technological advantage over firms. Besides, technological advances do not improve the financial performance. The apparel industries are depressed by large imports. New technology reduces the labour content, but does not always improve productivity. In general, the textile industries can benefit from investments in new technology which is chiefly produced in Europe and Japan to improve productivity and profitability with a reduction of labour content.

The apparel industries can reduce labour content to a certain point. However, this has not, so far, importantly improved productivity. In the aggregate, both industries will face large decreases in labour content. Some apparel industries must advantage from their potential in marketing by getting international marketing expertise. There are potential growth areas in the textile and apparel industry. Productivity in the textile industry has increased faster than the industry average over the past twenty years. The potential for further increases in productivity is high, but increased productivity does not essentially yield short run financial improvements.

Long-term planning is required, and a particular independence from the financial markets is beneficial. Privatization of textile companies is very common. Productivity increases are mainly geared towards reducing the labour content in production. Higher productivity machinery is chiefly supplied by overseas manufacturers. The lost its competitiveness in the development of textile machinery. Further developments include system-wide improvements in materials handling and more efficient work flows rather than just invention of new gadgets. Productivity increases in the apparel industry are slow. They all emphasize the reduction of labour content. The sewing process is the limitation to higher productivity increases.

There have been no revolutionary improvements in systems to join fabrics, including sewing systems. System wide improvements promise higher returns than "futuristic" technologies. Improved management and control systems can drastically improve productivity of the textile and apparel industry, overall. Inventory control, the optimization and speeding up of order-to- delivery time are deasive. The time from order placement to delivery can be decreased by improved cooperation of tow difficult industry segments.

Fragmentation of the Industry

The fragmentation of the industry must be decreased in the sense that firms integrate vertically to achieve economies of scale in productivity and flexibility with fast response to the market. Vertical integration is not necessary in the sense of finance and ownership. However, this means that hostility among the industry segments disappears. Most system-wide improvements require coordination between the industry parts without which the full impact of these technologies will not be realised. Productivity in the textile industry is the most dominant factor in the competition among producers. The entire productivity is somewhat less important in the apparel industry against foreign competitors since there are other factors like exchange rates and high labour costs which dominate.

Productivity advantages over competitors can only be reached with regular upgrading of machinery. Since the technologies in these industries, particularly in the weaving and spinning sectors, change rapidly, the machinery becomes obsolete in short time periods. The capital needs, for example, for approximately five year cycles in the spinning industry, are enormous. Only financially strong industries are able to upgrade their production technologies without assistance.

There are three important technology related factors which keep the textile and apparel industries from being competitive and dominant in the international markets.

1. The textile and apparel industries receive the same technologies as do competitors in the world markets. The textile and apparel industries have no technological benefit over their foreign competitors.
2. The textile and apparel industries are dependent on foreign suppliers for machinery.
3. The textile machinery industry is fastly declining and has lost ground in chief machinery markets in some areas, such as spinning and weaving. There are no substantial American machinery producers in the market in these two areas.

The development of textile technology cannotes that productivity in the textile industry is above the average of all manufacturing industries. Unfortunately, this is not true for earnings. The technologies, however, are not to blame for the lack of performance. For instance, loom speeds have almost doubled since 1970.

Tighter international markets, imports, and the Tack of appropriate marketing are more likely the cause of unsatisfactory financial performance of the textile and apparel industry. The use of the newest technologies is not restricted to industrialized nations.

Machinery Manufacturers

Developing nations are rapidly increasing their capacities with the newest technology available. Machinery manufacturers are likely to shift their emphasis to the Far East, due to higher growth prospects. Small advantages in productivity which enable firms to be more competitive are the key to an industry which competes on a cost basis.

Labour cost differentials still are a high disadvantage for manufacturers. However, a positive aspect is that in several segments of the textile industry capital intensity is very high and labour costs become less important due to automation. New technologies in the textile industry reduce labour content, and improve productivity. In the apparel industry, the labour production component is reduced without substantial productivity increases.

The limits to labour reductions in the apparel industry are set by the sewing operation. It is feasible to almost fully automate some textile processes. One can hope that the textile industry will be more successful in becoming capital intensive than the apparel industry. The technology is available, and there are considerable developments going on in all parts of the world. Generally, apparel technology still lags substantially in automation.

The development of technologies is not at an end. Automation and robotics will further increase productivity and reduce labour. During the past decade, however, the industrialized nations, lost ground in the world markets despite increases in productivity. While capacities were only unused in developing nations up to now, they increasingly attain full capacity utilization. There is a high potential for increases in the production quantities of developing countries. Major issues on behalf of the textile competitive situation are related to the level of the technologies in the different industry segments. The question is-whether textile mills have technologies on the newest level.

THE LEVEL OF TEXTILE TECHNOLOGY

In general, the level of textile technology is considerably lower than in Europe, but both continents have superior technology levels to the developing nations. The gap, however, is fastly closing. Developing nations, especially Korea, Taiwan, and Hong Kong are spending heavily on the newest technologies at a higher rate than the Western nations. These three Far Eastern countries can no longer be counted as developing nations anymore regarding their textile and apparel industries. The weaving industry is the largest spender on new technologies. These investments are concentrated among the thin biggest corporations.

The ten largest companies account for 85% of these expenditures. It appears that the upgrading of machinery is limited to large scale operations. Apart from upgrading textile and apparel machinery, there are three traits An current development that go through all the various manufacturing processes. These are the automation of all processes, monitoring of the complete manufacturing process, and the integration of all manufacturing technologies in flexible units and fewer steps. Productivity increases and reductions in the labour content are more likely feasible through-further development of the current technologies and system-wide improvements than through expensive "futuristic" technologies like moulding garments to individuals in zero-gravity environments. Most textile machinery is imported EEC countries and Japan. Imports of textile machinery are concentrated in the fabric and yam industries as well as in some other industries.

The American market is still the most important market for all machinery producers. However, some Swiss machinery manufacturers realize the limited growth in the textile industry and are shifting towards developing countries. West Germany and Switzerland together account for two-fifths of the world exports in textile machinery. Czechoslovakia and Japan have emerged as important competitors. The concentration is rather high in the machinery industry. The Swiss based Sulzer corporation recently acquired its strongest competitor, Ruti. Moreover, Sulzer-Ruti has close ties with Toyoda, the Japanese leader in looms as well as to British air-jet technology. These impressive market positions have been achieved with high R&D in their respective fields and traditional reliability in service. The American machinery producers basically lack any momentum in this regard. Most of the European success is also because of their service. All the big machinery producers have service facilities in the heart of the textile industry.

The whole staff speaks English. If essential, spare parts can be flown in within a reasonable amount of time. The success of the American textile industry depends heavily on these machinery manufacturers. However, this increasing dependency should be a major concern of the American producers. A key to competitive textile industries is to lower down the diffusion of new technologies. This would mean to emphasize in-house, proprietary technology. It is reasonable to believe that the textile companies are unable to invest in process R&D. Furthermore, the market positions of the textile machinery producers is such that a natural dependency is inevitable.

The apparel industry, however, can take advantage from developments in the electronic industries for further applications of computer controls. American resources are enormous, if used. In general, the textile and apparel industry is largely dependent on foreign machinery which is sold all over the world. The structure and performance of the various industry segments in the textile and apparel industry vary widely. New technologies influence the structure and performance of these industries differently due to the variety of the competitive forces. Also, the structure of the industries is likely to change rapidly with the introduction of new technologies.

Past data indicates that there have been important differences between the textile and apparel industry's profitability. The textile industry's profitability has been significantly below the apparel industry's profitability. A reason for the differences in earnings might be in the higher cyclicality of the apparel industry's earnings.

Apparel purchases are more volatile to the business cycles than the primary textile industry. One might hope, therefore, higher fluctuations in apparel earnings. Earning changes in the apparel industry influence the textile and fiber producer's earnings with a time lag but somewhat smoothed out. On the other hand, there are no differences in the average productivity of labour between the two industries. Contrary to popular belief, the apparel industry is not less productive than the textile industry. This is even more interesting when the different levels of capital and labour intensities are compared.

SIGNIFICANCE OF TEXTILE INDUSTRY

The textile industries are significantly more capital intensive. As a consequence, productivity is not an argument for the observed reductions in the labour force. It is quite the escape from cost disadvantages in the U.S., thus the labour cost differential. Productivity increases come as a "free gift" with further automation and robotics. Among the textile and apparel industries, onc can observe significant differences in the levels of labour intensity, capital intensity and technological volatility. The apparel and textile industry's levels of labour intensity are different, but not as widely spread as the capital intensity levels.

Gross value of fixed assets per employee is about five times as large in the textile industry as in the apparel industry. The capital requirements are, therefore, much higher in the textile industry. Besides, this enhances the industry's entry barriers. The apparel industry's entry barriers are very low, whereas, in the textile industry, there are considerable capital related entry barriers and scale related effects. Industry concentration in the textile industry is much higher than in the apparel industry. In the textile industry, there are more large firms dominating the market, whereas the apparel industry cooprises, smaller, but so many firms.

Interestingly enough, the industry's firm size adjusted concentration, and the scale assessment levels of the two industry groups are not importantly different. When the firm size differences are ruled out, the concentrations of the four largest firms are not different for the two industries. This implies, that in both industry groups, there are a few dominant firms on the market. The respective concentration levels in both are high.

In both industries, the four largest firms account for 50% of the respective markets. The relative levels of economies of scale in the two industry groups are similar. It is not the case that in one industry chief large or small scale operations dominate. However, one can observe a wide variety of economies of scale in both industries.

Regression analysis indicates that in the apparel industry, monopoly benefits (excessive profits after reinvestments and transfers to the shareholders) are literally not responsive to changes in the labour intensity. In the textile industry, monopoly profits are negatively related to labour intensity. These results clearly indicate, that for the apparel industry, the labour intensity is not directly liable for the profitability performance.

Apparel industries that use more labour as their production factor are no better off than apparel industries that are relatively more capital intensive. On the other hand, in the textile industry, the more labour intensive production facilities are clearly worse off. As a result, other factors, for example, the increasing competition from imports, are more likely to influence the profitability of the apparel industry. Obviously, apparel industries of various degrees of labour intensity have been equally capable of protecting themselves from competition. Textile industries which are less labour intensive benefit from their technological benefit. This is reflected in the fact that they are more likely to behave in an oligopolistic manner, and thus, with higher concentration. The trend in the textile industry should, therefore, be in increased expenditures in capital to constantly upgrade the technologies. Generally, industry concentration is invariant to profitability. Firms with big market shares face the same struggles in generating enough monopoly advantages as small share firms. The tendency, however, is that the apparel industries' profitability more positively responds to industry concentration.

Thus, apparel firms with high market shares tend to be more profitable and are more successful in the battle against imports than apparel firms with small market shares. The amount of economies or diseconomies of scale has no effect on the profitability of the industry. This means that the behaviour of the industries with respect to enlarging or downsizing the operations has no effect on the profitability.

The argument that larger plants are more competitive than smaller ones does not hold in both industries with respect to profitability. It is explicit from the industry structure profiles that no textile or apparel industry is identical in the way it can and will exploit new technologies, especially automation and robotics. Not all textile and apparel industries are able to drastically improve their competitive position with new technologies. In these cases, market forces are such that imports are at levels where essentially small improvements in cost and product differentiation have only marginal impact.

This is where critical market shares have already been captured by foreign firms. The most apparent examples are in knitting and in the whole apparel sector. In the relatively capital intensive industries, like the weaving and spinning industries, automation can and will enhance the competitive position of firms which can afford it. Also, the necessary and feasible technological changes are closer at hand in the latter industries, to be beneficial within a reasonable amount of time.

Winding technologies took big steps in the past years. About full automation is or can be reached soon. The spinning process still lags in full automation. However, immense improvements are under way in the basic spinning technologies. Rotor and air-jet technologies eliminated steps in the production process. The reduction of steps in the textile production process is the most important source of cost reductions. New weaving systems drastically speed up the fabric forming process.

High segmentation of the textile machinery industry, however, hinders; efficient development of joining technologies in the sense of improving the overall textile manufacturing process. Technological developments are merely further refinement of current machinery. Completely different ways are pursued by the newly emerging textile industries, the tufting and the non- woven industries. As in every early stage of the industry life cycle, proprietary technologies are developed in-house. The profits are apparent in the impressive domestic and international competitive positions of the U.S. firms which are at least partly a result of efficient technologies. The apparel industries have yet to overcome the technological disadvantage of the needle-sewing process which needs as much labour as sewing stations. Rumors of prospective revolutionary sewing robots tend to neglect the commercial value of such gadgets. Unless these technologies are cheaper than labour, their practical value is not evident. Therefore, materials handling is where efficient technological improvements have economic value. New technologies are likely to change the economies-of scale in manufacturing of the respective industries. The weaving industry is the most clear example. Air-jet weaving technology drastically enhanced economies of scale. However, if this happens in an uncertain market environment where smaller but various production batches are postulated, flexibility might be advantageous.

The apparent tradeoff between flexibility and big economies of scale is the subject of substantial research in suitable weaving technologies in Europe and in Japan. Changes in the industry structure can be hoped, once the development of joining technologies is at the Point where spinning and winding processes, as an example, can be performed without intermediate steps. One might hope more vertical integration caused by more efficient materials flow between the spinning and the winding process.

Other instances are likely to have the same effect as weaving directly from spinning frames. These ideas obviously are yet to come, but they will change the industry structure. Specialists will be less in demand and firms will vertically integrate to coordinale the workflow It is also expected that more vertical integration raises entry barriers. If this is not too late foreign competitors might find it more difficult to enter the markets.

On the other hand larger economics of scale distract from essential flexibility in the marketing and manufacturing sense. It is potent not to be undermined by quicker foreign suppliers. The degree to which automation is introduced must be carefully evaluated with respect to changing economies of scale flexibility, entry barriers and overall industry attractiveness. The mature textile and apparel industries operate with technologies which are chiefly foreign produced. Weaving and spinning machinery industries are concentrated in Europe and Japan. Diffusion of technologies can hardly be halted, such that first mover effects are crucial for the competition, but their effects are not long lasting.

LACK OF INFORMATION ON DEMAND AND SUPPLY ASPECTS

Most of the decisions a manager takes are related to demand and supply issues. But unfortunately very few are able to get it, as a result decisions taken carries risk and uncertainty. Excess inventory is one of the most common problems faced by managers which further results in long cycle-time, outdated stock, poor sale, low rates, and reduction in order visibility and finally leads to customer dissatisfaction.

Long Procurement Time

In a traditional textile industry, procurement process takes a much longer time. So, the retailers need to forecast demand and identify consumption trends at a much earlier stage. Lack of clarity about future can either result in early stock out, delay or overstock.

Supply Chain incompetency

With the urge for getting global, apparel and textiles are facing hurdles of inefficiency in carrying out various processes involved right from designing, developing samples, getting approval, manufacturing, dispatching to payment procedures. The total time taken can get extended to one year or even longer. If we calculate, production actually accounts for just ten to twenty percent of the total time. Rest of the time is taken for the information processing from one end to the other. The trajectory of development of Information Technology has intersected every application in textile industry. From enhancing performance of textile manufacturing and tighter process control, IT has inserted intelligence at every node of textile supply chain.

Step into the Global Trade

It is a fact that a company going global is opened with lot of opportunities as well as threats in terms of competition, changing trends, and other environmental changes. It necessitates managing every kind of information efficiently and at much faster speed.

INTERACTION OF INFORMATION TECHNOLOGY WITH TEXTILE SUPPLY CHAIN

Sharing of Information

Proper flow of information among supply chain member is very crucial. Such flow of information can influence the performance of overall supply chain operations. It includes data about customers and their demand, inventory status, production and promotion plan, shipment schedules, payment details, etc. Bar coding and Electronic data interchange are the two information technology tools which can facilitate information integration. Bar coding facilitates recording of detailed data by converting it to electronic form and can be easily shared among members through EDI system. EDI with its high efficiency is able to replace the traditional ways of transmission like telephone, mail and even fax.

EDI enables managers to analyse and apply it in their business decisions. It also helps in expediting order cycle that reduces investment in inventory. EDI based network enables Company to maintain quick response and closure relations with suppliers and customers, who are geographically dispersed. Manufacturers and retailers can share even new designs developed through CAD/CAM.

Supports Planning and Execution Operations

Planning and coordination are very important issues in supply chain management. The next step after sharing information is planning which includes joint design and implementation for product introduction, demand forecasting and replenishment. Supply chain members decide their roles and responsibility which is coordinated through the IT system. Various software tools like MRP, MRP-II, APSS facilitates planning and coordination between different functional areas within the organization.

Material Requirements Planning (MRP): It helps in managing manufacturing processes based on production planning and inventory control system. Proper implementation of MRP ensures availability of material for production and product for consumption at right time optimizes the level of inventory and helps in scheduling various activities. MRP system uses computer databases to store lead times and order quantity. MRP includes mainly three steps: first assessing the requirement of how many units of components is required to produce a final product; here it applies logic to implement Bill of Material (BOM) explosions. Second step includes deducting the stock in hand from gross to find out net requirement. Finally, scheduling manufacturing activities such that finished goods are available when required, assuming the lead time.

Manufacturing Resource Planning (MRPII) system is a logical extension of MRP system which covers the entire manufacturing function. This typically includes machine loading, scheduling, feedback and Software extension programmes in addition to material requirement planning. It provides the mechanism to evaluate the feasibility of a production schedule under a given set of constraints.

A textile company which has multipoint manufacturing and engaged in global business necessitates something more than MRP and MRP-II like Distribution Requirement Planning (DRP), it has ability to solve both capacity and material constraints and quickly propagates the effects of problems in both backward and forward direction throughout the supply chain. The Advance Planning and Scheduling (APSS) system includes both material focus of MRP and rapid response scheduling power of MRP-II.

Coordination of Logistics Flows

Workflow coordination can include activities such as procurement, order execution, implementing changes, design optimization, and financial exchanges which results in cost and time efficiency. The results are cost-effective, speedy and reliable supply chain operations. IT contributes towards the maximizing the value of textile supply chain through integrating supply chain operations within and outside the organization and collaborating the acts of vendors and customers based on shared forecasts.

Internet adds to IT contribution towards supply chain management through coordination, integration and even automation of critical business processes. New system of the supply chain game emerges as a result of business innovation fuelled by the Internet. Many supplying companies maintain demand data by style, size, fabric and colour to replenish inventory at retail outlet. Level of replenishing is predetermined by both parties after reviewing history of sales by product and buying behaviour of the community. New Business Models:

Data Mining and Data Warehousing

Data mining is the process of analysing data from different viewpoints and summarizing it into useful information that can be used as a basis of monitoring and control, enabling companies to focus on the most important aspects of their business. It allows users to analyse data from many different dimensions, categorize it, and summarize the relationships identified. In short it is the process of finding correlations or relationship among dozens of fields in large relational databases. Data warehousing is the repository of data and can be defined as a process of centralized data management and retrieval. Centralization of data maximizes user access and analysis.

E-commerce

E-commerce can be B2B (Business To Business) and B2C (Business To Customer). B2C commerce is the direct selling to consumers through Internet. While B2B marketplace can be defined as neutral Internet-based intermediaries that focus on specific business processes, host electronic marketplaces, and use various market-making mechanisms to mediate transactions among businesses. B2B appears to be more prospective than B2C.

E-retailing

The textile-retail giants are adding an Internet shopping-component to their offering. It has affected their distribution and warehousing infrastructure. As a result of going online, retailers have changed their supply chain strategy. High volume products with stable demand are stocked in local stores, while low-volume products are stocked centrally for online purchasing. Companies prefer a direct route to consumers by closely scrutinizing individual customer's tastes, preferences, habits, and buying patterns. Instead of waiting for consumers to visit their stores, retailers simply send them e-mails with offers. Internet has facilitated quick response system. With the use of web-enabled technology it is possible to have automatic customer replenishment system.

FUTURE OF THE TECHNICAL TEXTILES INDUSTRY

The future of technical textiles embraces a much wider economic sphere of activity than just the direct manufacturing and processing of textiles. The industry's suppliers include raw materials producers (both natural and artificial), machinery and equipment manufacturers, information and management technology providers, R&D services, testing and certification bodies, consultants, education and training organisations.

Its customers and key specifiers include almost every conceivable downstream industry and field of economic activity, including the architects, engineers, designers and other advisors employed by those industries. In between lie many other interested parties, including environmental, health, safety, business and free trade regulators, patent and intellectual property agents and lawyers, investors, bankers, regional investment agencies and providers of development aid.

The task of disseminating and communicating information to all these organisations and individuals is undertaken by a growing number of specialist and general-ist publications as well as by international and local trade exhibitions, fairs, seminars and conferences. The economic importance of technical textiles worldwide therefore undoubtedly far exceeds the $60 billion.

A Changing Strategic Surroundings

If the 1980s was a period when the technical textiles industry enjoyed a rapid and increasing awareness of its existence by the outside world (as well as within the mainstream textile industry), then the 1990s was an era of more mature commercial development and consolidation as fibre producers and textile manufacturers alike concentrated on overhauling and refocusing their businesses in the wake of world recession.

The new millennium promises even fiercer international competition which will see manufacturers striving to engineer costs downwards and develop global economies of scale in production and product development. Technical textiles will become better 'value for money' than ever before and this should open the way towards further applications as existing end-uses mature.

Individual companies will become less defined by the technologies and materials they use than by the markets and applications they serve. The summarises some of the key market areas and the functions which technical textiles perform, with examples of individual products in each category. It does not pretend to be an exhaustive list which would run into many thousands of products and would constantly be changing.

❐

2

The Principles and Elements of Textile Design

Textiles are frequently made to be decorative and are used to embellish and decorate both people and objects. The designers responsible for such textiles have to balance many factors when answering a design brief. What is the fabric for? How must it perform? Who is the customer? What are the economic restraints? How is the fabric to be produced?, etc. Research into how people select products shows that colour and appearance are two of the most significant factors, with handle, performance and price coming lower down in terms of importance.

Textile designers therefore need to have a good understanding and sensitivity to colour and aesthetics. The same design elements and principles apply to design as to fine art, and an understanding of and an ability to use these are as vital to the designer as to the fine artist. 'Design is about relating elements, whether they are similar or contrasting and visually arranging an interesting unity with them. Shapes, forms, colours and texture all combine to become a unified whole which is commonly called a design.' Art and the act of creating are highly personal activities. In the first instance it may seem impossible to objectively analyse works of art.

In different cultures and at different times, styles of art and even the media used to express art have varied enormously. There are, however, certain basic design features that appear to be natural and common to all art.

DESIGN PRINCIPLES

In every design or work of art there are some or all of the design elements— varieties of line, positive and negative shape, three-dimensional form, occupied and unoccupied space, colour, value and texture. The manner in which these elements are used and combined determines the quality of a piece of work.

Thoughtfully balancing, moving, repeating, emphasising and contrasting the design elements can achieve a unified piece of artwork or design.

Balance

Balance is a sense of stability when applied to opposing visual attractions or forces. There is a natural desire for balance, and in nature balance is ever- present. In formal balance, the design elements are almost equally distributed. A design or composition that is divided in half so that one side is the mirror image of the other is said to have symmetrical balance.

In radial balance, the design elements radiate from a central point as the spokes of a wheel or the natural form of a daisy. Asymmetry uses informal balance; a centre line or point is ignored, with the design elements being balanced visually, rather than in a symmetrical manner. The position of any particular shape in a composition contributes to its strength.

A shape in the exact centre of a picture plane is at perfect equilibrium. Moving the same shape off-centre can increase or decrease its importance. In any textile design, each shape affects everything else. Exciting balance or imbalance is usually only achieved after frequent arranging and rearranging. The study of composition has been a fascination for many artists and designers. The Pointillist artist Seurat was as equally absorbed in the study of composition as in the study of light.

Movement

Movement and the portrayal of movement have always fascinated artists and designers. By careful arrangement of the design elements, the illusion of movement can be created. In optical art and designs the sensation of movement may deeply affect the viewer's responses. Some paintings can provoke dizziness by making it difficult for the eyes to focus on a central point.

Associated with movement is time. Pictures and patterns are capable of holding our attention for varying amounts of time. Some designs may be so subtle that these are barely noticed, if at all, by the viewer, while others can hold attention for much longer periods.

Repetition

Repetition occurs when elements that have something in common are repeated. When a design consists of shapes that are exactly alike, repeated in a uniform and regular manner, then that design tends to seem more formal.

By varying the shapes and the spaces between them, a more informal interest is created. The repetition of some of the elements within a design repeat can hold designs together. Repeated shapes make patterns. Many textile designs, because of the method of manufacture, will automatically repeat.

Emphasis/Contrast

Unity exists when all the elements in a design work together harmoniously. In a unified design, each element plays an equally important part.

THE PRINCIPLE OF DIGITAL PRINTING

In digital printing, small droplets of dyes, in aqueous solution, are sprayed on the fabric to reproduce the pattern. The viscosity of the solutions is low and therefore, to strictly keep the pattern profiles (this problem originates from the capillarity of textile material) and allow a good definition of the pattern, the fabric must be prepared with a special pad-wetting process with thickeners and auxiliaries (typical of traditional printing) and then dried. The printing operation will be followed by a steaming process (to fix the dye) and washing, like traditional printing.

Digital printing has several advantages if compared to traditional printing systems: no costs to produce screens, rollers or other printing equipment (production costs range approximately from 210 to 230-520 euro per colour), and the possibility of printing patterns in a few hours (not days or weeks) in all the desired colour variants. Furthermore, limited yardages do not excessively increase costs and patterns can always be slightly modified or customised.

For environmental protection and cost reasons, it is also worth considering that this system applies controlled quantities of dyes, thickeners and auxiliaries, avoiding printing paste residues (usually excessive when prepared with traditional printing methods) and their consequent disposal.

An inconvenience due to ink-jet printing is the low output efficiency and difficult reproducibility (by changing program or printer), the reduction of the colour space and above all the poor penetration of the dye onto the fabric, with evident discrepancies between the two sides of the fabric. All these problems make this printing system suitable for specific uses.

DROP-SPRAYING TECHNIQUES

The Drop-on-Demand technique, i.e. the direct application of a drop of dye on the fabric is the most diffused digital printing technique applied to the textile field.

In particular, the nozzle technique used to spray the drop of dye determines the size of the drop itself, the spraying frequency, the accuracy, the evenness and partly also costs and reliability related to the machine. The type of nozzle used also influences the choice of dyes/inks used. Thermal nozzle (HP Technology, Bubble-jet): a small quantity of dye in aqueous solution is heated at 300-400°C inside a small container.

The steam bubble created causes the drop of ink to be forced through the nozzle and adhere to the fabric, while the quick cooling of the ink creates a concentration of dry ink particles and an immediate stop of the drop.

A very high jet frequency can be obtained with this system. This technique makes it possible to use plates with a very high number of nozzles at quite low cost but one of the problems lies in the application of special inks that can be used at high temperatures.

Furthermore the nozzles can be subjected to continuous and quite rapid deterioration due to deposits (originating from the decomposition of dyes and/or precipitation of salts) produced by high temperatures in the steaming unit. We can briefly conclude by saying that this technique is scarcely reliable due to the colour variations connected with deterioration, and also because when a single nozzle does not efficiently work in a printing head featuring a very high number of nozzles (even though a single nozzle is quite inexpensive) the whole printing head must be replaced thus entailing process interruptions and higher costs.

Piezoelectric nozzle (Epson, Canon, Roland, Mimaki etc. technology): this technique is essentially that of ejecting drops of ink contained in a small unit by effect of the deformation of a crystal subjected to the action of an electric field.

This technique is more precise and reliable that the previous one because crystals are much more strong and hard-wearing than resistances and also because the system reliability remarkably improves thanks to the elimination of the deposit problem; furthermore less sophisticated (and therefore less expensive) dyes/inks can be applied with this system.

This technique makes it possible to vary the size of the dye/ink drop by varying the intensity of the electric field. It is still impossible to use plates (printing heads) featuring a very high number of nozzles, and each head is much more expensive than the previous ones.

THE PROCESS PRINTING TECHNIQUE

This system essentially reproduces design patterns by means of a technique similar to digital printing (dietering): by using four (four-colour printing with 4 printing heads) or seven colours (seven-colour printing with 7 printing heads) and by mixing and/or spreading on the fabric dye drops of different colours (this step is controlled completely by special software) different shades can be accurately reproduced. The intensity can be adjusted:

- VDS Process (Variable Dot Size by analogue modulation): the drop size determines the intensity of the colour shade.
- FDS Process (Fixed Dot Size by digital modulation): the number of drops per surface unit determines the intensity of the colour shade.

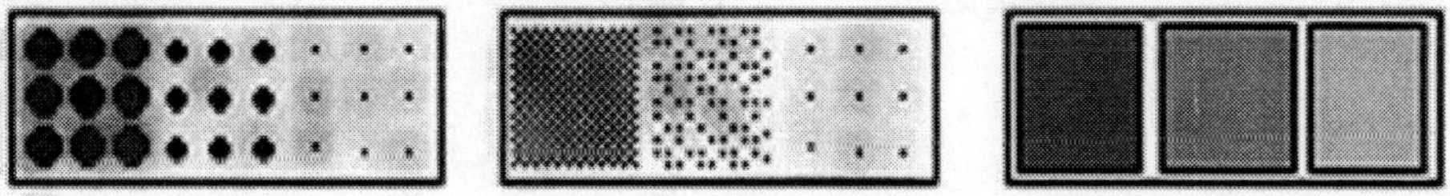

Process VDS ***Process FDS*** ***Spot***

This system allows (by using 4 or 7 standard colours and the same number of plates with nozzles) a quite easy reproduction of a wide coloured area, but creates problems in reproducing patterns with backgrounds in pastel shades (marked dotting, poorly uniform backgrounds), and very unsatisfactory penetration of pastel colours (poorer quantity of liquid ink). Some problem could arise also for the combination of shades and light colours.

It is worth considering that the manufacturers of these printing systems are always more oriented towards nozzles granting more and more sharply defined printing (1200-2000 dots per inch), with always smaller droplets: this is an excellent technique for paper printing but not for textile printing, since very high definitions are not necessary and cause reliability problems (nozzles with very small holes which often clog), poor penetration and slow printing.

SPOT PRINTING TECHNIQUE

The colours to be reproduced are prepared by mixing master batches (similarly to traditional printing) and suitably diluted (a special colour kitchen must be set up). Therefore it would be necessary to use as many inks as the colours of the pattern and as many printing heads as the colours. This technique allows the printing of the fabric with the same number (maximum number) of ink drops per surface unit, by eliminating dotting problems, unevenness and enhancing the penetration in design patterns with background in pastel colours.

Obviously patterns with a huge number of colours cannot be reproduced (each colour must have its corresponding printing head and an excessive number of printing heads would make the printer less reliable). This makes the printing process very difficult and requires using a special colour kitchen, and washing the printing heads at every pattern varying, thus causing time losses and serious problems for nozzles, particularly for piezoelectric nozzles (drop ejecting holes with diameters of 10-12 micron).

DESIGN PRINCIPLES AND ELEMENTS

Design features, the elements and principles of design, can be called the language of art and design. Pick up one of the many books on design and these elements and principles will be there, although they may be detailed slightly differently in each. This is, in part, due to the way that in any one work of art no one element or principle can exist in isolation. Designing can be defined as relating and visually arranging components or elements to create effects. Space, line, shape, form, colour, value and texture are the design elements with which artists and designers work to create a design. The design principles of balance, movement, repetition, emphasis, contrast and unity are what artists and designers do with the design elements to make the art form or design.

DESIGN ELEMENTS

Line

A line can be a mark made by a pen or drawing instrument or it can be any continuous mark that causes the eye to follow along its path. The viewer's eye travels along the path of a line because a line is longer than it is wide. A line moves, and as it does so it indicates direction. A straight line leads the eye swiftly across the picture plane but the eye travels more slowly when following the path of a jagged line. Lines appear in different ways. There are curved lines and straight lines.

These can be long or short, thick or thin, ragged, sharp, light, dark, simple or complex. Lines can be broken and yet have direction. Lines can be textured and can be coloured. Lines can be made from repeating similar elements, as diverse as dots or people, in a lengthways direction. Lines can be used to create form, to give depth. Lines can be carefully controlled to create optical sensations and can be used to project feelings of sensitivity and strength.

When someone looks at lines they try to fit them into something related to their previous experiences; for example, scribbled spirals may be interpreted as seashells, and a few lines can easily suggest an apple to someone who is familiar with this fruit. In some ways this can restrict the artist's or designer's freedom to make viewers see what is intended, although it does also open up new possibilities. Skilful artists and designers play with this tendency to see familiar forms in everything by using only a minimum of visual clues to evoke a far more elaborate response. Care must be taken, however, that abstract designs and patterns do not unintentionally suggest unpleasant or ugly forms to the viewer.

Shape

When a line turns and meets up with its start point, a shape is created. A shape or figure is a positive thing and occupies positive space. The area surrounding a shape is called the background or ground. It is a negative thing and occupies negative space. Shapes can be clearly defined with hard edges but often they are not clearly defined, which means that it is more difficult to see where shape ends and background begins. There are a great variety of shapes to be found in nature.

Many artists have drawn creative inspiration from natural shapes. Through their imagination, artists have invented new ways to use shape and communicate ideas. Shapes can be solid or opaque, linear, textured, coloured and outlined. Shapes can be transparent, revealing other shapes behind them. Similar shapes need not be identical, yet they can have a common relationship, which visually ties them together. Some shapes will command more attention than others, depending on their size, colour, value, texture, detail or their location in relation to other shapes. Tall shapes are elevating, long flat shapes express calmness, downwardpointing shapes activate the sense of falling.

Form

Form is structure. In art and design, form is the illusion of three-dimensional volume or mass seen in two dimensions. Careful observation of the forms around reveals that, in nature and in man-made objects, many forms can be described as combinations of the basic geometric structures; spheres, cylinders, cones, cubes and pyramids. Paul Cézanne, the impressionist artist, in his landscapes and still lifes, explored how these basic geometric shapes combined to make more complex shapes.

There are several methods that can be used to give an illusion of three- dimensional form and some of these are detailed below. Line, shape, colour, value and texture can all be used to suggest form by the artist on a picture plane, and by the textile designer within fabric.

Space

Space flows in, around and between forms or shapes. A flat surface has only two-dimensional space. This means that it has length and width but no depth. It is impossible to create actual depth or space on a flat surface but an illusion of space, distance or depth is possible. There are many methods used by artists and designers to create this sense of space, and to convince the observer that there is space and depth when, in fact, they are victims of a type of visual deception. Objects placed higher up can create the feeling of depth or distance.

Overlapping shapes can also create the feeling of depth, as can converging lines. If, in two-dimensional art and design, space exists purely as an idea or concept, it leaves the artist or designer free to compress or stretch it as they wish, to portray the particular feeling that is desired. Colours have an effect on space. Colours that are warm and bright appear closer, while dull or cool colours recede into the distance. A flat surface that is covered only with pattern can eliminate any feeling of space.

Colour

Under normal light conditions, well over 10 million different colours can be seen. Throughout history, the study of colour and the development of colour theories were frequently undertaken by artists and designers, and many artists have spent their lives attempting to understand colour.

Seurat wanted to apply a scientific system to the methods of the Impressionists, and his Pointillist theories, where dots of colour from a restricted colour palette were used to create the impression of a wide range of colour, clearly show his fascination with analysing colours. Colours communicate; some colours are associated with cold (blues and greys) and some with warmth (reds and oranges). Colour can convey the time of day, weather conditions and temperature, and even the time of year.

Colours can be designed to blend in with the environment or to stand out. Frank Lloyd Wright saw architecture as growing directly from the earth on which it stood and therefore used the colours of the surrounding areas in his buildings while Richard Rogers and Renzo Piano, the designers of Paris's Pompidou Centre, used colour, not to blend in, but to code the different pipe systems for heating and other services. In art and design work, the colour can be used in a natural or abstract way. Maps make use of both abstract and natural colour; natural colours are used when illustrating mountains, deserts and seas while maps showing political boundaries will use abstract colour.

Colour is a crucial part of all branches of design and design-based industries. Advertising agencies know that graphic information in colour will have a more profound effect than that in black and white. Colour grabs the attention span because memory recall from colour is quite pronounced. Colour is used to promote corporate identity. Blue is used by many banks to give the suggestion of reliability, while the appetite colours of red and yellow are used by fast food chains. Green is frequently used to denote environmental friendliness while more subtle greens convey a feeling of upmarket status. The American Express card was originally launched in yellow but was a flop; however, when its colour was changed to that of the American dollar bill it became a success.

The green livery of Harrods, the world-famous upmarket store in London, epitomises good taste and sophistication. Forecasting colour trends is itself an industry, and fashion colours change with the seasons. Underlying these cyclical trends, however, are some basic colour preferences. In colour popularity tests, blue is frequently placed first, with red second. Blue ties are most popular, with red ties in second place, and blue and red cars regularly occupy top positions, only being outdone by silver, a colour symbolising luxury and wealth.

The colour of a product influences the perception of it, and this is used extensively in marketing. Many people believe a red car will drive faster than a white one. Tests with coffee showed that coffee served in a red mug was preferred to the same coffee served in a yellow mug (considered too weak) and in a brown mug (too strong). Foodstuffs claiming to be pure and unadulterated often use blue and white packaging to communicate purity. However, in this age of environmental awareness it is predicted that more earthy colours will symbolise a natural product while white will be associated with chlorine and all that is environmentally unfriendly.

Products communicating strength adopt vibrant and contrasting colours; the greater the contrast, the stronger the associated power. Colour can be used to represent a product, with some colours idealising a product, and some using biological signals to communicate function. Yellow and black are used in nature as a warning symbol for reptiles and insects that have poisonous bites or stings and this colour combination is therefore often used to represent danger. Yellow and black is used on signs when the desire is to signal caution.

Colour Mixing

There are two ways to mix colour—'additive' and 'subtractive'. Additive colour is the mixture of coloured lights. The three primary colours of red, green and blue when mixed together in equal colours produce white light. Mixing the three additive primaries in differing amounts of coloured light can create any colour in the rainbow. Colour televisions use the principle of additive colour mixing. In subtractive colour mixing the principle is exactly the opposite.

The subtractive primary colours are cyan, yellow and magenta. When mixed together they subtract from the light producing black. When different pairs of the subtractive primaries are mixed, the colours red, green and blue are produced. These principles are used when we paint and in photography and colour printing.

Colour Systems

As the human eye can distinguish between 10 million colours, it is clear that to describe colour experiences by name is imprecise. While everyone knows what is meant by tomato red, different people have different ideas as to exactly what colours are meant by beige and sand; mauve and lilac. In order to accurately describe or pinpoint colours, a reference or colour system is required. All the attempts to notate colour can be traced back to the work of Sir Isaac Newton. In 1660 he re-created a spectrum by directing a narrow beam of white light through a prism; he went on to develop a colour wheel by taking the two ends and bending the spectrum into a circle.

This colour wheel evolved and changed over the centuries and in 1810 Otto Runge created a spherical model, with white at the North Pole and black at the South Pole and with Newton's colour circle forming its equator. In 1915 Williem Ostwald devised his double-cone colour solid; also in 1915, Albert Munsell developed another system of colour notation that added steps to the constituent hues. Munsell allowed his three-dimensional colour solid to respond in shape to the different potential strengths between hues, creating an asymmetrical colour solid. His colour model can be explained in three dimensions, in terms of hue, value and chroma. Hue is the 'colour' of a colour, i.e. its redness, greenness or yellowness, value refers to the amount of lightness or darkness, while chroma refers to its saturation or its colour strength. Anumber of commercial colour specification ranges have been developed from Munsell's work including the BS4800 and the Pantone and Colour Dimension systems. In textiles and clothing, the Pantone system is probably the most commonly used, and a whole range of products is available in its defined colours. These include ranges of marker pens, paper and even fabric samples.

Colour Psychology

There is a commonly held belief that red is exciting and green calming. But which red and which green? Research has shown that strong greens, yellows and blues are all seen to be as exciting as strong red. The same research also showed that pale and dark versions of the same hues have quite the reverse effect. Pink has a calming effect on violent people. A common belief is that blue increases the size of a room while red has the opposite effect. Recent research, however, has shown that it is not the colour itself that has this effect but rather its value, the amount of whiteness or blackness. However, with regard to temperature, colour does have a very definite effect. Red and yellow rooms are perceived to be warmer than blue and green rooms.

Value (Tone)

Between the whitest white and the blackest black there are countless degrees of light and dark values. Value is important to the designer. Shapes that are close in value or tone appear to merge together. Visually dark values appear to come forward and light values tend to recede, but the reverse can occur. Sharply contrasting values attract attention and the use of light against dark or dark against light can create the illusion of size difference. Value is probably the most elusive of all the design elements. The success or failure of a piece of work may rely on the use of values within it.

Texture

One definition of texture is the surface of a material as perceived by touch. Running a hand over a surface may find it to be smooth, rough, dull, glossy, hairy, sandy or bumpy. Texture is very important in textiles, and how fabric feels is an important consideration in product choice. Texture can be seen as well as touched and artists and designers can use a variety of techniques to convey textures when none is actually there. Repetition of design elements can often create a visual illusion of texture.

GRAPHIC OR MULTIMEDIA DESIGN

Graphic design is the knowledge of typography, composition/layout, print mediums, packaging, branding and identity, web design and motion graphics. A graphic designer produces corporate and brand identity, website design, motion graphics, multimedia, package design and prints. As a result of the rapidly changing computer technology, multimedia design is becoming a design occupation on its own. Multimedia designers produce video/film, animations and audio for commercial as well as educational use.

INDUSTRIAL OR PRODUCT DESIGN

Industrial design is the professional service of creating and developing concepts and specifications that optimize the function, value and appearance of products and systems for the mutual benefit of both user and manufacturer. Industrial designers maintain a practical concern for technical processes and requirements for manufacture; marketing opportunities and economic constraints; and distribution sales and servicing processes.

They work to ensure that design recommendations use materials and technology effectively, and comply with all legal and regulatory requirements. Some industrial designers are calling themselves "product design engineers", emphasizing the technological aspect of their background. In addition to supplying concepts for products and systems, industrial designers are often retained for consultation on a variety of problems that have to do with a client's image.

Such assignments include product and organization identity systems, development of communication systems, interior space planning and exhibit design, advertising devices and packaging and other related services. Their expertise is sought in a wide variety of administrative arenas to assist in developing industrial standards, regulatory guidelines and quality control procedures to improve manufacturing operations and products. Industrial designers are generalists, not specialists, in contrast to the other design professions.

FASHION DESIGN

Fashion design is applied in the garments industry as well in haute couture. As the name implies, fashion design is about designing apparel and fashion accessories. A fashion designer knows fashion illustration, pattern drafting, design, draping, clothing construction, textiles, fashion history and production techniques.

TEXTILE DESIGN

Textile design is the knowledge of (natural and synthetic) fibres and their properties, textile constructions including woven, knitted and non-woven, how colour and designs are applied, finishes and testing for quality and performance. A textile designer is good at sourcing and developing new fabrics for products, but is often specialising in designing woven or printed fabrics, carpets, towels, bed linen or knits.

JUTE

In Bangladesh, 25 % of the population (30-35 million people) is directly affected by jute production and many more by the industry. Jute manufacture is one of the most important industries, as important as ready-made garments, seafood processing and pharmaceuticals. India is the world's largest producer of jute and also its leading consumer of jute, selling 80% of the production on the home market. Bangladesh is the only other major producer of jute, exporting 80% of the yearly output. Bangladeshi jute is supposed to hold a high quality. Jute has, however, a low price image in the local market.

Jute is a natural fibre obtained as an extract from the bark of the jute plant. It can be harvested three times a year and provides a necessary break between rice crops helping to enrich the soil. The Bangladesh Jute Research Institute claims that jute can be a substitute for cotton.

Bangladeshi agriculture has as its foremost aim to provide food for the rapidly growing population. Rice is the main crop. In fact, Bangladesh hardly produces cotton and silk for its textile production, but has remained a net importer of yarn at least since 1947. Almost all yarns are imported; warp silk from China, cotton from China and India. If jute, which is locally grown, could be used for more of the textiles being produced in Bangladesh, this would be of advantage both to the farmers and to textile producers like jute mills, garment manufacturers, handloom weavers or craft businesses.

The jute industry is, unfortunately, a so-called "sunset" industry. Decline in sales and production volume has been a fact for many years now. Synthetic substitutes play a great role in the downfall of the jute industry, as many of the traditional jute products, i.e. packaging and carpets, now have been substituted by synthetics. The government policy of subsidizing the government-owned mills, has given the private-owned mills a difficult competitive situation while not avoiding a major breakdown of the government-owned production.

JUTE DIVERSIFICATION

Parallel to the sun setting over the jute industry, significant research and development (R & D) activities have taken place in many countries in the world during the last twenty years. As a result, many technologies and processes are now available for commercialization and more are coming out. The jute sector has previously concentrated its efforts on producing packaging (sacks and Hessian).

The diversification efforts have put an emphasis on:

1. Home textiles
2. Agro textiles
3. Composites.

The Bangladesh Jute Research Institute (BJRI) claims to have developed 37 new technologies, of which 15 are ready for commercialization on a pilot scale, among them jute blankets and prayer mats, knitwear, jute denim and blended jute/cotton thread. The BJRI is concentrating its efforts on research and leaves the commercialization to the private sector.

An example of jute diversification in the field of composites in Bangladesh is a student project at the Department of Materials and Metallurgical Engineering at Bangladesh University of Engineering and Technology (BUET). The aspiring engineers are experimenting with jute as a substitute for glass in "glass fibre", hoping to provide a useful material for (at least) the furniture producer who is lending the technology to the university. Realising there is a need to build bridges between the R & D environment and the jute industry, the Ministry of Jute with financial support from the European Commission, set up the Jute Diversification Promotion Centre (JDPC) in 2002.

Perhaps the most well-known diversification programme was the Jute Development Programme in India launched in 1992 by UNDP in order to search for and develop diversified, high value added jute-based products and then to encourage entrepreneurs to commercialise results through an incentive credit facility. This project managed to achieve production of blended yarns where jute was mixed with cotton, linen, ramie, viscose and polyester in union blends. Critical voices, say, however, that the UNDP program failed because "They helped the jute mills in design and development, but other aspects like investment in new machinery, changing attitude of workforce, marketing, market study, investing in new technology (and) machinery, etc. was missing from the project."

DIVERSIFICATION IS NOT NECESSARILY COMMERCIALIZATION

Several of the private-owned mills in Bangladesh have already to some extent diversified their production. The main challenge at present does not seem to be diversification as such, but commercializing the results of the already existing research from the R&D environments. The process of commercialization is a complex weave of trial and error; analyzing market potential, designing products, financing investments etc.

CO-OPERATION BETWEEN R&D INSTITUTIONS AND THE INDUSTRY

The contact between R&D and the businesses seem to be on an ad hoc basis, taking place when the businesses face technological questions they hope the research institutions can solve. The mills, as well as smaller companies, are rather critical towards the government-financed research institutions, claiming inefficiency and little willingness to meet the needs of the businesses.

Jute and the Small Businesses

Small businesses working with jute are mostly found in the crafts sector. This sector is large; it is supposed to be the second largest source of employment in the rural areas, even if the businesses are small. Most often the businesses are organised with a small number of employees (for instance 30-40) and a large number of connected craftspeople (for instance 300-400) from which the products are bought. In most developing countries and certainly in Bangladesh, the concept of the craftsperson as a "crafts-artist" is not known. The Bangladeshi craftspeople are production workers, not artists.

National Crafts Council of Bangladesh (NCCB) expresses a strong interest in jute as a material in crafts production. For the handloom businesses the use of blended threads in the production of fabric for both apparel and interiors are interesting. One business has already had success with fabric and apparel of jute/cotton mixes and claims that jute is a selling point. For crafts businesses in general both blended fabrics and pure jute, treated or not, are materials that can be utilized for product development. New products for export markets are especially demanded. This is an area where NCCB believes it is necessary to use international designers, hoping that donors will be willing to subsidize the cost.

Markets

For the smaller businesses, the local market is the most important one. It would be of great advantage for the smaller businesses if the jute mills succeeded in selling and producing larger volumes of, for instance, the soft fabric. The price would go down, making the fabric available for many more of the small businesses.

Then the fabric (and eventually also softer yarn) could be used for products not only aimed at the export markets, but also at the local and regional markets, giving income to a larger group of companies and, incidentally, work to more people. However, some high value niche export markets are approachable also with the present high prices, as has been proved in the Norad project, if the quality is high enough.

THE NORAD PROJECT "THE DEVELOPMENT OF THE JUTE INDUSTRY IN BANGLADESH"

The NORAD jute project started in 1997 and ended in June 2003. In the end, the participants were 2 mills, Sonali and Pubali, and four craft producers: two craft businesses, Esheeta and Swajan Crafts, and two NGOes, Concern and CORR - The Jute Works. The project has succeeded in producing a new, soft jute fabric in light and heavy weights and in different colours, lately also with prints. The market focus has been "home furnishings". The fabric and the home furnishing products have been presented every year, starting 2001, at the Heimtextil fair in Frankfurt, Germany. A greater quality consciousness has grown out of working with niche products for an upper-grade market.

The Dutch design company LA Colours worked as consultants in the project's first years. The project participants grant much of the honour for their success to the Dutch designers. The companies participating in the Norad project have now joined in the loosely knit "Jute Group". South Asia Enterprise Development Facility (SEDF) has been asked by Norad to make a market study, especially looking into the potential of the soft fabric that was a result of the Norad project.

The Jute Mills

Government owned mills dominate the jute sector, both in terms of employment, number of mills and capacity. The mills are large industrial plants, often employing thousands of people, most often using old technology.

In the 1950-ies and 60-ies, mainly four types of jute industries were set up:

1. Hessian and Sacking Cloth and Bags (spinning and weaving machinery)
2. Spinners (spinning machinery)
3. Carpet Backing Cloth (spinning and weaving machinery)
4. Jute Carpet Mills

According to E. Sigvaldsen et al´s report (2002), there are 47 spinning mills, 11 privately owned weaving mills and 30 government-owned weaving mill. The government does not compete in the spinning segment.

Strategy of Value-Adding

The focus of the jute mills presently seems to be on value-adding, of finding ways to add value to the products that can be made with (more or less) the existing technology. The mills are today more interested in finding new markets for thread and weave, and in diversifying – and adding value - within the framework of their existing production of thread and weave than starting on a radical diversification process involving great economic risk.

Yarn and weave represent the major part of the existing jute industry and possess an unused potential for product development. The large markets of agro- and geo textiles can be approached using (mainly) existing technology. The soft fabric will have to be further developed so that problems with shrinkage and colour fastness are solved. Thinner threads and blended threads are other areas of growth. The idea of developing fully vertically integrated manufacturing, e.g production of thread and yarn, fabrics, cutting and sewing is done in one place, has been taken up by some of the Bangladeshi jute producers. In a longer perspective, at least some of the mills show interest in expanding beyond the traditional thread and weave, for instance are non- woven textiles mentioned as an interesting opportunity.

Large Volume Markets

The jute mills need volume sales in order to keep their businesses going and will have to focus on markets accordingly. New products should (1) utilize large volumes of jute, (2) have a sustainable demand for large volume output in the foreseeable future and (3) be profitable. As pointed out by Vinay Chand in his report about the Norad jute project, the textile markets approachable for the treated fabric are large, - much larger than the specialised interior design markets where the products from the project's small businesses and NGOes can be sold. The jute mills are themselves pointing at large potential markets, expressing interest in producing geotextiles and agrotextiles.

Design in Bangladesh

"Why scramble to be the cheapest when using design can make you the best by transforming everything you do?"

DESIGN COUNCIL (UK)

The strong position of the garment industry in Bangladeshi economy - it is one of the largest export industries - does unfortunately not indicate that the country in general has a lot of excellent fashion or textile designers. Buyers from developed countries usually bring their own designs as well as their own materials to the Bangladeshi garments industry. The buyers focus on price and quality, not on contributing to create a thriving design profession in Bangladesh or elsewhere. In the jute industry, which is another important source of export income, one of the informants said outright that the employees can copy, but not design. In general, the manufacturing industry of Bangladesh seems to be very good at copying, but lacking in the understanding of how their competitiveness can be increased by using design as a strategic tool in reaching existing and new markets.

The main characteristics of the design situation in Bangladesh seems therefore to be a great capacity of copying as well as being able to produce cheap products that are designed elsewhere. Even if this "strategy" of copying and producing cheaply seems to function at the present level, it is not a strategy that will help Bangladeshi exports in the future. The role of Bangladesh will be reduced to the role of the re-active, the one player in the game who is not trying to win, but just - barely – trying to participate. Such an approach is understandable for a poor country, but is unfortunately doomed in the long run. If you are not winning markets shares, you are loosing them.

INSPIRATION FOR TEXTILE DESIGNS

Inspiration for textile designs can come from a variety of sources. It is possible to create textile design work by going straight to the process being used. For example, a weave designer may go straight to the weaving shed, choose warp yarns in colours that appeal and, with a knowledge of fabric structures, make an attractive fabric. Experience, however, has shown that such a method of designing often results in fairly mundane design. Innovative, exciting textile design starts with much more fundamental paperwork; drawings and paintings exploring colours, textures, shapes and patterns.

Drawing from objects in an imaginative and open way will inspire new colour combinations, textural ideas, shapes and arrangements of these. Inspiration for such paperwork, and ultimately for textile designs, can come from many things. Both natural and man-made objects can inspire. Whether the source material is natural or man-made, abstract or tangible, how themes and source material are used is a matter for debate. Drawing from man-made items such as architecture can raise the question as to whether or not the resulting design work is truly original. Drawing from architectural patterns can be seen, if the work is very literal, as merely copying someone else's designs—the proportions and shapes have been created by another person.

Working from nature, however, is usually seen as producing more original work. The designer may still be copying but is constantly making decisions and judgements about what to include and what to omit. Being influenced by the work of artists and other designers raises the question—when does a design influenced this way become a copy? Is a textile design that lifts elements from other designers or fine artists good or bad design? Fine art can inspire textiles; part of a menswear collection by the fashion designer Paul Smith in the late eighties was made in fabrics that were inspired by the paintings of Matisse.

Textiles can be created by fine artists; tapestries and silk scarves have been designed by artists and sculptors such as Picasso and Henry Moore. Textiles can have fine art directly applied; reproductions of the Mona Lisa have been applied to a variety of products, from tea towels to tee shirts. Much of textile design is derivative. Source books for designers often consist of designs from the past or from other cultures. William Morris, the famous nineteenthcentury writer and designer, often based his designs on Persian textile designs and many of the designs credited to him that are still best- sellers today were almost literal copies of the original Persian ones.

Does this knowledge change how Morris's work is perceived? Does using archive or historical sources allow copying to become acceptable? Whatever the inspiration or source for a textile design, the textile designer needs to have a good understanding of colour and aesthetics. A textile designer must be able to draw. They must understand and be able to use colour and pattern.

Pattern

Any textile designer needs to have a good idea of how their design is going to look as a finished fabric. One piece of paperwork could be worked through to become many different finished designs, woven, knitted or printed. All designers need to understand how designs can repeat. While many designs work as straight repeats, where the design element is repeated again and again, one on top of another, side by side, there are also half-drop repeats and tile repeats. Mirroring, where elements are reflected about either, or both, x and y axes, is another common way of repeating elements.

Fabrics may have sections within one complete repeat that show other repeat patterns, while some fabrics such as border designs will employ repeated designs only within certain sections of the fabric. It may be useful to mask-off certain areas of paperwork (or sample blankets and sample fabrics in the case of woven and knitted fabrics respectively), or use a frame to establish the most suitable sections to develop.

It is important to consider the repeat structure from an early stage in the design development, and various sketch plans of possible repeat structures should be evolved. Very often, trying to interpret paperwork too literally can be a problem, particularly for a print designer. By its very nature, weaving and knitting design requires elements to be extracted from the initial inspirational paperwork.

For print designers, this decisionmaking process of what to include and what to discard is equally important. The best designs are so often simple. This advice is as true for printed textile design as for any other type of design. Everything that does not contribute, everything that is not necessary, should be left out.

THE ACTIVITIES OF A TEXTILE DESIGNER

The overall purpose of a textile designer is to design and produce to an agreed timetable, an agreed number of commercially viable textile designs. Research into what designers do has identified several different activities.

The activities listed below relate to an in-house fabric designer engaged on branded, contract and general work:

- Deciding what to design.
- Producing original design ideas.
- Developing design ideas through to a form suitable for initial sampling.
- Supervising the production of original fabric samples and keeping suitable records.
- Submitting samples to customers, to company or to company selection systems.
- Adapting and modifying designs from sketches or fabrics submitted by customers (or obtained from within the firm or group) to meet a price or other restriction.
- Obtaining the acceptance of a certain proportion of the original sample fabrics by the customer.
- Controlling the production of sample ranges in consultation with the customer's technicians, technologists and buyers.
- Establishing production specifications.
- Ensuring the production of sample ranges by certain agreed dates.

- Reporting to the company on contacts with customers, competitors, exhibitions, developments by fibre and yarn producers, etc., in order to augment market intelligence.
- Controlling the systems and procedures for the storage and retrieval of designs and samples within the company.
- Working within an agreed departmental budget.
- Controlling the supply of materials and equipment for design and sampling.

All textile designers will certainly be involved in some of these and should have an understanding of all of them.

HOW DESIGN WORK IS DONE

Design ideas are developed through in different ways, depending upon how an individual designer likes to work, upon the product being designed and upon the manufacturing process/es. From initial paperwork, designers of constructed textiles may take their design ideas and develop them through on the loom or knitting machine.

Designers of printed textiles will usually develop their ideas right through on paper. 'Much design work is carried out in a very direct and informal way.

The degree of formality becomes a function of scale and the number of interests represented:'

- Design is an investigative process; it involves research. The first stage in any design exercise is normally an enquiry into what the client (or potential client) requires; their needs and expectations.
- Design is a creative process; it involves art and aesthetics. Designs can be copied or invented. Adesign problem is solved with the help of know-how, ingenuity, pattern recognition abilities, lateral thinking, brainstorming, etc.
- Design is a rational process; it involves logical reasoning in the checking and testing of proposed solutions, information analysis, experimentation, field trials, etc.
- Design is a decision-making process; it involves making value judgements.

The selection of particular combinations and configurations, layouts or shapes involves considerable uncertainties. These are resolved by estimating the values that are likely to be placed on the various major alternatives. In this respect the task of the designer is closer to that of a manager rather than a researcher, scientist or artist. Estimating the social consequences of various design alternatives also falls into this category. Solving design problems involves a mixture of the intuitive (having ideas) and the systematic (rational scientific appraisal). There is no single solution to a design problem, rather there are many solutions although some may be better than others.

The Design Process

The design process usually starts with a requirement or desire for a new item or product. Research will usually be carried out then to find out as much as possible about this need and about the role or function the new item or product is to have. Ideas generation is the next stage when various alternative initial ideas are conceived.

These initial ideas are then usually developed through until the designer is happy to offer them as proposals to meet the initial need. In the early stages, alternative ideas will often also be presented. These proposals will be considered and perhaps modified. A decision is then taken as to the best solution to the design problem and the necessary specifications and instructions will then be given.

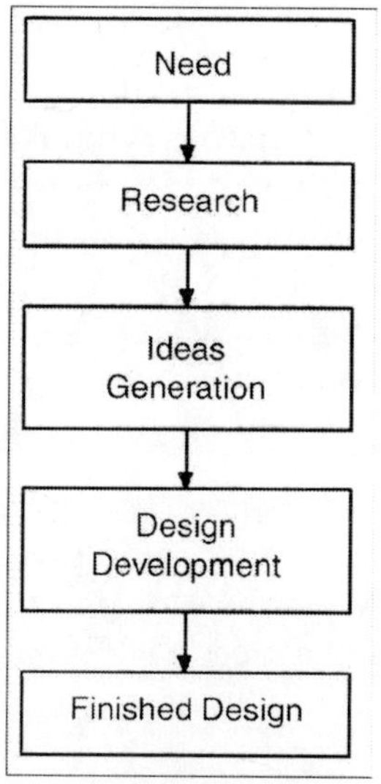

Fig.2.2: The Design Process.

Planning Design Work

Any design project will usually need to be completed by a certain date, and more often than not designers will find themselves working on more than one project at any one time. Efficient project management and efficient time of individuals working together over a period of time to achieve an agreed goal or outcome. Any project needs to be completed on time, to a standard and within a budget. A design project, as any other project, needs to be planned and managed efficiently.

The Planning Process

Planning can be described as managing and controlling events to achieve a goal and making the best use of resources. Planning is achieved by making decisions about what is to be achieved (aims) and how best to get there (who does what, when and how). While planning takes a little time, lack of planning can result in the waste of a lot of time, the expenditure of much money and the generation of considerable stress and tension. A plan gives what could be described as a set of route markers that allow checks to be made as work is undertaken to achieve the goals. Regular checking of current position against plan identifies any deviations from course which can then be remedied. The more detailed the plan, the more route markers there will be. A plan helps in the controlling of events rather than events determining direction. Very few jobs go exactly according to plan, but if there is no plan there is no way to keep control and track progress.

Objectives

An objective describes something to be achieved in the future. The essence of an objective is that it defines what is wanted without describing how this is going to be achieved. Without objectives people do not know where to invest their time or resources, and they can drift in an unco-ordinated way. When objectives are unclear, it is impossible to make effective plans and people will not be committed to action. Despite the obvious importance of objectives many people find it difficult to set them.

Identifying the Aims and Objectives of a Design Project

The aims and objectives of any design project are usually identified at a briefing meeting. This is when the designer finds out what is required of them. Many clients often have little idea of what they actually do want so it is up to the designer to get as much information as possible; this is usually done by asking questions.

Checklists

Using a checklist can be very helpful at many stages in the design process. For example, a checklist for a briefing meeting would simply be a list of questions, prepared beforehand, that the designer will use as a prompt. Enough knowledge of a situation is required to enable a checklist to be developed that covers the right questions. Use of a properly prepared checklist should ensure that the designer does not forget to ask for any necessary information and this should help avoid misunderstandings that might create problems later in the design process.

Project Planning Methods

Different methods can be used to help plan design projects. The simplest is to arrange elements of the plan in a logical sequence. Working from the brief, designers determine what is required to fulfil this and plan a logical sequence of events to take them through the design process to a design solution that satisfies the brief.

Backwards Planning

Often, the best way to ensure that design work achieves the requirements of the brief is to start by examining the expected final products or outcomes. These products or outcomes need to be listed and agreed. Having considered what it is that is to be achieved, the processes or work to achieve the outcomes can be determined. Finally, it must be decided what inputs are necessary to enable the work to be carried out successfully.

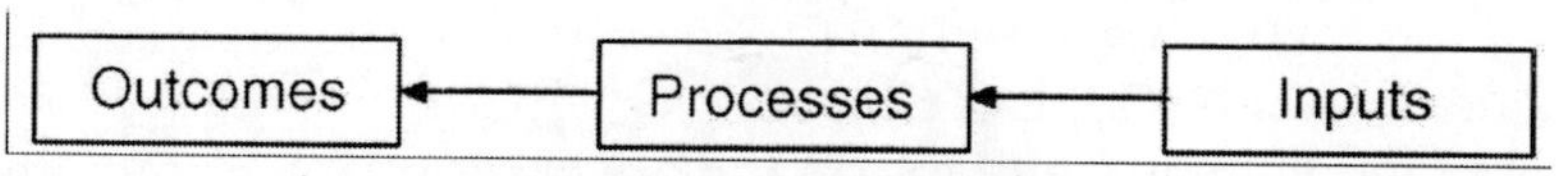

Fig.2.3: Backwards Planning

- *Outcomes:* The planned result of the project, equal to the aims and objectives of the project, to achieve the quality or standard required.
- *Processes:* The work needed to be done to achieve the output deliverables or outcomes.
- *Inputs:* The resources in terms of individuals and their skills, time, materials, equipment, techniques, etc., necessary to achieve the outcomes.

For example, a designer is asked to design a range of printed curtaining fabrics. The outcomes would be a specified number of fabric designs, with colourways, for a specific time, to sell at a specific price point. The processes would be initial research of the market (to see what is currently selling and what the competition are doing), the formulation of initial design ideas, the development of these ideas, the selection and production of the specified number of fabric designs (with recommendations for print base fabrics) to be included in the range, colourway development and selection, and the specification of final fabrics for production. The inputs would be the designer with the required skills and knowhow, the time they would require and the materials and equipment necessary.

Gantt Charts

A slightly more sophisticated way of planning is to use a Gantt chart. During a design project, several stages can be under way at the same time. A Gantt chart is a simple horizontal bar chart that graphically displays the time relationships of the stages in a project. Each step is represented by a line or block placed on the chart in the time period in which it is to be undertaken.

When completed, a Gantt chart shows the flow of activities in a sequence, as well as those that can be under way at the same time. Gantt charts can also be used to chart actual progress, by drawing lines in different colours to show the start and end dates of each step. This allows easy assessment of whether or not a project is on schedule.

Network Analysis

This is a generic term used for several project planning methods, of which the best known are PERT (Programme Evaluation and Review Technique) and CPA (Critical Path Analysis). These are more sophisticated forms of planning than Gantt charts and are appropriate for projects with many interactive steps.

Project Management

Managing a project involves co-ordinating activities so that they run according to plan. The progress of a project should be monitored and measured against the plan. When deviations occur, corrective action should be taken.

Time Management

All projects are time-bounded and for any practising designer it is desirable (if not essential!) to make the best use of the time available. Time management is simply making the best use of time to achieve what is necessary. To effectively manage time, goals and time limits need to be set. What is required? What has to be achieved and when? How efficiently do these goals have to be met? It is only against set targets that success can be measured. The way any individual uses time is unique to that individual. Some people use time as chunks into which they can fit certain activities, all neatly stacked. Others have no clear view of time, selecting activities at random or changing priorities to suit the current crisis. There are strengths and weaknesses in both ways and it is of value to consider both because many people will alternate between the two, depending on the jobs in hand.

The way designers use their time will be different, since everyone has their own pace of work and their own rhythms, with different peaks for different activities. Where possible, work should be done at times to suit an individual's own speed and their own way of organising and completing activities. Managing time costs time. To sit down and plan the best use of time is an investment.

It takes time to learn to use software packages for word processing and database management but their use is a huge investment for future time management. The time spent on any activities should be considered afterwards and evaluated. Can any lessons be learnt to plan more effective use of time in the future? The Pareto principle: 20% of what you do yields 80% of the results. Targets that will result in a high pay-off should be identified. Constructive avoidance is when time is spent on work that is neither important nor urgent in preference to urgent and important work.

Time management involves:

- *Planning tasks:* Getting information, assembling relevant facts, skills, experience, resources, establishing what is known or what needs to be known, processing the information, considering options and identifying the risks involved,
- *Stating what has to be done:* Scheduling what will be done, how, where, when and by whom.
- *Getting Things done:* Doing things and monitoring progress against checkpoints/standards, reviewing outcomes by assessing the results achieved in relation to the aims, determining if more needs to be done, analysing successes and difficulties so as to plan for improvement.

RANGE PLANNING

A range is a group of products offered for sale. These products will be the designer's answer to a brief. Having the right products in a range is very important in terms of how well that range will sell.

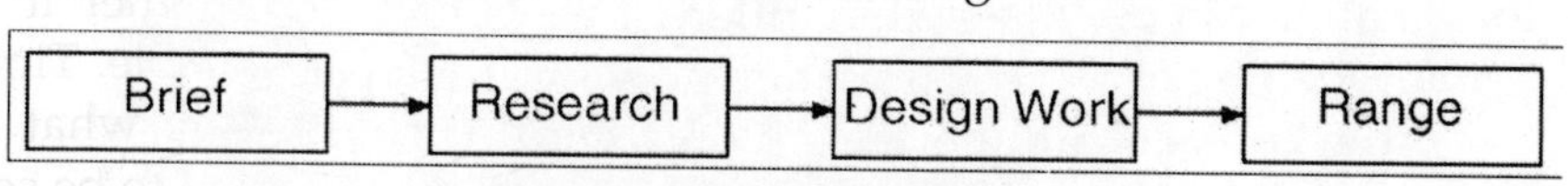

Fig.2.4: Range Development

Good design adds value to a product. With products of equal quality and price, the design will be what differentiates. What does the designer need to know or make decisions about when planning a range? Or, put at its most simplistic, how does a designer decide what to design? All designers are designing for the future and are influenced by trends in their product area.

The whole area of forecasting is one where much money is invested to 'get it right' and much money can be lost if a designer gets it wrong. As well as needing to understand forecasting, a designer needs to know other information when planning a range.

This includes:

- Type of products,
- Customer/market areas,
- Price points,
- Manufacturing capabilities,
- Quality required,
- Number of designs,
- Number of colourways.

It is usually the job of the design manager (or stylist) in a studio to plan the ranges. There will have been some discussion with sales, marketing and production about all or some of the factors listed above—essentially to build up a full picture of what criteria the range must answer. The type of designs depends on the products being designed for, the customer profile, price points for sales, manufacturing plant availability and quality.

The number of designs and colourways in a range is controlled by several commercial factors including the amount of capital the company wishes to tie up in the range, the raw materials that are needed, the amount of stock that can be carried, and the production capacity, i.e. the number of machines available for printing/knitting/weaving the range (some machines may be tied up with specific customer orders rather than general range production).

Research

After the briefing meeting, the next stage in the design process is usually research: finding information about products and markets, production processes and techniques, etc.

Information can be collected in different ways:

- By waiting to see if information presents itself (gathered by chance from contacts and perhaps by reading): This is unsatisfactory if there is any form of time limit on when the answer is required.
- By asking questions: This is appropriate if it is known who to ask and what to ask. Known as primary research or field research, this is where designers find information directly for themselves; by going out and looking at the shops and visiting trade fairs and exhibitions, by asking relevant individuals and groups, by using mailed questionnaires, by setting up focus groups and by interviewing people.
- By looking up what is required: This is appropriate if it is known where to look, how to look it up and what exactly is being looked for. Known as secondary or desk research, this is where information is gleaned from work already carried out by other individuals or groups. Such research might include looking

at market research information obtained through government censuses and large market research programmes.

Information Search

To ensure that the required information is found and time is not wasted, the collection of information should be systematic. The aim should be to find key information. Identify what is not known. As far as possible, vague requests for 'information on' some problem area should be broken down into questions defining what it is that is not known and what needs to be found out.

The questions that need to be answered should be identified and listed. The level of answer required should be established (there is a balance between the importance of what is being looked for and the time and effort spent looking) and a checklist of likely sources of reliable answers to questions can be prepared. It is sensible to keep control over any search for information by setting limits and deadlines and by using expert opinions and expert literature searchers to identify the most promising sources. It is important to stop as soon as there is enough information to move forward and it is essential to keep accurate references.

Getting Information from other Organizations

There are many occasions when designers need to find out information from other organisations. Sometimes, the information sought may have to be bought, sometimes it may be free—part of a marketing strategy on behalf of the supplier. However, whether visiting a new supplier to source yarn or buttons, or telephoning to check prices of fabrics, it is important that designers know exactly what they want so as not to waste time. Before any visit, the information required should be clearly identified.

It is essential for any designer to be prepared, and establishing a checklist of questions that need to be answered is a good way of making sure that all relevant information is obtained. When seeking information about market areas and products, it would be usual to employ professional market researchers. However, sometimes designers may prefer to carry out some market research themselves. In either case, well-constructed questionnaires can be very useful, and when market research is being carried out by professionals the designer's input should not be overlooked.

Questionnaires

Questionnaires should be designed in such a way that they take a minimum amount of time to fill in. A busy company director or buyer is much more likely to complete and return a questionnaire if it is clear to read, to the point and does not take up too much of their valuable time. Formulating questions in such a way that they can be answered by ticking boxes is much more likely to elicit a positive response than having questions that require written replies.

Ideas Generation

With some initial research undertaken, the designers need to be able to generate suitable ideas to help them answer the brief. Design ideas can come from almost any source, but sometimes designers may find difficulty in thinking of suitable sources and themes for work.

Brainstorming

Brainstorming is a very useful method of generating ideas and can be used at many stages in the design process. In its most formal sense, it is a group participation technique for generating a wide range of ideas in order to tackle a stated problem. In a less formalised way, an individual or pair can use a brainstorming session to generate ideas.

What follows is a description of brainstorming at its most formalised; such a rigid approach, however, may well inhibit ideas:

- A problem statement is formulated: Too vague or too restrictive a statement should be avoided.
- The group of people to participate in the session is selected. The group should ideally include some people familiar with the problem area. Small groups of about 4–8 people are best.
- Five or ten minutes are allowed for group members to write down their first ideas in reply to the problem statement.
- Group members are encouraged to continue writing down new ideas whilst each person in turn reads out one idea from their set. The session rules are:
  - No criticism is allowed of any idea.
  - Crazy ideas are welcome.
  - The more ideas the better.
  - Ideas should be combined and built upon.
- After the session, the ideas are evaluated.

THE DIVERSITY OF TEXTILE DESIGN AND TEXTILE DESIGNERS

The diversity of the textile and clothing industries is reflected in the many different types of designers needed. At every stage of manufacture of textiles there are colourists determining the fashion colours in which the fibres will be produced, yarn designers developing yarns to meet certain requirements, knitted-fabric designers, woven-fabric designers, carpet designers, print designers, embroidery designers, knitwear designers, designers of women's wear, men's wear and children's wear, accessory designers, designers of casualwear, sportswear, eveningwear, swimwear and designers for the mass market, haute couture and designer labels, etc.

The Purpose of the Textile Designer

The role of the designer can be quite complex but the overall purpose can be stated quite simply—the textile designer has to design and produce, to an agreed timetable, an agreed number of commercially viable fabric designs. Depending on the markets that he or she is designing for, several different activities are involved in fabric design and the number and type in which any designer is involved will vary according to the product and production methods used, and the type of company for which the work is done.

Stylists

Designers also put together ranges. For example a stylist might handle the development of a company's range of printed fabrics. A range is a group of fabrics (or products) designed, developed and edited to be shown and sold to the market each season. The stylist initiates the design work, organises and directs the development and colouration of intended designs (frequently using freelance designers), and co-ordinates with manufacturing personnel to have samples made.

These samples are shown to customers; the stylist then edits and finalises the group of designs that will form that season's range. Further down the chain, buyers and merchandisers in retail organisations do much the same range-building processes.

Colourists

Some designers work purely with colour, predicting colour trends and putting together palettes of colours for specific seasons and product groups. Other colourists will work further down the design process line, colouring designs produced by other designers to create different and alternative colourways.

Repeat Artists

Acompany producing printed textiles will often employ designers whose main function is to take designs and put these into a size and repeat appropriate to the intended enduse.

In-house and Freelance Designers

Designers may work for manufacturing companies as in-house designers, or they may work independently as freelance designers. In-house designers, or as they are sometimes called staff designers, are employed by a company usually on a full-time basis, although some may be employed part-time. Often they work within a manufacturing environment, although they can also be employed by retailers and by converters. Freelance designers may either work for independent studios or through an agent, producing designs on paper for which the studio/ agent receives a commission when the designs are sold to mills and converters. Alternatively, freelance designers may put together a portfolio of their designs, which they may sell directly to stylists.

The work they produce for their portfolio, while it will have at least to reflect trends, will be often very much what they themselves like and want to produce. While the designer may have a view of the type of customer who will buy their designs when the design is developed, there may be no specific customer waiting to buy their work on completion. Freelance designers may also develop design work according to a stylist's specification.

For example, a freelance print designer who is particularly good at intricate florals may well be approached by a stylist to work on a specific print idea that will form part of that company's new season's collection. The brief may include size details, colouring details and even the type of flowers to be painted. This work will be commissioned in advance. The designer develops their paperwork with the knowledge that when it is finished there is a buyer for it.

Freelance weave and knit designers will normally work on a specific project with a manufacturer. They will be commissioned to produce a range of fabrics, or, in the case of a knitwear designer, a range of knitted-garment designs. A third type of designer found within textiles is the consultant designer. A consultant is employed by a company to advise on design matters and may be given the task of managing the design programme.

A consultant designer will usually work for several companies at any one time, although their contract may be such as to impose restrictions on their working for closely related organisations. Very often consultants will do little actual working-through of design ideas themselves; rather they will make design policy decisions and direct other designers who may be in-house or freelance. All designer systems have advantages and disadvantages to the designers themselves and to the organisations for whom they work.

Just as many different people doing different jobs are given the name designer, so too are many rooms called design studios. The 'studio' can be anything from an area set aside on the factory floor to a large, smart office or even suite of offices. One designer or a whole team of designers can work in a studio and a few or many of the functions of, and stages in, the design process might be carried out there.

TIMING IN THE TEXTILE AND CLOTHING INDUSTRIES

Products are planned and produced well ahead of retail selling seasons in all areas of the textile and clothing industries. In August, and even July, autumn clothing appears in the shops. Before this clothing can be designed, fabrics must be designed and shown to clothing manufacturers, and orders placed, produced and delivered. Before then, new yarns and sometimes even new fibres must be developed. The scheduling and amount of time necessary for all of these steps are dependent on the amount of change occurring in the product, the volume being produced and the efficiency of the producing a-half in front of the retail season. Major changes such as the development of a completely new type of fabric will take even longer.

Seasonal Ranges

Manufacturers producing for the fashion industry will normally launch two main ranges a year; for the selling seasons Spring/Summer and Autumn/Winter. Sometimes, midseason ranges are also produced. Manufacturers of furnishing fabrics and household textiles normally produce one main range per year. In every segment of the market, the higher-volume manufacturers work further ahead of the retail season than the companies producing lower volumes (at the higher end of the market).

PRINTED AND CONSTRUCTED TEXTILES

Textile designers may be categorised by the types of product or fabrics for which they design. Printed textiles are often considered to include fabrics patterned by dyeing techniques as well as those where the design is applied to the fabric by a printing process. Constructed textiles include woven textiles, knitted textiles, lace and carpets.

From Sketchbook to Fabric Samples

The design process is about the realisation of ideas —ideas that are transformed into tangible products. The designer will start with some sort of brief describing the project. For the in-house designer, the briefing may be very informal as their experience within the company will usually mean that they will already have an understanding of the requirements of the range.

They may, indeed, be the person setting the brief! Hopefully, any brief, formally or informally delivered, will have all the information needed, but if not, the designer must be ready to ask questions. Who is the customer? What is the price range? What are the manufacturing possibilities in terms of machine availability? The designer needs to get as much information as possible. Designs come from a variety of different sources, and different designers will have different methods for developing design work from initial ideas.

Most designers keep some form of sketchbook —something they carry with them and use to record and store ideas to call upon as a source of inspiration in the future. This may contain drawings and photographs, magazine cuttings and fabric pieces. Often, a brainstorming session will be used to give inspiration and generate a wide variety of ideas. Some of the considered themes and ideas will be selected and subsequent artwork based around these. While the way these ideas are used will be individual to the designer, much of the process is similar for many different types of designers.

Yarn Design

Yarn designers have to know what machinery they have available to them and what that machinery is capable of producing. They will usually start with ideas collected on their travels; colour ideas, texture ideas, looks and moods that they see as becoming important in the future. They should have an understanding of their existing and potential customers and what they want. The development of a range of yarns may involve the creation of a completely new yarn using a newly-developed fibre. It may involve the tweaking and fine-tuning of existing production ranges to meet the requirements of a future market.

An existing yarn quality may require to be re-coloured so that it can be used to service a fashion market. Some ranges of yarns will run from season to season servicing a classic market area. For example, a range of knitwear yarn for a manufacturer of schoolwear will include the classic school colours—navy, maroon, grey, bottle green, bright red and bright blue.

The knowledge base that the yarn designer will have built-up is the springboard from which they work, in conjunction with technicians and development personnel, looking at the overall range, determining qualities and the types of yarns appropriate to their market area. The selling cost of the yarn must also be considered. Colour is very important and yarn designers will often subscribe to colour prediction publications to help them determine their colour palettes. The same colours or shades of colours will often run through the different yarn types. Co-ordination is as important in yarn design as in any other area, helping the customer to see how the product can be used and often prompting more sales.

Yarns may be designed to work with other qualities in the range. Sample yarns will be specified and made using different components and in different colourways until the designer is happy with the handle and appearance. The yarns may have to perform in specific situations and they will have to be tested to ensure that any such performance requirements are met.

Weave Design

After the briefing meeting where the work that is required is established, and after initial ideas have been collected, one of the first things that a weave designer will do is to establish a colour palette. This colour palette may change as design work develops but such changes are normally minimal. A colour palette will usually consist of groups of colours, chosen with regard to trends and predicted directions. The way these colours work together will be important. Adegree of flexibility is usually desirable as economic constraints will normally demand that stocks of yarns (both for sampling and production) are kept to a minimum. Once an initial colour palette has been decided upon, suitable yarns are then selected and frequently from the colours in which the yarn producers have decided to run their ranges; sometimes, however, colours will have to be specially dyed. From their initial paperwork, weave designers will usually take their design ideas and develop them on the loom. Sample warps will be made up and different weave, colour and yarn combinations tried. Shape and pattern are important but these might well evolve more with the weaves used.

The way woven designs repeat is determined by the way the yarns are threaded up and the way these threads are lifted. This is a very integral part of the weave design process, and a good understanding of fabric structures is vital to allow the weave designer to be as creative as possible within the constraints set by the type of loom that is being used and its patterning capabilities. Sample blankets, or 'section' blankets as they are also known, consist of different sections across a warp. These sections may vary in colour, yarn type and/or weave. Initial sample warps will often have several warp sections with different drafts, and different warp patterns and yarns.

Different lifting plans (which, along with the way the loom is threaded, determine the weave) will be tried out as will a variety of weft patterns and yarns, again in sections. As well as true designs where the planned warp will be woven with the intended weft, there will be many areas where crossings occur.

These are sections where warp and weft patterns combine more by chance than by design. Areas of interest will be developed and hopefully an initial sample blanket will provide plenty of ideas for subsequent development. Having considered initial ideas, further sample blankets will be developed; these will show full repeats of the proposed fabric designs and will often have sections in alternative colourways. Some weave designers will work on computer-aided design (CAD) systems, using these to try out ideas before the weaving stage.

Many of the sophisticated weave CAD systems currently available, as well as showing representations of what the fabric will look like, also have facilities to show proposed weave designs in situ, on garments and on other products. However, in practice it is still usual to weave actual fabric samples of those ideas which best meet the brief. The way fabric feels, its handle, is still a very important factor in fabric selection.

With a selection of ideas chosen, the making particulars or fabric specifications will be recorded so that these designs may be produced again. The yarns and colours used, the draft (the way the loom is threaded), weave, lifting plan (the way the warp threads are raised), warping and picking plans (colour and yarn arrangements in the warp and weft directions) all need to be recorded, as do any subsequent process such as applying a fire-retardant finish or raising. Throughout the weave design process, the designer is constantly having to make decisions, on colour, yarn, weave, size of repeat, etc. These decisions are made from a knowledge base that includes intended selling price, customer preferences, the range as a whole, co-ordination requirements, performance requirements, and so on.

Knit Fabric and Knitwear Design

Again, as in weave design, the design of a new season's range will usually start with the development of a colour palette. This will come from initial ideas generated in response to information from a briefing meeting. Suitable yarns will then be selected. The working through of design ideas is very much restricted by the type of knitting machine being used and the type of structures that can be created on it. Inspiration from drawn work will influence the textures, colours and proportions of a knitted fabric. Creating visual representations of sketchbook work is only possible when machinery with jacquard patterning capabilities is used.

Some designers will put their initial design ideas straight into graph form, ready for translation by a knitting mechanic. Others may do more paperwork, perhaps developing fabric and garment styling ideas side by side. The fabric ideas worked out, the designer will then usually decide which yarns should be tried in which fabrics. It is usual to knit several swatches to enable the designer to see how any fabric looks in different yarn and colour combinations. For the knitwear designer, concerned with the design of final garment as well as the fabrics, styling ideas must then be worked out.

The designer of cut and sewn knitwear will probably sketch out styling ideas, and the next stage will be to cut a pattern. A first sample will be cut out and made up, pressed, measured and tried for fit. Any necessary alterations will be made and a second sample made to check that these alterations and the final specifications are correct.

To help knitted fabric and knitwear designers, there are specific CAD systems available which allow representations of fabrics to be viewed before knitting. They also often allow fabric ideas to be mapped onto garments, and these facilities should cut down on actual sampling time. In practice, this is not always the case as the ease of changing things on the computer often results in requests for more initial work giving more choice. Once the garments and colour ways that will form the range are decided upon, the range is then ready for presentation to sales teams and customers.

Print Design

The print design process can take many different forms. With modern technology, sketchbook work can be taken and re-created on fabric very much as it appeared originally. Print designers, after initial research, will usually work their ideas through on paper. Any medium can be used in the artwork for print design, but materials with which designers can achieve facsimiles of particular desired effects in manufactured fabrics allow design problems to be more accurately resolved in the studio before the design is put into production. Print designs are sometimes worked in repeat from the start but often they are designed in balance and put in repeat later.

A balanced design is called a 'croquis' (a French word meaning sketch). A croquis should give the impression that would be seen if a frame were placed over any section of the finished cloth. Although not in repeat, a croquis will give the feeling of being in repeat. The most common repeat structures are simple block repeats, half drops and bricks. Print designs for apparel fabrics are usually designed in croquis form with the repeat sizes varying enormously. Upholstery and curtain fabrics have standard repeat sizes so these are often designed as a repeat pattern with the size being carefully considered from the beginning.

Often, the involvement of a print designer will end with the production of the design on paper, the preparation of colour separations and the approval of these usually being undertaken by the printer. However, in-house print designers will usually be responsible for approving the strike-offs (sample prints on fabric). Again many print designers (particularly those working for large multinational companies and corporations) will often find themselves working with CAD systems.

Such print systems allow designers to develop and expand design ideas readily. Design ideas can be scanned in, and repeat, cut-and-paste and other functions allow ideas to be manipulated quickly. Many systems also have colour separation facilities to aid in the preparation of screens. Some systems even allow sample fabrics to be produced, and this is a very valuable tool, making it much easier for print designers to take their ideas right through to fabric.

Design Adaptation and Modification

As well as producing ranges, textile designers will have to adapt and modify existing designs, design ideas and sketches submitted by customers. Here, textile designers are using their creative and technical skills to translate ideas into reality. They must, of course, be careful not to copy or adapt designs that have copyright, or are registered, without the express permission of the copyright holder or design originator.

Examples of Textile Design Briefs/Problems

An in-house designer working for a manufacturer of printed fabrics may be asked by a customer selling babywear to develop a small design with chickens as the motif. The babywear company may also employ a designer and they might have put together rough sketches and colour ideas to give an idea of what is wanted. In this case the brief will be fairly specific. A company may have seen a range of designs for duvet covers that they like. However, they may be unhappy with the colourways being offered.

An in-house designer working for the printer may be asked to re-colour the designs, producing colourways that are considered more suitable. Perhaps these will have to co-ordinate with a range of lampshades being developed in a specific range of plain shades. A knitwear manufacturer might find themselves approached by a company which has a sweater that they are manufacturing overseas and are currently importing.

The company is, however, experiencing real problems with quality and late deliveries. Essentially the company wants the knitwear manufacturer to re-create their sample sweater to a specific price point. The designer's job in this case would be to source suitable yarns and develop specifications for the production of a garment that is essentially the same as the original sweater in terms of quality and appearance but which also meets the pricing requirements.

A company might have a fabric that is currently selling very well — their 'bestseller'. The marketing director and his team require a 'new' version of this fabric, perhaps more up-to-date and with a co-ordinate. They are happy with the existing colourways but are open to suggestions regarding colour and scale. As their market area is becoming increasingly competitive they would also like to see the new version having elements of 'added value' if at all possible. This might mean repositioning the product in the marketplace or developing a new product that acts as a co-ordinate with the current best seller. In this case the textile designer's job is to develop a fabric using the existing colourway that fulfils the company requirements. ❐

3

Digital Textile Printing and Dyeing Process

Textile Printing and dyeing processes include pretreatment, dyeing/printing, finishing and other technologies. Pre-treatment includes desizing, scouring, washing, and other processes. Dyeing mainly aims at dissolving the dye in water, which will be transferred to the fabric to produce colored fabric under certain conditions. Printing is a branch of dyeing which generally is defined as 'localized dyeing' i.e. dyeing that is confirmed to a certain portion of the fabric that constitutes the design. It is really a form of dyeing in which the essential reactions involved are the same as those in dyeing.

In dyeing, colour is applied in the form of solutions, whereas colour is applied in the form of a thick paste of the dye in printing. Both natural and synthetic textiles are subjected to a variety of finishing processes. This is done to improve specific properties in the finished fabric and involves the use of a large number of finishing agents for softening, crosslinking, and waterproofing. All of the finishing processes contribute to water pollution.

In the textile dyeing industry, bleaching is an important process. It has three technologies: sodium hypochlorite bleaching; hydrogen peroxide bleaching and sodium chlorite bleaching. Sodium hypochlorite bleaching and sodium chlorite bleaching are the most commonly used processes. Normal concentration of chlorine dioxide in bleaching effluent is 10-200 mg/L. As chlorine dioxide is a strong oxidant, it is very corrosive and toxic as well. The typical printing and dyeing process is shown in Fig. and the main used fibre dyes at present have been shown in Table.

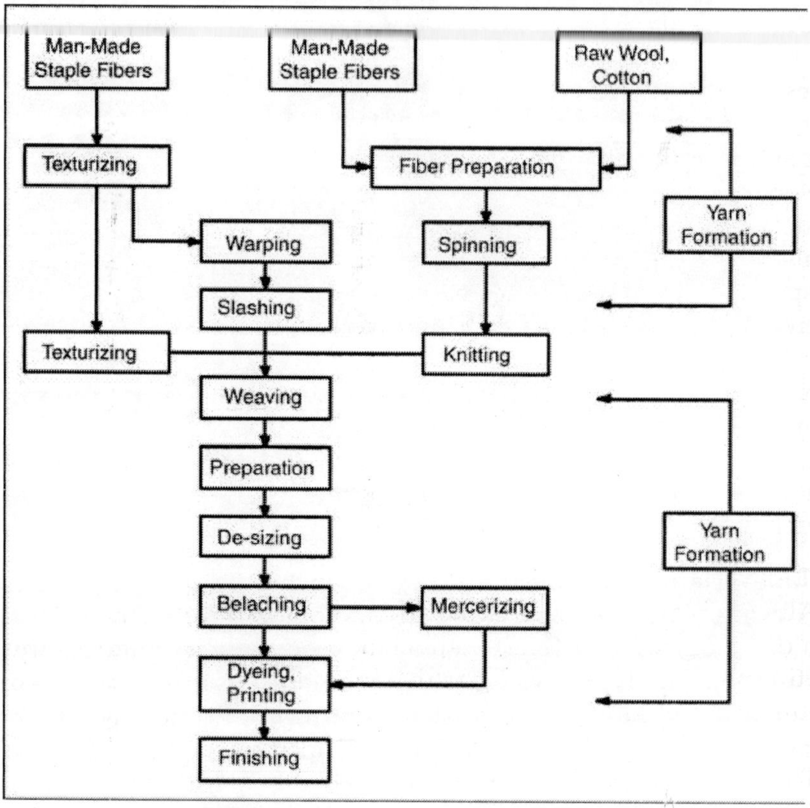

Fig.3.1: Various Steps Involved in Processing Textile in a Cotton Mill.

Table.3.1: *The Varieties of Common Used Fibre*

The Variety of Fibre	The Commonly Used Dyes
Cellulose fibre	Direct dyes, Reactive dyes, Vat dyes, Sulfide dyes, Azo dyes
Wool	Acid dyes
Silk	Direct dyes, Acid dyes
Polyester	Azo dyes, Disperse dyes
Polyester-cotton	Disperse/ Vat dyes, Disperse/Insoluble dye
polyacrylonitrile fibre	Cationic dyes, Disperse dyes
polyacrylonitrile fibre -wool	Cationic dyes, Acid dyes
vinylon	Direct dyes, Vat dyes, Sulfur dyes, Acid dyes

DIGITAL TEXTILE PRINTING

Digital textile printing, often referred to as direct to garment printing, DTG printing, and digital garment printing is a process of printing on textiles and garments using specialized or modified inkjet technology. Inkjet printing on fabric is also possible with an inkjet printer by using fabric sheets with a removable paper backing.

Today major inkjet technology manufacturers can offer specialized products designed for direct printing on textiles, not only for sampling but also for bulk production. Since the early 1990s, inkjet technology and specially developed water-based ink (known as dye-sublimation or disperse direct ink) has offered the possibility of printing directly onto polyester fabric. This is mainly related to visual communication in retail and brand promotion (flags, banners and other point of sales applications). Printing onto nylon and silk can be done by using an acid ink. Reactive ink is used for cellulose based fibers, such as cotton and linen. Using inkjet technology in digital textile printing allows for single pieces, mid-run production and even long-run alternatives to screen printed fabric.

OTHER METHODS OF PRINTING

Although most work is executed throughout by one or other of the seven distinct processes, combinations of them are frequently employed. Sometimes a pattern is printed partly by machine and partly by block; and sometimes a cylindrical block is used along with engraved copper-rollers in the ordinary printing machine.

The block in this latter case is in all respects, except that of shape, identical with a flat wood or coppered block, but, instead of being dipped in colour, it receives its supply from an endless blanket, one part of which works in contact with colour-furnishing rollers and the other part with the cylindrical block. This block is known as a surface or peg roller. Many attempts have been made to print multicolour patterns with surface rollers alone, but hitherto with little success, owing to their irregularity in action and to the difficulty of preventing them from warping. These defects are not present in the printing of linoleum in which opaque oil colours are used, colours that neither sink into the body of the hard linoleum nor tend to warp the roller.

'Inkjet Printing on Fabric' is a way anyone can print on fabric using their home printer. Specially treated Cotton, as well as various types of Bamboo and Silk fabric sheets, are available in various sizes. The fabric sheets have a paper backing which enable the fabric to go through the inkjet printer. Family photos printed on fabric are used to make memory quilts, pillows, notebook covers, wall hangings, ornaments and many other products.

The printing of yarns and warping is extensively practiced. It is usually carried on by a simple sort of surface printing machine and calls for no special mention. Lithographic printing, too, has been applied to textile fabrics with somewhat qualified success. Its irregularity and the difficulty of printing all over patterns to repeat properly, have restricted its use to the production of decorative panels, equal in size to that of the plate or stone, and complete in themselves.

Preparation of Cloth for Printing

Goods intended for calico printing ought to be exceptionally well-bleached, otherwise stains, and other serious defects, are certain to arise during subsequent operations. The Chemical preparations used for special styles will be mentioned in their proper places; but a general prepare, employed for most colours that are developed and fixed by steaming only, consists in passing the bleached calico through a weak solution of sulfated or turkey red oil containing from 21/2 per cent, to 5 per cent, of fatty acid. Some colours are printed on pure bleached cloth, but all patterns containing alizarine red, rose and salmon shades, are considerably brightened by the presence of oil, and indeed very few, if any, colours are detrimentally affected by it.

Apart from wet preparations the cloth has always to be brushed, to free it from loose nap, flocks and dust that it picks up whilst stored. Frequently, too, it has to be sheared by being passed over rapidly revolving knives arranged spirally round an axle, which rapidly and effectually cuts off all filaments and knots, leaving the cloth perfectly smooth and clean and in a condition fit to receive impressions of the most delicate engraving. Some figured fabrics, especially those woven in checks, stripes and crossovers, require very careful stretching and straightening on a special machine, known as a stenter, before they can be printed with certain formal styles of pattern which are intended in one way or another to correspond with the cloth pattern.

Preparation of Colours

The art of making colours for textile printing demands both chemical knowledge and extensive technical experience, for their ingredients must not only be properly proportioned to each other, but they must be specially chosen and compounded for the particular style of work in hand. For a pattern containing only one colour any mixture whatever may he used so long as it fulfils all conditions as to shade, quality and fastness; but where two or more colours are associated in the same design each must be capable of undergoing without injury the various operations necessary for the development and fixation of the others.

All printing pastes whether containing colouring matter or not are known technically as colours, and are referred to as such in the sequence. Colours vary considerably in composition. The greater number of them contain all the elements necessary for the direct production and fixation of the colour-lake. Some few contain the colouring matter alone and require various after- treatments for its fixation; and others again are simply mordants thickened. A mordant is the metallic salt or other substance that combines with the colouring principle to form an insoluble colour-lake, either directly by steaming, or indirectly by dyeing.

All printing colours require thickening, for the twofold object of enabling them to be transferred from colour-box to cloth without loss and to prevent them from running or spreading beyond the limits of the pattern.

Selecting Thickening Agents

The printing thickeners used depend on the printing technique and fabric and dyestuff used. Typical thickening agents are starch derivatives, flour, gum arabic, guar gum derivatives, tamarind, sodium alginate, sodium polyacrylate, gum Senegal and gum tragacanth, British gum or dextrine and albumen. Hot water soluble tickening agents as native starch are made into pastes by boiling in double or jacketed pans, between the inner and outer casings of which either steam or water may be made to circulate, for boiling and cooling purposes. Mechanical agitators are also fitted in these pans to mix the various ingredients together, and to destroy lumps and prevent the formation of lumps, keeping the contents thoroughly stirred up during the whole time they are being boiled and cooled to make a smooth paste. Most thickening agents used today are cold soluble and require only extensive stirring.

Starch Paste

This is made from wheat starch, cold water, and olive oil, and boiled for thickening. Non modified Starch was the most extensively used of all the thickenings. It is applicable to all but strongly alkaline or strongly acid colours. With the former it thickens up to a stiff unworkable jelly, while mineral acids or acid salts convert it into dextrine, thus diminishing its viscosity or thickening power. Acetic and formic acids have no action on it even at the boil. Today mostlymodified carboxymethylated cold soluble starches are used which have a stable viscosity and are easier to rinse out of the fabric and give reproducible "short" pasty rheology.

Flour paste is made in a similar way to starch paste. At the present time it is rarely used for anything but the thickening of aluminum and iron mordants. In the impressive textile traditions of Japan, several techniques using starch paste resists of rice flour have been perfected over several centuries.

Gums

Gum arabic and gum Senegal are both very old thickenings, but their expense prevents them from being used for any but pale delicate tints. They are especially useful thickenings for the light ground colours of soft muslins and sateens on account of the property they possess of dissolving completely out of the fibers of the cloth in the washing process after printing and have a long flowing, viscous rheology, giving sharp print and good penetration in the cloth. Today guar gum and tamarind derivates offer a cheaper alternative.

British gum or dextrin is prepared by heating starch. It varies considerably in composition sometimes being only slightly roasted and consequently only partly converted into dextrine, and at other times being highly torrefied, and almost completely soluble in cold water and very dark in colour. Its thickening power decreases and its gummy nature increases as the temperature at which good thickening with from 2 to 3 lb of gum to one gallon of water, but the darkest and most highly calcined require from 6 to lb per gallon to give a substantial paste. Between these limits all qualities are obtainable. The darkest qualities are very useful for strongly acid colours, and with the exception of gum Senegal, are the best for strongly alkaline colours and discharges. Like the natural gums, neither light nor dark British gums penetrate as well into the fiber of the cloth so deeply as pure starch or flour, and are therefore unsuitable for very dark strong colours.

Gum tragacanth, or Dragon, is one of the most indispensable thickening agents possessed by the textile printer. It may be mixed in any proportion with starch or flour and is equally useful for pigment colours and mordant colours. When added to starch paste it increases its penetrative power, adds to its softness without diminishing its thickness, makes it easier to wash Out of the fabric and produces much more level colours than starch paste alone. Used by itself it is suitable for printing all kinds of dark grounds on goods that are required to retain their soft clothy feel. A tragacanth mucilage may be made either by allowing it to stand a day or two in contact with cold water or by soaking it for twenty-four hours in warm water and then boiling it up until it is perfectly smooth and homogeneous. If boiled under pressure it gives a very fine, smooth mucilage (not a solution proper), much thinner than if made in the cold.

Starch always leave on the printed cloth somewhat harsh in feel (unless modified carboxymethylated starches are used) but are well suited to obtain very dark colours. Gum Senegal, gum arabic or modified guar gum thickening are yielding beautifully clear and perfectly even tints comparing to starch, but give lighter colours and are washedaway too much during the rinsing or washing of the printed fabric and are thuss less suited for very dark colours. (The gums are apparently preventing the colours from combining fully with the fibers.) So a printing stock solution is mostly a combination of modified starch and gum stock solutions usually made by dissolving 6 or 8 lb of either in one gallon of water.

Albumen

Albumen is both a thickening and a fixing agent for insoluble pigments such as chrome yellow, the ochres, vermilion and ultramarine. Albumen is always dissolved in the cold, a process that takes several days when large quantities are required. The usual strength of the solution is 4 lb per gallon of water for blood albumen, and 6 lb per gallon for egg albumen. The latter is expensive and only used for the lightest shades. For most purposes one part of albumen solution is mixed with one part of tragacanth mucilage, this proportion of albumen being found amply sufficient for the fixation of all ordinary pigment colours. In special instances the blood albumen solution is made as strong as 50 per cent, but this is only in cases where very dark colours are required to be absolutely fast to washing. After printing, albumen thickened colours are exposed to hot steam, which coagulates the albumen and effectually fixes the colours.

TEXTILE PRINTING

Textile printing is the process of applying colour to fabric in definite patterns or designs. In properly printed fabrics the colour is bonded with the fiber, so as to resist washing and friction. Textile printing is related to dyeing but, whereas in dyeing proper the whole fabric is uniformly covered with one colour, in printing one or more colours are applied to it in certain parts only, and in sharply defined patterns. In printing, wooden blocks, stencils, engraved plates, rollers, or silkscreens can be used to place colours on the fabric. Colourants used in printing contain dyes thickened to prevent the colour from spreading by capillary attraction beyond the limits of the pattern or design.

Traditional textile printing techniques may be broadly categorised into four styles:

- Direct printing, in which colourants containing dyes, thickeners, and the mordants or substances necessary for fixing the colour on the cloth are printed in the desired pattern.
- The printing of a mordant in the desired pattern prior to dyeing cloth; the colour adheres only where the mordant was printed.
- Resist dyeing, in which a wax or other substance is printed onto fabric which is subsequently dyed. The waxed areas do not accept the dye, leaving uncoloured patterns against a coloured ground.

Resist and discharge techniques were particularly fashionable in the 19th century, as were combination techniques in which indigo resist was used to create blue backgrounds prior to block-printing of other colours. Most modern industrialised printing uses direct printing techniques.

ORIGINS

Woodblock printing is a technique for printing text, images or patterns used widely throughout East Asia and probably originating in China in antiquity as a method of printing on textiles and laterpaper. As a method of printing on cloth, the earliest surviving examples from China date to before 220.

Textile printing was known in Europe, via the Islamic world, from about the 12th century, and widely used. However, the European dyes tended to liquify, which restricted the use of printed patterns. Fairly large and ambitious designs were printed for decorative purposes such as wall-hangings and lectern-cloths, where this was less of a problem as they did not need washing. When paper became common, the technology was rapidly used on that for woodcut prints. Superior cloth was also imported from Islamic countries, but this was much more expensive. The Incas of Peru, Chile and the Aztecs of Mexico also practiced textile printing previous to the Spanish Invasion in 1519; but owing to the imperfect character of their records before that date, it is impossible to say whether they discovered the art for themselves, or, in some way, learned its principles from the Asiatics.

During the later half of the 17th century the French brought directly by sea, from their colonies on the east coast of India, samples of Indian blue and white resist prints, and along with them, particulars of the processes by which they had been produced, which produced washable fabrics.

Technology

Textile printing was introduced into England in 1676 by a French refugee who opened works, in that year, on the banks of the Thames near Richmond. Curiously enough this is the first print-works on record; [This is an old story from a reference in the late 1800s but it has never been proven and is generally not believed to be the case any more. There are no French names on the list of fabric printers and dyers at that time. Later a few French Huguenots arrived but that was after the British had a flourishing calico printing industry established.] but the nationality and political status of its founder are sufficient to prove that printing was previously carried on in France. In Germany, too, textile printing was in all probability well established before it spread to England, for, towards the end of the 17th century, the district of Augsburg was celebrated for its printed linens, a reputation not likely to have been built up had the industry been introduced later than 1676.

As early as the 1630s, the East India Company was bringing in printed and plain cotton for the English market. By the 1660s British printers and dyers were making their own printed cotton to sell at home, printing single colours on plain backgrounds; less colourful than the imported prints, but more to the taste of the British. Designs were also sent to India for their craftspeople to copy for export back to England. There were many dyehouses in England in the latter half of the 17th century, Lancaster being one area and on the River Lea near London another.

Plain cloth was put through a prolonged bleaching process which prepared the material to receive and hold applied colour; this process vastly improved the colour durability of English calicoes and required a great deal of water from nearby rivers. Again, there were many dyehouses, the one I am most familiar with was that started by John Meakins, a London Quaker who lived in Cripplegate.

When he died, he passed his dyehouse to his son-in-law Benjamin Ollive, Citizen and Dyer, who moved the dye-works to Bromley Hall where it remained in the family until 1823 Ollive & Talwin, Joseph Talwin & Company, Talwin & Foster... Samples of their fabrics and designs can be found in many museums in England and the United States, including the Victoria and Albert Museum in London and the Smithsonian Copper-Hewett in New York.

On the continent of Europe the commercial importance of calico printing seems to have been almost immediately recognized, and in consequence it spread and developed there much more rapidly than in England, where it was neglected and practically at a standstill for nearly ninety years after its introduction.

During the last two decades of the 17th century and the earlier ones of the 18th new works were started in France, Germany, Switzerland and Austria; but it was only in 1738 that calico printing was first, practiced in Scotland, and not until twenty-six years later that Messrs Clayton of Bamber Bridge, near Preston, established in 1764 the first print-works in Lancashire, and thus laid the foundation of the industry. At the present time calico printing is carried on extensively in every quarter of the globe, and it is pretty safe to say that there is scarcely a civilized country in either hemisphere where a print-works does not exist.

From an artistic point of view most of the pioneer work in calico printing was done by the French; and so rapid was their advance in this branch of the business that they soon came to be acknowledged as its leading exponents. Their styles of design and schemes of colour were closely followed-even deliberately copied by all other European printers; and, from the early days of the industry down to the latter half of the 20th century, the productions of the French printers in Jouy, Beauvais, Rouen,

Alsace-Lorraine, &c., were looked upon as representing all that was best in artistic calico printing.

This reputation was established by the superiority of their earlier work, which, whatever else it may have lacked, possessed in a high degree the two main qualities essential to all good decorative work, viz., appropriateness of pattern and excellency of workmanship. If, occasionally, the earlier designers permitted themselves to indulge in somewhat bizarre fancies, they at least carefully refrained from any attempt to produce those pseudo-realistic effects the undue straining after which in later times ultimately led to the degradation of not only French calico printing design, but of that of all other European nations who followed their lead.

The practice of the older craftsmen, at their best, was to treat their ornament in a way at once broad, simple and direct, thoroughly artistic and perfectly adapted to the means by which it had to be reproduced. The result was that their designs were characterized, on the one hand, by those qualities of breadth, flatness of field, simplicity of treatment arid pureness of tint so rightly prized by the artist; and, on the other, by their entire freedom from those meretricious effects of naturalistic projection and recession so dear to the modern mind and so utterly opposed to the principles of applied art.

METHODS OF PRINTING

There are seven distinct methods at present in use for producing coloured patterns on cloth:

Hand Block Printing

This process, though considered by some to be the most artistic, is the earliest, simplest and slowest of all methods of printing. In this process, a design is drawn on, or transferred to, a prepared wooden block. A separate block is required for each distinct colour in the design. A blockcutter carves out the wood around the heavier masses first, leaving the finer and more delicate work until the last so as to avoid any risk of injuring it during the cutting of the coarser parts. When finished, the block presents the appearance of flat relief carving, with the design standing out.

Fine details are very difficult to cut in wood, and, even when successfully cut, wear down very rapidly or break off in printing. They are therefore almost invariably built up in strips of brass or copper, bent to shape and driven edgewise into the flat surface of the block. This method is known as coppering. To print the design on the fabric, the printer applies colour to the block and presses it firmly and steadily on the cloth, ensuring a good impression by striking it smartly on the back with a wooden mallet. The second impression is made in the same way, the printer taking care to see that it fits exactly to the first, a point which he can make sure of by means of the pins with which the blocks are provided at each corner and which are arranged in such a way that when those at the right side or at the top of the block fall upon those at the left side or the bottom of the previous impression the two printings join up exactly and continue the pattern without a break.

Each succeeding impression is made in precisely the same manner until the length of cloth is fully printed. When this is done it is wound over the drying rollers, thus bringing forward a fresh length to be treated similarly. If the pattern contains several colours the cloth is usually first printed throughout with one, then dried, and printed with the second, the same operations being repeated until all the colours are printed. Block printing by hand is a slow process it is, however, capable of yielding highly artistic results, some of which are unobtainable by any other method.

Perrotine Printing

The perrotine is a block-printing machine invented by Perrot of Rouen in 1834, and practically speaking is the only successful mechanical device ever introduced for this purpose. For some reason or other it has rarely been used in England, but its value was almost immediately recognized on the Continent, and although block printing of all sorts has been replaced to such an enormous extent by roller printing, the perrotine is still largely employed in French, German and Italian works. The construction of this ingenious machine is too complex to describe here without the aid of several detailed drawings, but its mode of action is roughly as follows: Three large blocks (3 ft. long by 3 to 5 in. wide), with the pattern cut or cast on them in relief, are brought to bear successively on the three faces of a specially constructed printing table over which the cloth passes (together with its backing of printers blanket) after each impression.

The faces of the table are arranged at right angles to each other, and the blocks work in slides similarly placed, so that their engraved faces are perfectly parallel to the tables. Each block is moreover provided with its own particular colour trough, distributing brush, and woollen colour pad or sieve, and is supplied automatically with colour by these appliances during the whole time that the machine is in motion.

The first effect of starting the machine is to cause the colour sieves, which have a reciprocating motion, to pass over, and receive a charge of colour from, the rollers, fixed to revolve, in the colour troughs. They then return to their original position between the tables and the printing blocks, coming in contact on the way with the distributing brushes, which spread the colour evenly over their entire surfaces. At this point the blocks advance and are gently pressed twice against the colour pads (or sieves) which then retreat once more towards the colour troughs.

During this last movement the cloth to be printed is drawn forward over the first table, and, immediately the colour pads are sufficiently out of the way, the block advances and, with some force, stamps the first impression on it. The second block is now put into gear and the foregoing operations are repeated for both blocks, the cloth advancing, after each impression, a distance exactly equal to the width of the blocks. After the second block has made its impression the third comes into play in precisely the same way, so that as the cloth leaves the machines it's fully printed in three separate colours, each fitting into its proper place and completing the pattern. If necessary the forward movement of the cloth can be arrested without in any way interfering with the motion of the block, san arrangement which allows any insufficiently printed impression to be repeated in exactly the same place with a precision practically impossible in hand printing.

For certain classes of work the perrotine possesses great advantages over the hand-block; for not only is the rate of production greatly increased, but the joining up of the various impressions to each other is much more exacting fact, as a rule, no sign of a break in continuity of line can be noticed in well- executed work. On the other hand, however, the perrotine can only be applied to the production of patterns containing not more than three colours nor exceeding five inches in vertical repeat, whereas hand block printing can cope with patterns of almost any scale and continuing any number of colours. All things considered, therefore, the two processes cannot be compared on the same basis: the perrotine is best for work of a utilitarian character and the hand-block for decorative work in which the design only repeats every 15 to 20 in. and contains colours varying in number from one to a dozen.

Engraved Copperplate Printing

The printing of textiles from engraved copperplates was first practiced in the United Kingdom by Thomas Bell in 1770. The presses first used were of the ordinary letterpress type, the engraved plate being fixed in the place of the type. In later improvements the well-known cylinder press was employed; the plate was inked mechanically and cleaned off by passing under a sharp blade of steel; and the cloth, instead of being laid on the plate, was passed round the pressure cylinder. The plate was raised into frictional contact with the cylinder and in passing under it transferred its ink to the cloth. The great difficulty in plate printing was to make the various impressions join up exactly; and, as this could never be done with any certainty, the process was eventually confined to patterns complete in one repeat, and was made obsolete by roller printing.

Roller Printing, Cylinder Printing, or Machine Printing

This elegant and efficient process was patented and worked by Bell in 1785 only fifteen years after his application of the engraved plate to textiles. Bell's first patent was for a machine to print six colours at once, but, owing probably to its incomplete development, this was not immediately successful, although the principle of the method was shown to be practical by the printing of one colour with perfectly satisfactory results. The difficulty was to keep the six rollers, each carrying a portion of the pattern, in perfect register with each other. This defect was soon overcome by Adam Parkinson of Manchester, and in 1785, the year of its invention, Bells machine with Parkinson's improvement was successfully employed by Messrs Livesey, Hargreaves, Hall & Co., of Bamber Bridge, Preston, for the printing of calico in from two to six colours at a single operation.

The advantages possessed by roller printing over other contemoporary processes were three: firstly, its high productivity, 10,000 to 12,000 yards being commonly printed in one day of ten hours by a single-colour machine; secondly, by its capacity of being applied to the reproduction of every style of design, ranging from the fine delicate lines of copperplate engraving and the small repeats and limited colours of the perrotine to the broadest effects of block printing and to patterns varying in repeat from I to 80 in.; and thirdly, the wonderful exactitude with which each portion of an elaborate multicolour pattern can be fitted into its proper place without faulty joints at its points of repetition.

Stencil Printing

The art of stencilling is very new. It has been applied to the decoration of textile fabrics from time immemorial by the Japanese, and, of late years, has found increasing employment in Europe for certain classes of decorative work on woven goods for furnishing purposes.

The sheet is now laid on the material to be decorated and colour is brushed through its interstices. It is obvious that with suitable planning an all over pattern may be just as easily produced by this process as by hand or machine printing, and that moreover, if several plates are used, as many colours as plates may be introduced into it. The peculiarity of stencilled patterns is that they have to be held together by ties, that is to say, certain parts of them have to be left uncut, so as to connect them with each other, and prevent them from falling apart in separate pieces.

For instance, a complete circle cannot be cut without its centre dropping out, and, consequently, its outline has to be interrupted at convenient points by ties or uncut portions. Similarly with other objects. The necessity for ties exercises great influence on the design, and in the hands of a designer of indifferent ability they may be very unsightly. On the other hand, a capable man utilizes them to supply the drawing, and when thus treated they form an integral part of the pattern and enhance its artistic value whilst complying with the conditions and the process.

For single-colour work a stencilling machine was patented in 1894 by S. H. Sharp. It consists of an endless stencil plate of thin sheet steel that passes continuously over a revolving cast iron cylinder. Between the two the cloth to be ornamented passes and the colour is forced on to it, through the holes in the stencil, by mechanical means.

Screen-printing

Screen printing is by far the most used technology today. Two types exist: rotary screen printing and flat (bed) screen printing. A blade squeezes the printing paste through openings in the screen onto the fabric.

PRINTING TECHNIQUE

A screen is made of a piece of mesh stretched over a frame. A stencil is formed by blocking off parts of the screen in the negative image of the design to be printed; that is, the open spaces are where the ink will appear on the substrate.

Before printing occurs, the frame and screen must undergo the pre-press process, in which an emulsion is 'scooped' across the mesh and the 'exposure unit' burns away the unnecessary emulsion leaving behind a clean area in the mesh with the identical shape as the desired image. The surface (commonly referred to as a pallet) that the substrate will be printed against is coated with a wide 'pallet tape'.

This serves to protect the 'pallet' from any unwanted ink leaking through the substrate and potentially staining the 'pallet' or transferring unwanted ink onto the next substrate. Next, the screen and frame are lined with a tape. The type of tape used in for this purpose often depends upon the ink that is to be printed onto the substrate. These aggressive tapes are generally used for UV and water-based inks due to the inks' lower viscosities. The last process in the 'pre-press' is blocking out any unwanted 'pin-holes' in the emulsion. If these holes are left in the emulsion, the ink will continue through and leave unwanted marks. To block out these holes, materials such as tapes, specialty emulsions and 'block-out pens' may be used effectively.

The screen is placed atop a substrate. Ink is placed on top of the screen, and a floodbar is used to push the ink through the holes in the mesh. The operator begins with the fill bar at the rear of the screen and behind a reservoir of ink. The operator lifts the screen to prevent contact with the substrate and then using a slight amount of downward force pulls the fill bar to the front of the screen. This effectively fills the mesh openings with ink and moves the ink reservoir to the front of the screen.

The operator then uses a squeegee (rubber blade) to move the mesh down to the substrate and pushes the squeegee to the rear of the screen. The ink that is in the mesh opening is pumped or squeezed by capillary action to the substrate in a controlled and prescribed amount, i.e. the wet ink deposit is proportional to the thickness of the mesh and or stencil. As the squeegee moves toward the rear of the screen the tension of the mesh pulls the mesh up away from the substrate (called snap-off) leaving the ink upon the substrate surface. There are three common types of screenprinting presses. The 'flat-bed', 'cylinder', and the most widely used type, the 'rotary'.

Textile items printed with multi-colour designs often use a wet on wet technique, or colours dried while on the press, while graphic items are allowed to dry between colours that are then printed with another screen and often in a different colour after the product is re-aligned on the press.

Most screens are ready for recoating at this stage, but sometimes screens will have to undergo a further step in the reclaiming process called dehazing. This additional step removes haze or "ghost images" left behind in the screen once the emulsion has been removed. Ghost images tend to faintly outline the open areas of previous stencils, hence the name.

They are the result of ink residue trapped in the mesh, often in the knuckles of the mesh (the points where threads cross). While the public thinks of garments in conjunction with screenprinting, the technique is used on tens of thousands of items, including decals, clock and watch faces, balloons, and many other products. The technique has even been adapted for more advanced uses, such as laying down conductors and resistors in multi-layer circuits using thin ceramic layers as the substrate.

Stenciling Techniques

A method of stenciling that has increased in popularity over the past years is the photo emulsion technique:

1. The original image is created on a transparent overlay, and the image may be drawn or painted directly on the overlay, photocopied, or printed with a computer printer, but making so that the areas to be inked are not transparent. A black-and-white positive may also be used (projected on to the screen). However, unlike traditional platemaking, these screens are normally exposed by using film positives.
2. A screen must then be selected. There are several different mesh counts that can be used depending on the detail of the design being printed. Once a screen is selected, the screen must be coated with emulsion and put to dry in a dark room. Once dry, it is then possible to burn/expose the print.

3. The overlay is placed over the screen, and then exposed with a light source containing ultraviolet light in the 350-420 nanometer spectrum.
4. The screen is washed off thoroughly. The areas of emulsion that were not exposed to light dissolve and wash away, leaving a negative stencil of the image on the mesh.

Another advantage of screenprinting is that large quantities can be produced rapidly with new automatic presses, up to 1800 shirts in 1 hour. The current speed loading record is 1805 shirts printed in one hour, documented on 18 February 2005. Maddie Sikorski of the New Buffalo Shirt Factory in Clarence, New York (USA) set this record at the Image Wear Expo in Orlando, Florida, USA, using a 12-colour M&R Formula Press and an M&R Passport Automatic Textile Unloader. The world speed record represents a speed that is over four times the typical average speed for manual loading of shirts for automated screen printing.

Screen Printing Materials

Caviar beads: a glue is printed in the shape of the design, to which small plastic beads are then applied – works well with solid block areas creating an interesting tactile surface. Cracking ink: the ink produces a cracked surface after drying. Discharge inks: used to print lighter colours onto dark background fabrics, they work by removing the dye in the garment – this means they leave a much softer texture. They are less graphic in nature than plastisol inks, and exact colours are difficult to control, but especially good for distressed prints and underbasing on dark garments that are to be printed with additional layers of plastisol.

- *Expanding ink (puff):* an additive to plastisol inks which raises the print off the garment, creating a 3D feel.
- Flocking: consists of a glue printed onto the fabric and then foil or flock (or other special effect) material is applied for a mirror finish or a velvet touch.
- Four colour process or the CMYK colour model: artwork is created and then separated into four colours (CMYK) which combine to create the full spectrum of colours needed for photographic prints. This means a large number of colours can be simulated using only 4 screens, reducing costs, time, and set-up. The inks are required to blend and are more translucent, meaning a compromise with vibrancy of colour.
- *Glitter/Shimmer:* metallic flakes are suspended in the ink base to create this sparkle effect. Usually available in gold or silver but can be mixed to make most colours.

- *Metallic:* similar to glitter, but smaller particles suspended in the ink. A glue is printed onto the fabric, then nanoscale fibers applied on it.
- *Plastisol:* the most common ink used in commercial garment decoration. Good colour opacity onto dark garments and clear graphic detail with, as the name suggests, a more plasticized texture. This print can be made softer with special additives or heavier by adding extra layers of ink. Plastisol inks require heat (approx. 150°C (300°F) for many inks) to cure the print.
- PVC and Phthalate Free: relatively new breed of ink and printing with the benefits of plastisol but without the two main toxic components. Has a soft texture.
- Suede Ink: Suede is a milky coloured additive that is added to plastisol. With suede additive you can make any colour of plastisol have a suede feel. It is actually a puff blowing agent that does not bubble as much as regular puff ink. The directions vary from manufacturer to manufacturer, but generally up to 50% suede can be added to normal plastisol.
- Water-Based inks: these penetrate the fabric more than the plastisol inks and create a much softer feel. Ideal for printing darker inks onto lighter coloured garments. Also useful for larger area prints where texture is important. Some inks require heat or an added catalyst to make the print permanent.

Versatility

Screenprinting is more versatile than traditional printing techniques. The surface does not have to be printed under pressure, unlike etching orlithography, and it does not have to be planar. Different inks can be used to work with a variety of materials, such as textiles, ceramics, wood, paper, glass, metal, and plastic.

As a result, screenprinting is used in many different industries, including:

- Balloons
- Clothing
- Decals
- Medical devices
- Printed electronics, including circuit board printing
- Product labels
- Signs and displays
- Snowboard graphics
- Textile fabric
- Thick film technology

Semiconducting Material

In screen printing on wafer-based solar photovoltaic (PV) cells, the mesh and buses of silver are printed on the front; furthermore, the buses of silver are printed on the back. Subsequently, aluminum paste is dispensed over the whole surface of the back for passivation and surface reflection. One of the parameters that can vary and can be controlled in screen printing is the thickness of the print. This makes it useful for some of the techniques of printing solar cells, electronics etc.

One of the most critical processes to maintain high yield. Solar wafers are becoming thinner and larger, so careful printing is required to maintain a lower breakage rate. On the other hand, high throughput at the printing stage improves the throughput of the whole cell production line.

Screen Printing Press

To print multiple copies of the screen design on garments in an efficient manner, amateur and professional printers usually use a screen printing press. Many companies offer simple to sophisticated printing presses. Most of these presses are manual. A few that are industrial-grade-automatic printers require minimal manual labour and increase production significantly.

PRODUCTION OF TEXTILE INDUSTRY POLLUTION

Textile Printing and dyeing processes include pre-treatment, dyeing and printing, finishing. The main pollutants are organic matters which come from the pre-treatment process of pulp, cotton gum, cellulose, hemicellulose and alkali, as well as additives and dyes using in dyeing and printing processes. Pre-treatment waste water accounts for about 45% of the total, and dyeing/printing process waste water accounts for about 50%~55%, while finishing process produces little. In China, chemical fibre accounts for about 69% of total in which polyester fibres accounts for more than 80%. Cotton accounts for 80% of the natural fibre production. Therefore, the dyeing waste water analysis of production and pollution is based on these two fibres. Pre-treatment of cotton includes desizing and scouring.

The main pollutants are the impurities in the cotton, cotton gum, hemicellulose and the slurry, alkali in weaving process. The current average COD concentration in the pre-treatment is 3000 mg/L. The main pollutants in dyeing/printing are auxiliaries and the residual dyes. The average concentration of COD is 1000 mg/L and the total average concentration is 2000 mg/L after mixing. Pre-treatment of polyester fibres mainly involves in the reduction with alkali. The so-called reduction is treating the polyester fabric with 8% of sodium hydroxide at 90 °C for about 45 minutes. Some polyester fabrics will peel off and decompose into terephthalic acid and ethylene glycol so that a thin polyester fabric will have the feel of silk. This process can be divided into continuous and batch type.

Taking the batch type as an example, the concentration of COD is up to 20000 mg/L-60000 mg/L. The waste water from reduction process may account for only 5% of the volume of waste water, while COD accounts for 60% or more in the conventional dyeing and finishing business. The chroma is one pollutant of the waste water which causes a lot of concerns. In the dyeing process, the average dyeing rate is more than 90%. It means that the residual dyeing rate in finishing waste water is about 10%, which is the main reason of contamination.

According to the different dyes and process, the chroma is 200 to 500 times higher than before. pH is another factor of the dyeing waste water. Before the printing and the dyeing process, pH is another factor,the pH of dyeing waste water remains between 10 to 11 when treated by alkali at high temperature around 90°C in the process of desizing, scouring and mercerization. Polyester base reduction process mainly uses sodium hydroxide, and the total pH is also 10 to 11. Therefore, most dyeing water is alkaline and the first process is to adjust the pH value of the textile dyeing waste water.

The total nitrogen and ammonia nitrogen come from dyes and raw materials, which is not very high, about 10 mg/L. But the urea is needed while using batik techniques. Its total nitrogen is 300 mg/L, which is hard to treat. The phosphorus in the waste water comes from the phosphor detergents. Considering the serious eutrophication of surface water, it needs to be controlled. Some enterprises use trisodium phosphate so that the concentration of phosphorus will reach 10 mg/L.

So, this phosphorus must be removed in the pre-treatment. In the production process, suspended substance comes from fibre scrap and undissolved raw materials. It will be removed through the grille, grid, etc. The suspended solids (SS) in the outflow mainly come from the secondary sedimentation tank, whose sludge has not been separated completely which will reach 10-100 mg/L as usual. Sulfide mainly comes from the sulfur, which is a kind of cheap and qualified dye.

Due to its toxicity, it has been forbidden in developed countries. However, in China, some enterprises are still using it, so it has been included in the waste water standards. The sulfide in the waste water is about 10 mg/L. There are two main sources of hexavalent chromium. Cylinder engraving makes the waste water containing hexavalent chromium.

However, this technology has not been used. Another possible source is the use of potassium dichromate additive in hair dyeing process. Aniline mainly comes from the dyes. The colour of the dye comes from the chromophore. Some dyes have a benzene ring, amino, etc., which will be decomposed in the waste water treatment process. The potential specific pollutants from textile Printing and dyeing is shown in Table.

Table.3.2: Specific Pollutants from Textile and Dyeing Processing Operations

Process	Compounds
Desizing	Sizes, enzymes, starch, waxes, ammonia. Disinfectants and insecticides residues, NaOH, surfactants,
Scouring	soaps, fats, waxes, pectin, oils, sizes, anti-static agents, spent solvents, enzymes.
Bleaching	H2O2, AOX, sodium silicate or organic stabiliser, high pH.
Mercerizing	High pH, NaOH
Dyeing	Colour, metals, salts, surfactants, organic processing assistants, sulphide, acidity/alkalinity, formaldehyde.
Printing	Urea, solvents, colour, metals.
Finishing	Resins, waxes, chlorinated compounds, acetate, stearate, spent solvents, softeners.

TEXTILE DYEING WASTE WATER RISK

Discharged waste water by some industries under uncontrolled and unsuitable conditions is causing significant environmental problems. The importance of the pollution control and treatment is undoubtedly the key factor in the human future. If a textile mill discharges the waste water into the local environment without any treatment, it will has a serious impact on natural water bodies and land in the surrounding area. High values of COD and BOD5, presence of particulate matter and sediments, and oil and grease in the effluent causes depletion of dissolved oxygen, which has an adverse effect on the aquatic ecological system.

Effluent from textile mills also contains chromium, which has a cumulative effect, and higher possibilities for entering into the food chain. Due to usage of dyes and chemicals, effluents are dark in colour, which increases the turbidity of water body. This in turn hampers the photosynthesis process, causing alteration in the habitat.

BIOCHEMICAL AND PHYSICOCHEMICAL COMBINATION PROCESSES

In recent years, as the application of new technologies in textile and dyeing industry, a large number of difficult biodegradable organic matter such as PVA slurry, surface active agents and new additives enter into the dyeing waste water, which result in the high concentration of the organic matter, complex and changeable composition and the obvious reduction of the biodegradability. The COD_{Cr} removal rate of the simple aerobic activated sludge process which was used to treat the textile dyeing waste water has decreased from 70% to 50%, and the effluent can not meet the discharge standards.

More seriously, quite a number of sewage treatment facilities can't normally operate even stop running. Therefore, the biochemical and physicochemical combination processes has been gradually developed. And its application is increasingly widespread. The types of the combination process are various, and the main adoptions currently are as following:

Hydrolytic Acidification-contact Oxidation-air Floatation Process

This combination process is a typical treatment process of the textile dyeing waste water, which is widely used. The waste water firstly flows through the bar screen, in order to remove a part of the larger fibres and particles, and Then flows into the regulating tank. After well-distributed through a certain amount of time, the sewage flows into the hydrolysis acidification tank to carry out the anaerobic hydrolysis reaction.

The reaction mechanism is making use of the anaerobic hydrolysis and acidification reaction of the anaerobic fermentation to degrade the insoluble organic matter into the soluble organic matter by controlling the hydraulic retention time. At the same time, through cooperating with the acid bacteria, the macromolecules and difficult biodegradable organic matter would be turned into biodegradable small molecules, which provide a good condition for the subsequent biological treatment.

Next, the sewage enters into the biological contact oxidation tank. After the biochemical treatment, the waste water directly enters into the flotation tank for flotation treatment, which is adopted the pressurized fulldissolved air flotation process.

The polymer flocculants added in flotation tank react with the hazardous substances, which can condense the hazardous substances into tiny particles. Meanwhile, sufficient air is dissolved in the waste water. And then the pressure suddenly is released to produce uniformly fine bubbles, which would adhere to the small particles.

The density of the formation is less than 1kg/m^3, which can make the formation float and achieve the separation of the solid and liquid. The anaerobic hydrolysis acidification tank equipped with semi-soft padding and the biological contact oxidation tank equipped with the new SNP-based filler. The following physicochemical treatment uses the dosing flotation tank, which has four characteristics. Firstly, the deciduous biofilm and suspended solids removal rate can reach 80% to 90%. Secondly, the colour removal rate can reach 95%.

Due to its toxicity, it has been forbidden in developed countries. However, in China, some enterprises are still using it, so it has been included in the waste water standards. The sulfide in the waste water is about 10 mg/L. There are two main sources of hexavalent chromium. Cylinder engraving makes the waste water containing hexavalent chromium

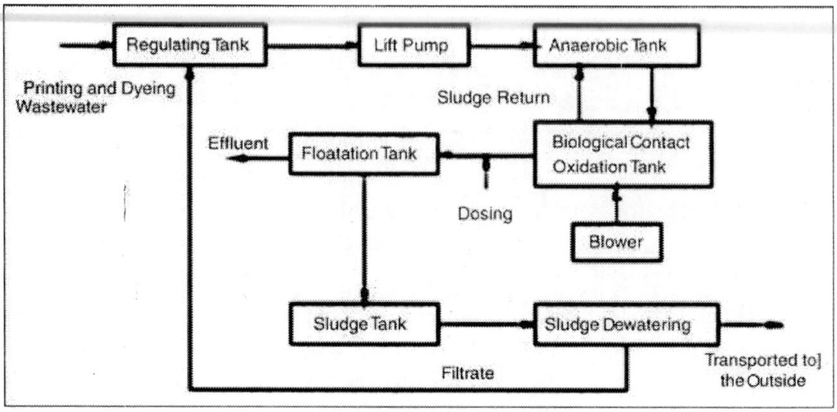

Fig. The Process Flow Diagram

Thirdly, the hydraulic retention time in the flotation tank is short, which is only about 30 min, while the precipitation tank is about 1.15 h to 2 h, so the volume and area of the flotation tank is small. Finally, the sludge moisture content is low, only about 97% to 98%, which can be directly dewatered. But the flotation treatment need an additional air compressor, pressure dissolved gas cylinders, pumps and other auxiliary system. The operation and management is also relatively complicated. After the treatment of this process, the COD_{Cr} removal rate can be up to 95% or more. The actual effluent quality is about: pH=6~9, colour<100times, SS<100mg/L, BOD 5 <50mg/L, COD_{Cr}<150mg/L (Honglian Li, 2006).

Anaerobic-aerobic-biological Carbon Contacts

The treatment process is a mature and widely used process in waste water treatment in recent years. The anaerobic treatment here is not the traditional anaerobic nitrification, but the hydrolysis and acidification. The purpose is aiming at degrading some poorly biodegradable polymer materials and insoluble material in textile dyeing waste water to small molecules and soluble substances by hydrolysis and acidification, meanwhile, improving the biodegradability and $BOD5/COD_{Cr}$ value of the waste water in order to create a good condition for the subsequent aerobic biological treatment.

At the same time, all sludge generated in the aerobic biological treatment return into the anaerobic biological stage through the sedimentation tank. Because of the sludge in the anaerobic biochemical stage has sufficient hydraulic retention time (8h~10h) to carry out anaerobic digest thoroughly, The whole system would not discharge sludge, that is the sludge achieve its own balance (Note: only a small amount of sludge accumulate in the anaerobic stage, but do not have to set up a special sludge treatment plant).

Anaerobic tank and aerobic tank are both installed media, which is a biofilm process. Biological carbon tank is filled with activated carbon and provided oxygen, which has the characteristics both of suspended growth method and fixation growth method. The function of pulse water is mixing in the anaerobic tank.

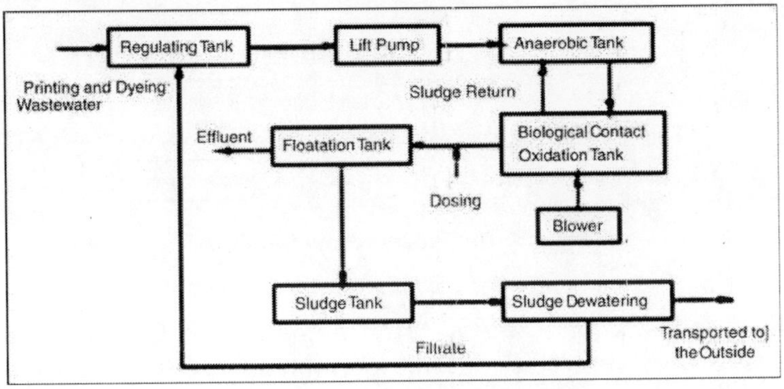

Fig.3.2: The Process Flow Diagram

The hydraulic retention time of various parts is about:

- *Regulating tank:* 8h~12h; anaerobic biochemical tank: 8h~10h
- *Aerobic biochemical tank:* 6 ~8h; biological carbon tank: 1h~2h
- *Pulse generator interval:* 5min~10min.

According to the textile dyeing waste water standard ($COD_{Cr} \leq$ 1000mg/L), the effluent can achieve the national emission standards, which can be reused through further advanced treatment. For the five years operation project, the results show that the operation is normal, the treatment effect is steady, there is no efflux of sludge and the sludge was not found excessive growth in the anaerobic biochemical tank.

Coagulation-ABR-oxidation Ditch Process

The treatment has been adopted widely currently, such as a textile dyeing waste water treatment plant in Jiangmen of Guangdong Province. The characteristics of the textile dyeing plant effluent are the variation in water, the higher of the alkaline, colour and organic matter concentration, and the difficulty of the degradation (BOD_5/COD_{Cr} value is about 0.25). The workshop waste water enter into the regulating tank by pipe network to balance the quantity and quality, after wiping off the large debris by the bar screen before the regulating tank. The adjusted waste water flow into the coagulation reaction tank, at the same time, the $FeSO_4$ solution was added into it to carry out chemical reaction. Finally, the effluent flows into the primary sedimentation tank for spate separation, meanwhile enhancing the BOD_5/COD_{Cr} ratio.

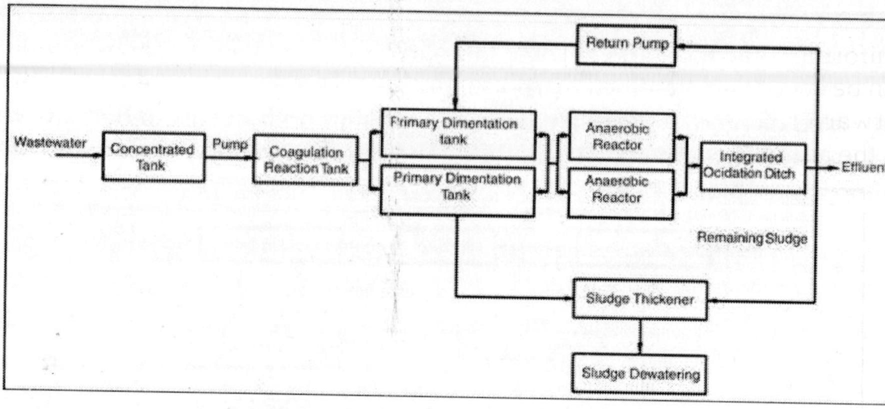

Fig.3.3: The Process Flow Diagram

The effluent of primary sedimentation tank flows into the anaerobic baffled reactor (ABR) by gravity. After the anaerobic hydrolysis reaction, it enters into the integrated oxidation ditch for aerobic treatment, and then goes into the secondary sedimentation tank for spate separation. The upper liquid was discharged after meeting the standards, but the settled sludge was returned to the return sludge tank, most of which was returned to ABR anaerobic tank by pump. The remaining sludge was pumped to the sludge thickening tank for concentration. Since the using of this sewage treatment process, the treatment effect is stable. The removal rate of each index is high.

Table.3.3: Average Quality of Each Process Effluent

Process	PH	CODcr (mg/L)	BOD5 (mg/L)	SS (mg/L)	Colour (times)
Waste water	9-13	1800-2000	400-500	250-350	500
Coagulation effluent	6-9	1327	344	157	102
ABR effluent	6-9	532	292	94	48
Aerobic secondly sedimentation effluent	6-9	80	15	14	30

UASB-Aerobic-Physicochemical Treatment Process

For the high pH value dyeing waste water treatment systems, we should adjust the pH value to the range from 6 to 9 before entering the treatment system. While towards the difficultly biodegradable textile dyeing waste water, effective measures should be taken to increase the biodegradability. At the same time, the volume of the regulating tank must be increased (this is repeatedly demonstrated in engineering practice) to guarantee the water quantity, quality and colour achieving a relatively uniform towards changeable dyeing waste water. Good inflow condition can be created for following process though this method. Therefore, we put forward the "UASB-aerobic-physicochemical method" treatment process in the actual project, and the technological process is shown in Fig.

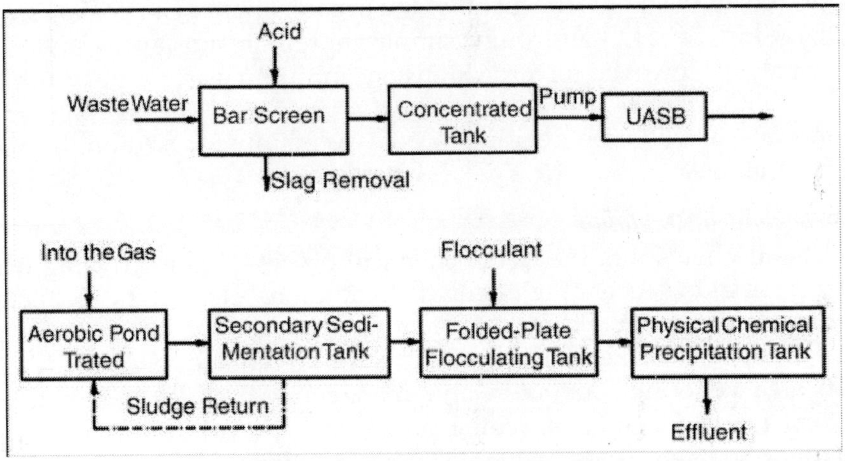

Fig.3.4: The Process Flow Diagram

At present, the treatment process has been applied in a number of textile dyeing factory, such as a Jiangyin textile dyeing factory, which sewage component is complex. Before the sewage enters into the regulating tank, the suspended particles in which must be removed by bar screen, at the same time, an appropriate amount of acid was added to adjust the pH value of the sewage. Then adjusting the water quantity and quality to make it uniformed.

After pretreatment, the textile dyeing waste water carries out anaerobic reaction firstly in UASB reactor to improve the biodegradability of waste water and the decolorization rate, and then flows into the aerobic tank. In the aerobic tank, the organic matter in sewage is removed. Finally, in order to ensure the effective removal of the suspended particles particular the activated sludge, some flocculants was added in the sedimentation tank to improve its effect.

CUTTING-EDGE TREATMENT PROCESS

Photochemical Oxidation

Photochemical oxidation has many advantages of the mild reaction conditions (ambient temperature and pressure), powerful oxidation ability and fast speed, etc. It can be divided into 4 kinds, which are light decomposition, photoactivate oxidation, optical excitation oxidation and photocatalysis oxidation. Among them, the photocatalysis oxidation has been more researched and applied currently. This technology can effectively destroy a lot of organic pollutants whose structure is stable and difficult to biologically degrade. Compared with the physical treatment in traditional waste water treatment process, the most obvious advantages of this technology are significant energy efficiency, completely pollutants degradation and so on. Almost all of the organic matter can be completely oxidized to CO_2, H_2O and other simple inorganic substances under the light catalyst. However, towards high concentration waste water, the effect of the photocatalysis oxidation process is not ideal. The research about photocatalysis oxidation degradation of dye mainly focused on the study of photocatalyst.

Electrochemical Oxidation

The mechanism of the electrochemical process treating dyeing waste water is making use of electrolytic oxidation, electrolytic reduction, electrocoagulation or electrolytic floating destruct the structure or the existence state to make it bleached. It has the advantages of small devices, small area covering, operation and management easily, higher COD_{Cr} removal rate and good bleaching effect, but the precipitation and the consumption of electrode material is great, and the operating cost is high.

The traditional electrochemical methods can be divided into power flocculation, electrical float, electro-oxidation, micro-electrolysis and the electrolysis method. With the development of electrochemical technologies and the appearing of a variety of highefficiency reactor, the cost of treatment will decrease largely. Electro-catalytic advanced oxidation process (AEOP) is a new advanced oxidation technology developed recently. Because of its high efficiency, easy operation, and environmental friendliness, it has attracted the attention of researchers. Under normal temperature and pressure, it can produce hydroxyl radicals directly or indirectly through the reactions in the catalytic activity electrode, thus the degradation of the difficultly biodegradable pollutants is effective. It is one of the main directions in future research.

Ultrasonic Technology

Using ultrasonic technology can degrade chemical pollutants, especially the refractory organic pollutants in water. It combines the characteristics of advanced oxidation technology, incineration, supercritical water oxidation and other waste water treatment technologies. Besides the degradation conditions are mild, degradation speed is fast and application widely, it can also use individually or combined with other water treatment technologies. The principle of this method is that the sewage enters into the air vibration chamber after being added the selected flocculants in regulating tank.

Under the intense oscillations in nominal oscillation frequency, a part of organic matter in waste water is changed into small organic molecule by destructing its chemical bonds. The flocculants flocculation rapidly companied with the colour, COD_{Cr} and the aniline concentration was fall under the accelerating thermal motion of water molecules, which play the role of reducing organic matter concentration in waste water. At present, the ultrasonic technology in the research of water treatment has achieved great achievements, but most of them are still confined to laboratory research level.

High Energy Physical Process

Highenergyphysicalprocessisanewwastewatertreatmenttechnology. When the highenergy particle beam bombard aqueous solution, the water molecules would come up with excitation and ionization, produce ions, excited molecules, secondary electrons. Those products would interact with each other before spreading to the surrounding medium. It would produce highly reactive HO• radicals and H atoms, which would react with organic matter to degrade it. The advantages of using high-energy physics process treat dyeing waste water are the small size of the equipment, high removal rate and simple operation. However, the device used to generate high energy particle is expensive, technically demanding is high, energy consumption is big, and the energy efficiency is low and so on. Therefore, it needs a lot of research work before put into actual project.

ASPECTS OF ROBOTIC MATERIALS HANDLING IN TEXTILES

By the time of the Bronze Age, looms had been invented that used many rigid materials, such as wood and horn, to position warp yarns in a more or less stationary configuration so that one could more efficiently insert the filling amongst the warps to produce the woven textile. Whorls and spindles had been invented to help in the forming of yarn and its packaging. The over-all processes of textile manufacturing had become sufficiently institutionalized to where textile manufacture was a treat fireside routine engaged in by members of the family, mainly the females.

These textile-making processes included the transfer of the crude fiber into yarns, initially with the aid of the whorl at the spinning wheel. The yarns then were placed into the hand loom as warps and later onto the bobbins that were loaded in the shuttle, which was thrown backwards and forwards through the yarns of the warp shed to insert the filling into the fabric. The primary power related to this operation involved the human effort of beating up the yarn thus inserted into the fabric which, in turn, was wound up onto the takeoff device. As the art of weaving progressed, it soon became apparent that more yarns were required to supply a loom installation than could be made by a single family.

A loom at the hearthside needed a large number of daughters constantly engaged in the production of yarn to keep the fabric production from the loom at the level needed by the family needs. This state of affairs obtained largely up to the inception of the Industrial Revolution.

There was, however as tonishing time when a premature motion towards a factory workplace occurred in ancient Rome. It was related to the production of woollen goods mainly for togas, wherein women from various households met collectively in a workplace to produce yarn and woollen fabric for clothing of the citizens of Rome. This movement was interrupted with the fall of the Empire and it needed several hundreds of years to elapse before this early movement towards the factory, was to become the generally accepted way of life. The reintroduction, of the workplace at the end of the Middle Ages sparked the renewal of the movement towards the modern industrial society.

As the introduction of a factory workplace was renewed by the Industrial Revolution, the factory quickly became related to a region with easy access, to power to run axles, which in turn gave some of the energy for yarn twisting and for loom operation especially filling insertion and the beating up of the filling as it was inserted into the warp sheet.

The factory provided the requisite space allocation for yarn production so that a balanced production could be achieved. In France and other parts of Western Europe, spinning halls were introduced for the specific making of yarn, in which young girls were utilised as labourers. They kept production rates uniform among a large number of spinning positions by timing their wheels as they sang multipart rounds, such as "Pop Goes the Weasel."

As this extra space was given, so too were mechanisms for the handling of the yarn and conveying it from a point of manufacture to a point of use, that is, the point of insertion into the fabric. While much human labour was still utilized in connection with the early factories of the textile industry, the development of factories took place in concert with the introduction of nonhuman handling devices wherever technological ingenuity was sufficient.

It is this feature of the early textile workplace that contained the germ of automation and robotics as we know the processes today. By the time that Jacquard looms had developed to the point where one could produce highly- patterned woven tapestries utilising machinery, the textile manufacturing process had been integrated with what were, in crux, early computers; these machines utilised punched cards to give the complex motions that were imposed upon the loom heddles.

With this programmed control of weaving machinery, figured tapestries and brocades were obtained which, in few cases, closely approximated the finer handwrought works of art that had been produced mainly in the nunneries of Western Europe. With the expansion of manufacturing processes immediately preceding World War II and throughout that period, techniques were perfected for using labour together with advanced machines in the creation of rudimentary "self-thinking" processes.

It was a fairly simple matter to devise lathes and grinding machines with human operators for the production of cylindrical shaped objects, live projectiles and machine screw threads. A simple extension of this process rapidly evolved in which the product was formed automatically and then transferred to an inspection station that confirmed the precision of the production. On the ground of a "go/no-go" measurement, the product was either accepted within a given channel or, failing the "go" measurement, transferred into a reject channel.

It was a simple matter at that point to automatically transfer the product back to the manufacturing site and subject the item to reshaping if that were feasible. Those items which were produced outside appropriate tolerance levels were, of course, rejected permanently. It was not a difficult matter to extend the go/no-go production inspection scheme to the point where the role of the human operator was progressively minimized to that of an overseer, who made sure that the automatic setting and conveying steps in the processes were operating properly in their appropriate sequence.

From this kind of process development, it was a relatively short time until there was developed not merely a go/no-go inspection surveillance of'the production, but instruments that could be utilised to measure chemical and/ or mechanical disturbances outside of an accepted tolerance. The measurement was utilised to activate appropriate mechanisms to move the process back within accepted tolerances. The role of the human was thus removed from the production process, and what several have termed the second industrial revolution was clearly recognized.

The second industrial revolution produced devices which replaced not only the muscle of man, as took place at the starting of the first industrial revolution but also replaced man's mental capacity and ability to follow with appropriate non-human mechanisms, so that now the production essentially was completely automatic. A "generalized robot" had been built to replace man's immediate role in the processes of manufacture, In the textile industry, one of the first clearcut examples of this total replacement involved the recognition of off-specification product quality.

The process was equipped with a means for "feeding-back" that recognition to a station which adjusted the controls so as to obtain the needed specification. This early textile process control involving feedback is found in the control of temperature and of size bath concentration, which are used to coat the warp yarns to be used in the loom. This kind of process control with its inherent feedback and essentially labour-free character was clearly in place by the end of the 1950s.

By this time the, second industrial revolution was gathering momentum throughout America. In the textile sector again, semi-automatic production control, developed in small steps in connection with production of synthetic yarns, gives a second example of production with feedback control. This took place in connection with the control of the viscose dope in the production of viscose filaments. In the art of filament handling, there are a number of processes that comprise the maneuvering of filaments after processing to further enhance the yarn-like character of the filament product. This involves the processes of texturizing which, in general, again involve not only automatic handling, but also a programmable sequence of temperatures that is imposed on the yarn as it is maneuvered through the processing equipment in order to achieve the desired snarled, interlaced, character. Such machines are elaborate robot factories.

They not merely handle material and call for various thermal treatments of it, but they can be programmed to produce a great variety of processes, thus giving the textile manufacturer an enormous inventory of yarn-like items made completely from the synthetic filament technology of the 20th century. Also in the case of filament yarns, a bundle of filaments appropriately interlaced by means of air jets produces a structure that can be subjected to twisting, plying or air texturizing to produce a looped and whorled structure that can be plied, plaited and/or twisted further.

This yields a continuous filament structure that has surface characteristics resemble to those of the conventionally spun yarn produced from staple fiber. Along with these developments of filament technology, newer types of spinning processes have evolved, comprising conventional staple products. The open-end spinning process involves the introduction of staple fiber by means of an air stream into a yarn forming chamber that provides intermingling between the filaments and a twisting of the product to produce a yarn which is similar to more conventionally spun yarns.

The primary mechanisms in these machines with their robotic characteristics are due to European manufacturers of textile machinery. The beginning of these processes comprises suction cups or mechanical fingers that can be moved over the surfaces of the fiber bale to progressively "eat" the material off the bale and convey it through air handling passages to the card. The product of the carding and drawing prodesses is fed into the open-end spinning machinery. All of these instances give rise to a certain perspective concerning the current art in the handling of textile materials.

It has attempted to give not only a retrospective review of many aspects of the production of textiles, but also to indicate that, as the history of textile production has unfolded, the introduction of advanced machinery occurred. Ultimately that machinery was such that it performed in several aspects as if it were "thinking", so as to produce a product without the advantage of essential human labour.

This is a somewhat more complex view of the robot than that discussed. Accordingly, one is forced to consider that a highly articulated mechanical device with appropriate sensing elements to permit it to "see" as well as to "think" perhaps is only a simplification of the more modern production techniques which will develop in the future.

In the textile industry it is already feasible to see places where the robot and the production mechanism may be thoroughly integrated. Regarding certain modern plants the conventional spinning frame is encircled by a travelling device which has articulated motion and is capable of sensing whether or not a given yarn is broken or a bobbin has been filled.

At these times the device plucks the filled bobbin and places it on a conveying belt to the production output station or ties up the ends which have broken as a consequence of a failure in the spinning process. Alternatively, mechanical devices for conveying yarn packages to looms can be seen in the automatic guided vehicle inevitably small cars moving on a track operated electronically by computers. These are activated when the loom senses that it is about to run out of yarn supply, and an inventory system is tapped automatically.

The necessary yarn is placed upon the car, which then is sent in response to the request of the loom station to that loom where the yarn is required to sustain continued production. A variation of this process, using much of the same equipment, is activated when the loom has produced a full beam of fabric, at which time the loom is doffed and the finished fabric rolled onto the conveying trolley and transported to the production shipping point. This process can be realised as integrated into a finishing or other later processing plant.

All of this more highly integrated production turns the total plant into a complicated robot which consumes raw material at its receiving dock in the form of fiber or filament and manipulates it through mechanical conveyance and sensing stations, the results of which are fed into computers which iii turn activate extra conveying and moving devices to manipulate the fiber into yarn and ultimately into fabric. The prime human content of all of this is that of the overseer of the process.

From the economic point of view, this new-labour factor (that of the robot factory) has a fixed cost with 'a particular maintenance requirement, and the new human labour need involved in the production is now that of a more complex reasoner or decision maker who monitors the overall activity of the production unit.

The opportunity for this decision maker to engage in entrepreneurial activity is comparatively limited, but there still is an essential and major difference in this human labour input, compared with that of the labour that operated factories at the beginning of the Industrial Revolution.

The second industrial revolution has, in fact, separated that which is machine-like from that which is intellectually more stimulating from human labour content; it has permitted the human component to perform in a somewhat more elevated environment and transferred the drudgery of the process to that of a nonhuman robot slave. The techniques for the production of material things underwent a substantial change at the starting of the first Industrial Revolution. The first revolution can be thought of as the introduction of automatic transfer of power from process unit to process unit conveying work material from machine to machine, or performing automatically certain work tasks utilizing a power source which is available in the workplace.

The second revolution culminates in the recognition of automatic devices which are programmable to stimulate through feedback loops several aspects of this power transmission to complete process modifications upstream of the sensing measurement. In this sense the two industrial revolutions can be thought of as end-points of a scale of production which has been incessantly varying throughout history from the first toward the second. The manner in which human labour is used has changed substantially. In the starting it needed the collection of workers from their homes into the factory workplace and the organization of these workers within the scheme of production.

The second revolution leads to a displacement of several of the worker positions in the production process but introduces the need for more highly skilled service employees to keep the process operating at the desired level. In the earliest phases of robot introduction into textile processes much of the traditional yarn making and weaving process details are maintained in the newer technological scheme, and the automatic devices with their feedback loops are simply embroidered around the existing processes, thereby reducing the number of human labourers that earlier were employed in the chain of production.

Devices for the automatic retying of yarn ends on spinning frames where breaks have occurred at particular spindles represents one of the simplest instances of the substitution of automatic equipment for human labour. In recent past, robot-like devices with limited articulation have been mounted on carriages which move around spinning frames and offer not only automatic relying of broken ends, but also give doffing and the starting of spinning by the throwing on of yarn onto an empty take up package.

In this way the production of yarn can be made entirely automatic from sliver to the wound-up package. It in turn can be conveyed automatically to a next stage in the production chain. Extra robots are under development that will permit the packaged yarn to be picked up from a supply source and conveyed from the point of yarn manufacture to the point of use within a weaving or knitting process or the like.

The robot transfers the yarn, puts it into the next stage of the textile production chain and starts the production process. These motions need substantial amounts of movement through space and a series of sensing devices that control the subsequent motions. Another textile-related aspect of the second industrial revolution is found in the elaborate automation involved in the maintenance of material inventories. As an example, a picking device can traverse a predetermined set of fiber bales to produce the essential tufts and convey them aerodynamically to the card for the formation of sliver which is then fed into spinning devices, for instance, open-end spinning processes.

The automatic feeding of these devices can be structured in such a way that one can sample statistically the contents of a series of bales so as to achieve the eventual in blending from a given supply of baled staple fiber. Similarly in the case of continuous filament yams it is feasible to receive at the input of a factory site the large cheeses or straight wound packages, which are transferred to a series of trolleys. When an appropriate encoding is provided at the loading station these convey the yarn to an appropriate spot within the inventory area, to be withdrawn on demand. Such production units are now available wherein hundreds of looms can be found on a given weaving shed floor with relatively small amounts of human labour, on the order of ten workers per 300 looms.

The looms are regularly supplied on demand by trolleys working from an inventory containing the necessary yarn components for the fabrics being woven within the factory at a given time. The human labour content is primarily that of correcting various weaving errors which originate from yam irregularities and giving machine maintenance. In some cases this minimal labour force must sense the approaching need of a given machine for input supplies and signal that need to the inventory delivery system. This type of automatic production of necessity needs either the automatic sensing that a beam has been filled with woven fabric or that the pirn supply for the feeding of the shuttles is running low and needs resupply. All of the processes briefly alluded to above represent textile processes that have developed through the first and second industrial revolutions and thereby contain a minimum of human labour. Further, labour which is inherent to the processes tends to be of a rather very trained and sophisticated variety.

Individuals must understand the nature of the automatic sensing devices and the feedback loops, and the controls which are passed through such loops, as the processes for self regulation continue to operate throughout the production cycle. Further the complex mechanical and electrical mechanisms which are included in this production system comprise both elementary mechanisms and highly sophisticated electronic and electromechanical devices. One can quickly infer from this that the processes for programming these processes are indeed complex and comprise a complicated set of inputs which can and are changed from time to time as the production is tuned towards higher and higher quality levels or towards greater and greater productivity with some acceptable fault level.

Automation Activity

Due to the attention being provided to Japanese automation activity, an impression exists that United States sewn products and equipment industries are not active in trying to improve productivity through automation. This is not true. Since the 1960s there have been a variety of attempts to attack both particular and common joining problems. Joining limp fabric semi- automatically or automatically presents a variety of problems which have been and are a constant challenge to equipment manufacturers and the industry as a whole. It is almost not possible to detail the wide variety of efforts which have been made in this area.

Basically it appears that the Japanese have proceeded to collect patent information worldwide, organize it and make an orderly assault on creating a sewing system. In making this assault, teams of government technicians, university staffs and industry engineers roamed the world gathering main sewing system information. A high proportion of what they are studying is of U.S. origin. Why then haven't the American engineers mechanics innovators succeeded in developing a sewing system? What have they been doing all this time? What do they require to achieve success?

New Techniques of Sewing

Assembling apparel, shoes, tents, curtains, furniture and auto seat covers are but a few of the several activities in which thread or thread substitutes are utilised to join seams. Joining parachute. seams represents a substantial difference in handling techniques than joining a styled outerwear jacket even though both products may use the same material and kind of joining equipment.

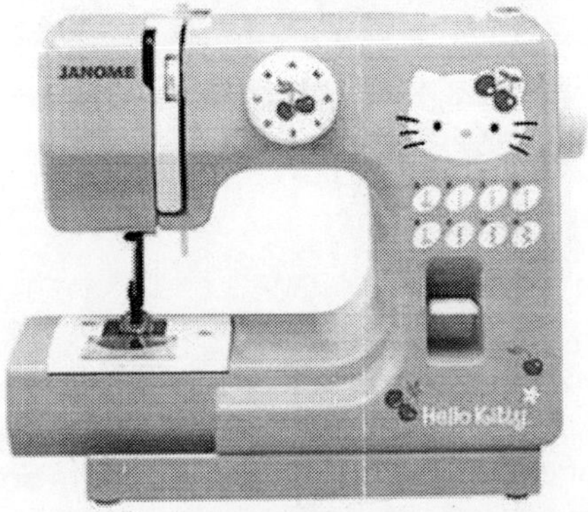

Fig.3.5: New Techniques of Sewing

As joining activities are investigated, the response to solving problems tends to become product oriented. That is, the problems of assembling a product are fragmented into a series of digestable steps. Ordinarily, production people and industrial engineers solve assembly problems by copying the way they have been earlier solved. Equipment firms provide a quick reference point for establishing sewing production lines. When production lines are set up under time restraints, the opportunity for creative innovation is limited. The sewn products industries have consistently sought to provide better equipment to satisfy both individual and broad industry needs. Modifications of equipment generated by the mechanic/innovator to solve readily problems are often incorporated into later versions of that equipment by the equipment manufacturer.

Handsewing, either actual or with machines, which requires highly skilled operators may be perceived as either a problem or an opportunity to seek solutions. Solutions have tended to create particular equipment, sometimes of limited general usefulness.

Adding of Feeds

The Federal Stitch Catalog lists a succession of alternative stitch formations in common use. Machine suppliers compound this complexity by adding a variety of feed and material handling mechanisms. Needle suppliers give a wide range of alternate shapes and sizes for use on different products and materials. Accessory suppliers display a wide range of folders and button handlers to enhance material handling and joining quality. Joining is a highly complex activity which deals not only with several equipment alternatives but also with problems of seam strength, decorative stitching, and in some cases, the creation of air tight seams.

When the complexities of sewn joining are considered in a world of changing fibers, fabrics, wovens, non-wovens, knit and molded goods, it is not surprising that fully automated factories have yet to develop in the sewn products industries. But, this does not imply that some steps toward a higher level of automation have not occurred. The problem is being studied.

Handling

Probably the most frustrating facet of joining parts together evolves from the wide variety of materials used in creating sewn products. A substantial portion of existing equipment activity is devoted to developing or improving existing material handling devices.

Almost every study proves that moving and positioning materials to, under, and away from the joining process is the chief labour time-consumer within the sewn industries. The Japanese Apparel Automation Project selected thirty material pick-up devices for study in their "System J" project. Twenty- one of these devices were patented in the USA, five in West Germany, two in Great Britain and two in Japan.

From this study, a new technique comprising of a modified pick-up device and "stiffening of material" was developed. What is significant in this study, insofar as the American apparel industry is concerned, is that better than two- thirds of all the inventions considered in this report were developed in the United States. The Japanese preliminary study represents a relatively small portion of all the handling devices which might be used for bringing together and positioning parts to be sewn, bonded or otherwise joined. Omitted are overhead and belt conveyors, sensors and switches, indexing equipment and several other devices, in full or pertial use within the sewn products industry.

Matching

Matching one part to another in the joining process is being approached by the machine industry in a variety of ways. Most of the methods use an operator to feed a clamp or clamping point which in turn actuates a series of positioning and joining actions. These semi-automated activities are controlled, cam and electronic controlled, or electronic controlled. Because the methods use equipment to actuate the joining operations, an operator can generally handle more than one machine. Skill levels are reduced while productivity is increased. In some cases a series of activities are combined in one sewing centre. Pieces of equipment are combined to do more than one sewing operation or to accomplish intricate jobs semi-automatically.

Methods of Accomplishing

As properties of materials change, the methods of accomplishing product design features also change, While there is nothing new in shaping materials through steaming, pressing, stretching or moulding the characteristics of several materials allow for a broader use of these techniques today. Moulding of products ranges from bra cups through wet suits to automobile seat covers. Several of the moulding or shaping techniques include adhesive supporting materials to improve joining bonds and to improve retention of shape. When these techniques are considered as significant displacement of other sewing activities, another range of complexity faces the designer/production/ engineering activity.

Shaping or forming products instead of sewing them has seen broader use over the past 15 years, and is achieving increasing acceptance. Items like slacks, uniforms and dresses have been formed in whole or in part. Patents have been granted in the United States, Great Britain, West Germany, Japan and Czechoslovakia for making semi-complete and complete garments. Techniques as varied as spot welding by heating a bow on lingerie through utilising sound to cut buttonholes are starting to achieve acceptance. Mixture of natural and manmade fibers offer the innovative designer opportunities to create new looks and better products through the use of moulding and bonding techniques.

Limited Production

Most sewing products firms are small and tend to produce limited volumes of goods for splintered markets. Tiny firms with limited management are not likely to make investments in equipment research and development. The fragmentation of this industry is, in itselt, a barrier to joint equipment manufacturer luser efforts. The sewn products industries represent a low investment sector of the economy. seldom no investment is made in equipment; the manufacturer rents it. In this environment of small, diverse users catering to limited markets, high speed and high volume equipment has a doubtful market. Sewn products research and development activity is largely conducted by the chief sewn products firms.

This R&D generally takes one or more of four forms:

- In-house R&D,
- In cooperation with an equipment firm,
- Employment of a research firm capable of producing a prototype
- Employing a university.

Two other forms of R&D investigative activity have been sponsored by apparel and equipment firms:

- The Technical Advisory Committee (TAC) which comprises members of American Apparel Manufacturers Association (AAMA)
- The now defunct Apparel Research Foundation (ARF) which consisted of 375 dues-paying members and which received some R&D money from the Government.

Apparel Research and Development R&D

Apparel R&D tends to be cyclical and specific. Departments are created and funded when business is good. Projects are generally highly product oriented, usually devoted to either improving quality, reducing cost or both. A high proportion of these projects are basically short term in nature. This kind of R&D can often lead to a competitive edge in the market place. Generally, the risk of investing in this kind of R&D is relatively low since targets tend to be specific, limited in scope and well planned. In the earlier example of separating, picking up and positioning materials, 21 of the patents reviewed by the Japanese were U.S. patents.

One patent was held by a research firm, one by an individual, and the rest by equipment firms. Review of patent records in other areas indicates a similar pattern of activity. It should be kept in mind that several large firms, such as Farah and Haggar, do not usually seek patents yet pursue a reasonably active R&D programme.Besides, several smaller firms whose mechanic/ innovator develops a device pass the item to an equipment firm to receive a production item. This increases the equipment firm's patent volume and reduces the activity attributable to the sewn products industries.

Used Equipment Firm Cooperation Firm

This form of R&D again is generally specifically directed at an opportunity. The user is a major prospect for the equipment firm, but ordinarily the equipment firm also perceives a market beyond the user. Projects evolving from user/equipment firm cooperation provide for user testing and user first call on the equipment. Success in these joint ventures has been spotty, with most of it in the area of combining jobs. Probably the best known joint venture is that of Union Special and Cluett/ Pfaff in developing semi-automatic assembly of shirts. This venture covered a span of several years and resulted in several innovative machines which are now on the market.

There were some ideas which did not work out at that time, primarily because the electronics were not available. In recent year, Kellwood/Union

Special, Lee/Jet Sew, and Haynes/Union Special provide a sample of firms working together on specific problems ranging from automatic bottom hemming to combining three jobs into one. Both development and failures resulted. However, most of the projects obtain most of the objectives.

DYES APPLIED TO FIBRE CLASSES

Dyes for Cellulosic Fibres

Cellulosic fibres can be dyed readily using a number of dye classes. The less crystalline regenerated cellulosics dye more readily than the more crystalline natural cellulosic fibres such as cotton. Cellulosics can be dyed or printed using direct, reactive, basic, vat, sulfur, or azoic dyes. Cellulosics can also be coloured using pigment-binder systems. Mordanting of direct and basic dyes on cellulosics improves overall fastness. Since the hydroxyl groups in cellulosics are less reactive than many functional groups found in protein fibres, reactive dyes such as the dichlorotriazine or dichloroquinoxaline dyes are often used on cellulosic fibres due to their higher reactivity. The general stability of cellulosic fibres to basic solutions permits them to be effectively dyed by vat, sulfur, and azoic dyes without significant damage.

Dyes for Cellulose Ester Fibres

Acetate and triacetate fibres can be effectively dyed using disperse dyes. The rate of dyeing is more rapid with the more hydrophobic triacetate fibres than with acetate. Under special conditions, azoic and vat dyes may be used to dye these fibres. Acetate fibres also have affinity for selected acid and direct dyes. Since acetate loses its luster above 85°C, dyeings must be carried out at or below this temperature. Addition of pigments or solvent-soluble dyes to the acetate or triacetate spinning "dope" prior to fibre spinning leads to coloured fibres possessing excellent colourfastness, although the colours available are limited.

Dyes for Protein Fibres

Protein fibres are the most readily dyed fibres due to the numerous reactive functional groups present. They can be dyed with a wide range of dyes under acid, neutral, or slightly basic conditions. Since the keratin fibres are less crystalline and oriented than secreted fibres such as silk, they tend to dye more rapidly and more readily to deeper shades. Under acid conditions amino groups in the protein fibres are protonated to form NH; groups. In this form, they are able to attract dyes containing acid anions including acid, direct, mordant, and reactive dyes. Special premetallised acid dyes of sufficient solubility are used to dye protein fibres to fast colours.

The functional groups available in protein fibres are more reactive than hydroxyl groups in cellulosic fibres. Reactive dyes of more limited reactivity have been developed especially for protein fibres. Protein fibres complex very readily with multivalent metalcations. Acid dyes and mordant dyes may be rendered very fast by mordanting with metal salts, and chromium salts are especially effective as mordants. At neutral or slightly acid pH, protein fibres may be dyed with cationic or basic dyes; however, the fastness of the dyed fibre is poor without mordanting with tannic acid or other mordants for cationic dyes.

Azoic and vat dyes find only limited use on protein fibres due to the damaging effect that basic solutions of these dyes have on protein fibres. Sulfate esters of reduced vat dyes can be used effectively on protein fibres, however. Natural dyes from many sources have good affinity for protein fibres and are used extensively in the crafts area and often in conjunction with mordants.

Dyes for Polyamide Fibres

With the exception of the aramid fibres, the polyamides dye readily with a wide variety of dyes. Since the polyamides contain both acid carboxylic and basic amino end groups and have a reasonably high moisture regain, the fibres tend to dye like protein fibres such as wool and silk. Since the molecular structure is somewhat more hydrophobic, more regular, and more densely packed in the polyamides than in protein fibres, they also exhibit to some degree the dyeing characteristics of other synthetic fibres such as polyesters and acrylics.

Due to their highly regular molecular structure and dense chain packing, the aramid fibres resemble polyester and are dyed only by small dye molecules such as disperse dyes. Polyamides such as nylon 6, 6,6, and Qiana can be readily dyed with dyes containing anionic groups, such as acid, metallised acid, mordant dyes, and reactive dyes and with dyes containing cationic groups such as basic dyes.

Acid dyes on nylon can be mordanted effectively for additional fastness; however, the colourfastness of basic dyes is poorer and more difficult to stabilise by mordanting. Vat and azoic dyes can be applied to nylons by modified techniques, and polyamides can be readily dyed by disperse dyes at temperatures above 80°C. Aramids can only be dyed effectively with disperse dyes under rigourous dyeing conditions. The biconstituent fibre of nylon and polyester can be effectively dyed by several dye types due to the nylon component, but for deep dyeings disperse dyes are preferred. Nylon 6 and 6,6 are produced in modifications that are light, medium, or deep dyeable by acid dyes or specially dyeable by cationic dyes.

Dyes for Polyester Fibres

Owing to their high crystallinity and hydrophobicity, the polyester fibres are extremely difficult to dye by normal dyeing techniques unless the fibre has been modified, as in the case of modified terephthalate polyesters. A limited amount of polyester is solution dyed through incorporation of dye or pigment into the polymer melt prior to spinning. It is more common to use this technique to incorporate fluorescent brightening agents into polyester. Only smaller, relatively nonpolar dye molecules can effectively penetrate polyester; therefore disperse dyes have been the dye class of choice for the fibre. Azoic dyes and pigment-binder systems have also found limited use on polyesters. Polyester modified with appropriate comonomers can be dyed at lower temperatures or with acid or basic dyes depending on the nature of the modifying groups.

Dyes for Acrylic Fibres

The nature and distribution of acrylonitrile and comonomer or comonomers in the acrylic fibres affect the overall dyeability and the classes of dyes that may be used in dyeing these fibres. Both acrylic and modacrylic fibres can be dyed using disperse dyes, with the more hydrophobic and less crystalline modacrylic being more dyeable with this dye class. The polar cyanide groups in the acrylonitrile unit of these fibres have some affinity for acid dyes and particularly mordanted systems containing copper or chromium ions. Addition of an acid or basic comonomer such as acrylic acid or vinyl pyridine as comonomer imparts improved dyeability with basic and acid dyes, respectively, for these fibres. Vat dyes can be used on acrylic fibres to a limited extent.

Dyes for Polyolefin Fibres

Polyolefin fibres are hydrophobic, and the molecular chains within the fibre are tightly packed. Therefore it is extremely difficult to dye polyolefin fibres or to increase their affinity to dyes. Coloured inorganic salts or stable organometallic pigments have been added to the polymer melt prior to fibre spinning to colour the fibres. Also, nonvolatile acids or bases or materials such as polyethylene oxides or metal salts have been added to the polymer prior to fibre formation to increase the affinity of the fibre for disperse, cationic, acid, or mordant dyes. Polyolefin fibres can be chemically grafted with appropriate monomers after fibre formation to improve their dyeability.

Dyes for Vinyl Fibres

The vinyl fibres, with the exception of vinal and vinyon-vinal matrix fibres, are extremely hydrophobic and difficult to dye, and consequently they can be dyed only through pigmentation of the polymer melt before fibre formation or through dyeing with disperse dyes. Vinal and vinyon-vinal matrix fibres dye readily with dyes used on cellulosics including direct, mordant, reactive, vat, and sulfur dyes.

Dyes for Elastomeric Fibres

Since the elastomeric fibres are often a component in the core of blended yarns, colouration is not important in all applications. Rubber fibres cannot be dyed readily and are coloured through mixing of pigments into the rubber prior to extrusion into fibres. Spandex fibres are more dyeable and can be dyed with acid, reactive, basic, or vat dyes. Anidex can be dyed with disperse or basic dyes. The nylon component of spandexnylon fibres can readily be dyed with acid, basic, disperse, or vat dyes.

Dyes for Mineral and Metallic Fibres

The mineral and metallic fibres are essentially undyeable, and special techniques must be used to impart colour to the fibres. Thermally stable ceramic pigments can be added to molten glass prior to fibre formation, or pigment- binder systems may be applied to the surface of the mineral and metallic fibres. Glass fibres can also be sized with a protein which then can be insolubilised and dyed with conventional protein dyes. Glass fibres are coloured by coronising, which involves preheating of the glass substrate to high temperatures to remove all organic materials followed by colouration with a pigment-binder system. The metallic fibres may also be coloured through anodising the metal filament present or through pigmentation- of the plastic layer coating the metal. The nature of the metal in the organometallic fibres determines their ultimate colour.

APPLICATION METHODS AND FACTORS AFFECTING DYEING

Dyes may be applied to textile structures in a number of ways and at a number of points within the textile construction process. Dyeing or printing techniques can be used. Dyeing methods involve application of dye solutions to the textile, whereas printing can be considered a specialised dyeing technique. In printing the concentration of dye is higher, and the dye medium is thick and viscous to limit dye migration on the fabric, permitting formation of a design or pattern.

Fibre or stock dyeing involves dyeing of the loose fibres or fibre top or sliver before yarn formation. Colourants can be added to man-made polymers before they are formed into fibres to ensure uniform colouration throughout the fibre. This technique is referred to as "solution" or "dope dyeing." Yarns or skeins can be dyed, and piece dyeing of textile fabrics can be carried out. Resist techniques such as tie-dyeing or batik limit dye migration to certain parts of the fabric.

Discharge processes use bleaches or other chemicals to remove dye from selected areas of a dyed or printed fabric. The above processes are used for application of dyes to textile substrates in the form of fibre sliver or top, yarn, or fabric by batch or continuous methods. Fibre or stock dyeing of sliver or top is usually conducted in large vats with movement of the dye liquor through the fibres to assure intimate contact of the dye liquor with the fibres. Yarn or skein dyeing is conducted by suspending skeins of yarn in an agitated dyebath with possible additional movement of the skeins during dyeing.

Yarns can also be wound as packages on perforated spindles or spools and immersed in the dyebath. The dye liquor is then circulated back and forth through the packages. Fabric rolls can also be dyed by this package dye technique. Package dyeing is often carried out in closed systems at elevated temperatures and pressures. Jig dyeing involves passage of a fabric piece back and forth from one spindle to another through a dyebath, whereas a dye beck containing a winch is used to move a continuous fabric piece through the dye liquor. The techniques are all batch processes.

The pad-batch method is a specialised batch technique for application of reactive dyes to cellulosic fibres. In the pad-batch method, cellulosic fabric is passed through a concentrated solution of reactive dye, followed by storage of the wet fabric in a vapor tight enclosure for 24 to 48 hours at room temperature, to permit time for diffusion and reaction of the dye with the fabric substrate prior to washing off unreacted dye. The process leads to significant energy savings compared to conventional processes. Various specialised techniques have been developed for application of disperse dyes to polyester. Unless the dyeing is carried out at 100 °C or above, the rate of dyeing is very slow.

Dyeing with disperse dyes from aqueous solutions at 120°-130°C to achieve rapid dyeings is common but requires the use of closed high-pressure equipment. Recently, jet dyeing has been introduced, which permits not only high-temperature dyeing but also impingement of the dye onto the moving fabric through use of a venturi jet system. Also, carriers can be introduced to permit dyeing of polyester at atmospheric pressure and below 100°C. Carriers are usually aromatic organic compounds that can be emulsified in water and which have affinity for the polyester.

The carriers penetrate the polyester, open up the molecular structure of the fibre, and aid in passage of the disperse dye across the dye solutionfibre interface and within the fibre. Suitable carriers include aromatic hydrocarbons such as diphenyl and methyl naphthalene, phenolics such as the di- and trichloro-benzenes, aromatic esters including methyl salicylate, butyl benzoate, and diethylphthalate, and benzaldehydes. Carriers must be removed after dyeing, and the presence of carriers in mill effluents presents a problem because of their toxicity. Continuous dyeing is carried out on a dyeing range where fabric or carpet is continuously passed through a dye solution of sufficient length to achieve initial dye penetration.

The dye on the fabric or carpet is fixed by subsequent s teaming of the substrate. Recently, foamed dye formulations have been applied to fabrics, thereby effectively reducing the dye liquor to fabric ratio and reducing energy and effluent treatment costs. A novel approach to continuously dyeing polyester with disperse dyes involves sublimation of disperse dye under heat and partial vacuum into polyester by the technique called "thermosol dyeing." Polyester containing disperse dye applied to the fibre surface is heated near 200°C under partial vacuum for a short period of time.

At this temperature, the molecular motion within the polyester is high, permitting the dye vapor to penetrate into the fibre. On cooling, the disperse dye is permanently trapped and fixed within the fibre. The above processes are graphically represented in figure.

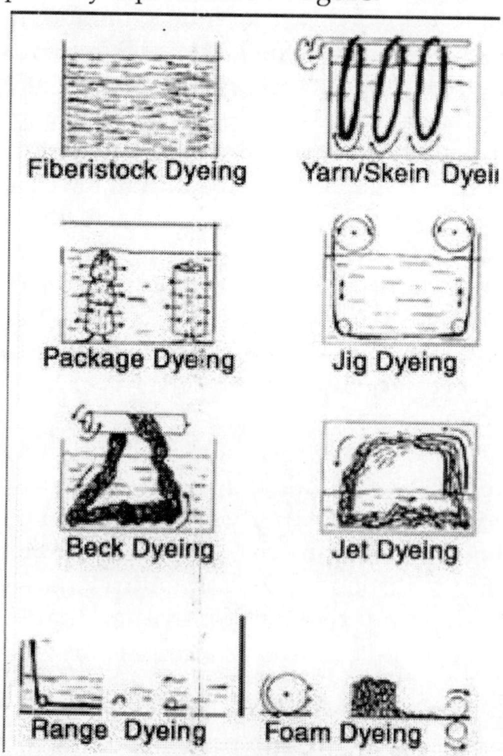

Fig. Dyeing Processes.

In printing, the printing paste is applied through use of direct transfer dye using a block or engraved roller or through application using a partially marked flat or rotary screen and squeegee system. Printing of polyester by disperse dyes can be accomplished by heat transfer printing, which is a modification of thermosol dyeing. In this process disperse dyes are printed onto paper followed by bringing the polyester fabric and printed paper together under pressure with sufficient heating to cause diffusion of disperse dyes into the polyester. Block, flat screen, and heat transfer processes are batch processes, whereas engraved roller and rotary screen printing are continuous processes.

Special techniques using dyeing solutions which give printed style fabrics have been developed. In these processes, multiple jets of different dye solutions are sprayed in programmed sequence onto the fabric as it passes under the jets to form patterns with definition very nearly 1ike that of prints. Specialised techniques for formation of patterns on carpets have been developed. In one process dye solution is metered and broken or cut into a pattern of drops which are allowed to drop on a dyed carpet passing underneath to give a diffuse overdyed pattern on the carpet. Representations of the printing and printed style processes are found in figure.

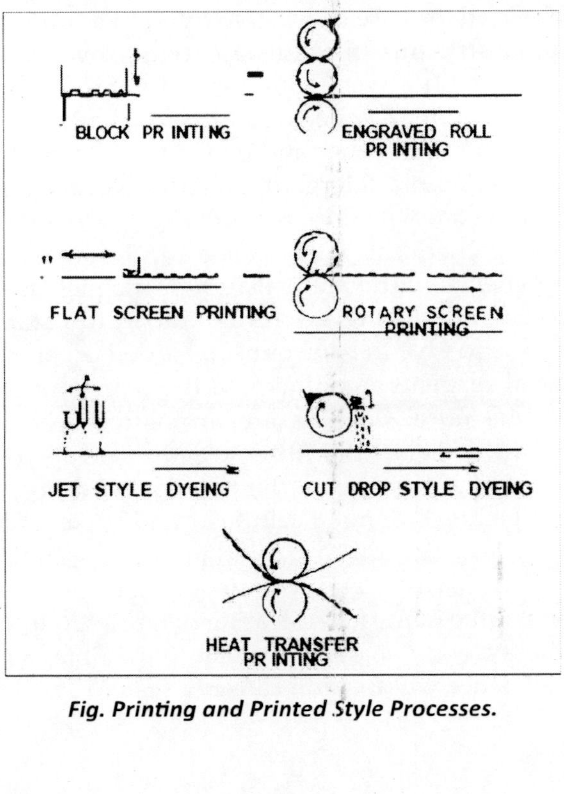

Fig. Printing and Printed Style Processes.

Physical factors such as temperature and agitation and auxiliary chemicals added to the dyebath or printing paste can alter the rate of dyeing and/or the total dye absorbed by the fibre. In dyeing, the rate of dyeing of the fibre is dependent on the rate of migration of dye in solution to the fibre surface, the rate of diffusion of dye at the fibre interface, and the rate of diffusion of dye in the fibre matrix. Agitation of the dyebath effectively eliminates the effect of dye diffusion to the fibre in the dyebath.

The rate of dye passage across the fibre-liquid interface is rapid in most cases; therefore the rate of dyeing is solely determined by the rate of dye movement within the fibre matrix. As the temperature of dyeing is raised, the rate of "strike" of dye onto the fibre and diffusion in the fibre increases, whereas the total amount of dye present in the fibre at equilibrium decreases. In other words, heating a dyebath speeds dyeing but decreases the total dye exhausted on the fabric.

Dyeing is usually carried out at a temperature above the glass transition temperature of the fibre, since the molecular segments of the polymers within the fibre have more mobility and permit more rapid dye diffusion above that temperature. A number of chemical reagents are added to the dyebath to alter in some manner the course of dyeing.

Acids or bases may be added to the dyebath to induce charge formation in the fibre in order to increase dye diffusion or to promote reaction of the dye with the fibre as in the case of reactive dyes. In addition, bases may be used to open up the structure of cellulosics to improve dyeing or to aid in dissolving of vat and sulfur dyes. Common inorganic salts such as sodium chloride or sodium sulfate may be added to a dyebath and act as leveling agents to retard the rate of dyeing and give a more even dyeing. Surface-active agents such as anionic detergents can act as leveling agents and also permit the rapid and complete fibre wetting needed to give even dyeing.

Water softening chemicals such as sodium hexameta-phosphate are added to bind or chelate hardwater calcium or magnesium ions that may interfere with dyeing. Reducing agents are added to vat and sulfur dyes to react with the dye to give the leuco form. Added organic solvents and/or certain chemical reagents may increase the dye solubility and rate of penetration into the fibre. Carriers are aromatic derivatives added in disperse dyeings to open up the fibre structure of polyester and other thermoplastic fibres and to increase the rate of dye diffusion. Urea has a similar effect in speeding dyeing of cellulosic and protein fibres.

In printing pastes, natural and synthetic gums and thickeners are necessary to provide viscosity and thickness to the dye paste and to limit dye migration across the fabric face. Heating of fabrics following printing is necessary to achieve good dye penetration into the fibre, and superheated steam is preferred, since wet fixation causes a faster rate of dye migration than dry heating methods. The fastness of the dyeing will be dependent on the location of the dye within the fibre, chemical and physical forces holding the dye to the fibre, and the stability of the dye-fibre combination to environmental factors. Dye distributed evenly throughout the fibre in small aggregates is preferred, whereas surface or ring dyeing leads to poor washfastness.

COLOUR, DYES, DYEING AND PRINTING

Colour Theory

Colour is defined a s the net response of an observer to visual physical phenomena involving visible radiant energy of varying intensities over the wavelength range 400 to 700 nanometers.

The net colour seen by the observer is dependent on integration of three factors:

1. The nature of the light source,
2. The light absorption properties of the object observed, and
3. The response of the eye to the 1ight reflected from the object.

The relative intensities of the various wavelengths of visible 1ight observed by the eye are translated by the mind of the observer resulting in the perception of colour. In colour measurement, the human eye is replaced by a photocell which detects the light energy present at various visible wavelengths. Visible 1ight is a narrow band of electromagnetic radiation from 400 to 700 nm detected by the human eye. Radiation falling below 400 nm is ultraviolet radiation, and that falling above 700 nm is infrared radiation; both are unseen by the human eye.

If pure light of a given wavelength is ob served, it will have a colour corresponding to that wavelength. Pure wavelengths of light are seen when white light is refracted by a prism into a "rainbow" spectrum of continuous colour. Light sources such as sunlight, incandescent light, and fluorescent light are continuums of various wavelengths of light with the relative amounts of the various wavelengths of light being dependent on the overall intensity and type of light source. Sunlight at noon has very nearly the same intensity of each wavelength of 1ight throughout the visible spectrum, whereas at dusk sunlight is of lower intensity and has greater quantities of the longer, red wavelengths than of shorter, blue wavelengths. Fluorescent lights generally contain large amounts of shorter, blue wavelengths, while incandescent tungsten lights contain a large component of longer, red wavelengths compared to noon sunlight.

Differences in intensity and wavelength distribution between light sources has a profound effect on the colour observed for a dyed textile, since the textile can absorb and reflect only that 1ight available to it from the source. When a dyed fabric appears different in colour or shade under two different light sources, the phenomenon is referred to as "flare." When two fabrics dyed with different dyes or dye combinations match under one light source but not under another, the effect is called "metamerism."

When light from a source strikes a dyed textile surface, different portions of the light of the various wavelengths are absorbed by the dye, depending of the structure and light absorption characteristics of the dye. Light not absorbed by the dye on the textile is reflected from the surface as diffuse light. The colour seen is a composite of all the wavelengths reflected from the fabric.

Table.3.4: Colours After Absorption/Reflectance

Wavelength of Light Absorbed (nm)	Light Absorbed by Dyed Textile	Colour Seen by the Observer
400-435	Violet	Yellow-green
435-480	Blue	Yellow
480-490	Green-blue	Orange
490-500	Blue-green	Red
500-560	Green	Purple
560-580	Yellow-green	Violet
580-595	Yellow	Blue
595-605	Orange	Green-blue
605-700	Red	Blue-green

If significant direct reflectance of light from the fabric occurs, the fabric exhibits a degree of a gloss. If little or no light throughout the visible range is absorbed by the fabric and the majority of light is reflected, the fabric appears white. If the fabric absorbs all of the light striking it, the fabric is black. If uniform light absorption and reflectance across the visible wavelengths occurs at some intermediate level, the fabric will be a shade of grey.

The dye absorbs discrete packages or quanta of light, and the dye molecule is excited to a higher energy state. This energy is normally harmlessly dissipated through increased vibration within the dye molecule as heat, and the dye is then ready to absorb another quantum of light. If the dye cannot effectively dissipate this energy, the dye will undergo chemical attack and colour fading or colour change will occur or the energy will be transferred to the fibre causing chemical damage. Organic molecules that contain unsaturated double bonds are capable of absorbing light within a given wavelength range.

If these double bonds are conjugated and alternate within the molecule, they are able to mutually interact with one another as a cloud of n electrons.

If sufficient conjugation exists, the molecule will partially absorb light in the lower energy visible wavelength range and will be considered a dye or a pigment. In general, dyes are coloured molecules soluble or dispersible in water or solvent media which can penetrate the fibre on colouration, whereas pigments are not dispersible and must be mechanically entrapped in or locked to the fibre by a binding resin.

A series of colourless dyes exist which are called "fluorescent brighteners." These dyes absorb little light in the visible region, but absorb radiation at unseen ultraviolet wavelengths and then emit this radiation at long blue wavelengths to provide an optical bleaching effect on fabrics. Fluorescent dyes combine fluorescence with visible light absorption characteristics to give extremely bright colours, since unseen ultraviolet light is also being made visible to the eye.

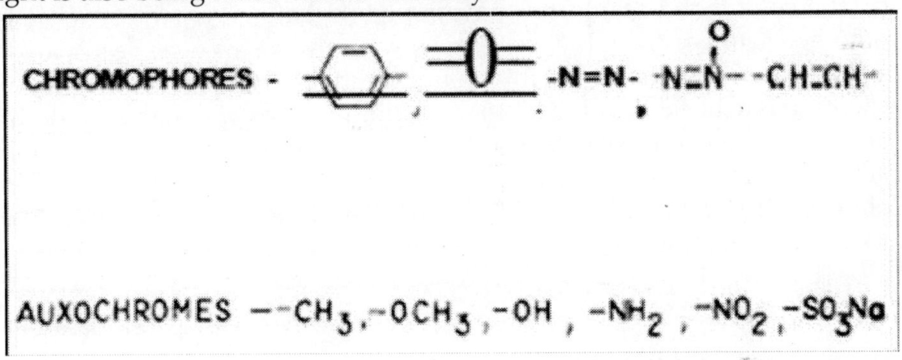

The unsaturated groups which can be conjugated to make the molecule coloured are referred to as "chromophores." Groups which enhance or alter the colour within a conjugated system through alteration of the electron density are referred to as "auxochromes." A series of typical chromophores and auxochromes follows:

The third component in colour is the observer, which can be the human eye or a photodetector in a colour instrument. Most colour measurement systems are based on a standard 1ight source and a "standard observer" for quantitative measurement of colour. The human eye doesn't respond uniformly to colour throughout the visible region, but gives maximum response in the middle visible wave lengths.

In summary, then, the colour observed is a composite of three factors:

1. The light source,
2. The object, and
3. The observer.

A change in any one of these three factors will affect the net colour observed.

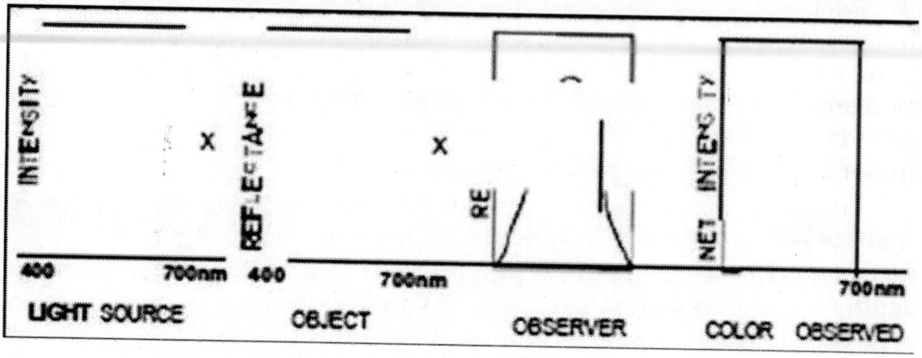

Fig.3.8: Observed Colour as a Corrposite of three Factors.

The colour of a textile can be completely defined by the reflectance colour spectrum of the fabric as seen above; however, since spectra are of limited value in defining given colours or shades, and numerical colour systems have been developed to quantitatively or qualitatively define colour. Knowing the relative position of two colours within the colour space permits one to determine differences between the two colours. Colour is often defined by the following terms: hue, chroma or saturation, and lightness or value.

These colour terms are defined as follows:

- *Chroma or saturation:* Basic difference between colour and the closest primary hue.
- *Lightness or va1ue:* Re1ative degree of 1ightness.
- *The Munsell system:* Uses standard hues and numerical values for chroma and lightness to define colour.

An array of chips of equal colour difference as defined by many observers has been prepared that make up the Munsell Book of Colour. The primaries consist of all major hues plus purple arranged logically to form a horizontal circle. The value or lightness makes up the vertical axis varying from 0 to 10 with 0 being black, 10 being white, and the intermediate numbers being varying shades of grey. The chroma is the degree of deviation from the "true" primary and can vary from 0 to 14, with the larger numbers being closest to the "pure" colour.

To determine the Munsell value for a given colour, the Munsell colour book is consulted to determine the colour designation. For example, if a colour had a designation of 5BG SIB, the sample would be a blue green with a value or lightness of 5 and a chroma of 8. In such a way colour can be characterised, but it is not possible to assign strict numerical values to colour differences between two dyed samples by use of the Munsell system.

Additive colour systems used in colour measurement determine the amount of three colour primary lights necessary to define a given colour using a standard light source and observer. Subtractive systems are used by dyers and colourists, since the net colour reflected from a dye bath or dyed fabric is more meaningful in matching dyeings and depends on the amount of the three subtractive primaries present.

The primaries defined by CIE are not real colours, but are imaginary primaries used to define all colours in the colour space. The amount of each of these primaries in a given colour are used to define the shade and depth of shade for that colour. Since the tristimulus values are difficult to plot, the values are normalised and reduced to trichromatic coefficients according to the equations x = X/X+Y+Z and y = YjX+ Y+Z.

Then the shade of a sample is defined by x and y, and the relative lightness by the Y value which is equivalent to the total reflectance of the dyed textile as observed by the human eye. Colour differences between two samples are determined by the equation $\Delta E = (\Delta x^2 + \Delta y^2 + \Delta y^2)1/2$. The colour space can be mathematically presented in a number of ways and numerous colour difference formulas and systems exist.

Recently, the CIE has established a colour and colour difference system based on rectangular colour coordinates called CIELAB. This system use s L rather than Y for lightness, since L is more closely related to the response of the human eye, with black being assigned 0 and white being assigned 100. A and B provide the shade value of the colour in rectangular coordinates with A+ being red and A- being green, and with B+ being yellow and B- being blue.

Thentheequation$\Delta E = (\Delta L^2 + \Delta A^2 + \Delta B^2)1/2$willgivethecolourdifference. Al so cylindrical coordinates of L, C, and HO, C is the distance from neutral grey shade (C A^2+B^2) and H° is the arc tangent B/A expressed on a 360° scale where A + 0°, B + = 90°, A– = 180°, B– = 270° may be used if desired by three methods:

1. Measurement of the decrease in dye concentration in solution with time by ultraviolet-visible spectroscopy,
2. Determination of the dye concentration on the fabric dyed for a given time by dye extraction and ultraviolet-visible spectroscopy, or
3. By measurement of the reflectance spectra of the dyed fabric followed by application of the Kubelka-Munk relationship in which,

$$\frac{K}{S} = \frac{(1-R)^2}{2R}$$

DYES AND DYE CLASSIFICATION

Dyes as coloured unsaturated organic molecules must have affinity for fibres to be effectively applied. The dyes on fibres are physically bound to the fibre by one or more physical forces including hydrogen bonding, van der Waal s, or ionic forces and in certain cases chemically bound by covalent bonds. Dyes may be classified in a number of ways, including colour, intended use, trade name, chemical constitution, and basis of application. Of these classification methods, chemical constitution and basis of application have been most widely used.

Chemical constitution indicates the major chromophores present in the dye but does not indicate more than such structural aspects of the dye. A classification scheme for dyes has been developed and evolved for use by dyers which is based on the method of application and to a lesser degree on the chemical constitution of the dye class. Dyes classified by this scheme are assigned standard designations according to dye class, colour, and overall constitution by the Society of Dyers and Colourists in the Colour Index.

Dyes Containing Anionic Functional Groups

A number of dyes, including acid, direct, mordant, and reactive dyes, contain functional groups that are sodium salts of sulfonic or carboxylic acids. These functional groups provide water solubility to the dyestuff. The dyes differ in sub-classification in their affinity for fibres and/or the presence of special functional groups.

Acid Dyes

The acid dyes are large dyes containing one or more sulfonic or carboxylic acid salt functional groups. These dyes are dyed onto fibres from acid solution, since positive charge development within the fibre in acid solutions acts as a driving force for dye diffusion and migration into the fibre. Only fibres which develop a positive charge in the presence of acid, such as wool, silk, and other protein fibres, nylon, and certain modified synthetics, are readily dyed by acid dyes, Acid dyes on fibres are reasonably colourfast to light and laundering, but mordanting will improve the overall fastness properties of the dye. The colour of the dye may be affected somewhat by mordanting; however, pre-metallised acid dyes are a special class of acid dyes which have been reacted with a mordant prior to dyeing and which have sufficient solubility to be dyed under conditions normally used for acid dyes.

One method of classifying acid dyes involves dividing them into three groups according to their application and wetfastness. Leveling acid dyes dye evenly to a moderate degree of fastness. For wool and protein fibres they are small molecules requiring highly acidic dyebaths for good exhaustion.

For nylon, leveling dyes are somewhat larger molecules and are applied from weakly acidic dyebaths. Milling dyes have better wash fastness, but generally give duller shades and lack good leveling characteristics. They are larger than leveling dyes and are applied from dilute acetic acid solutions. Acid milling or super milling dyes are applied from neutral solutions and have poor leveling characteristics due to their larger molecular size. They generally are applied to wool and have high wetfastness and light fastness.

Direct Dyes

Direct or substantive dyes are a special class of dyes which penetrate cellulosic fibres readily and have good affinity for these fibres due to their size and shape. Whereas acid dyes are large and bulky, direct dyes are long, narrow, and flat in molecular structure, which allows them to readily enter the cellulose structure and interact with the cellulose in such a way as to provide good fibre affinity.

Direct dyes often contain one or more azo groups connecting aromatic chromophores, thereby providing a straight chain dye molecule. Since charge cellulosics, the dyes are usually applied from basic solutions in which cellulosics are more stable and more likely to swell.

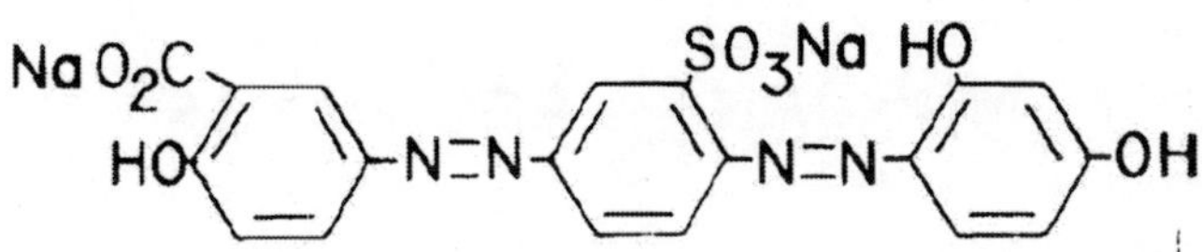

DIRECT RED 185

Direct dyes fall into three main categories. Class A direct dyes level well even in the presence of high salt concentrations, while Class B direct dyes have poor leveling properties which can be improved by proper adjustment of salt concentration.

Class C dyes have poor leveling properties, but exhaust well on raising the temperature of the dyebath in the absence of salt. The direct dyes are reasonably colourfast on cellulosic fabrics, but fastness can be improved by mordanting with metal salts, cationic fixing agents, or formaldehyde or through reaction with diazonium compounds or diazotisation of the dye and reaction with a coupling compound.

Mordant Dyes

Mordant dyes are acid dyes that have special sites other than acid salt anion groups that can react with a metal salt mordant. Mordant dyes are "tailor- made" to chelate with metal ions to form a strong organometallic complex of limited solubility and greater colourfastness. The fibre may be dyed initially and then mordanted, dyed and mordanted simultaneously, or mordanted and then dyed. Of the three methods, post-mordanting is preferred. Salts of chromium, aluminum, copper, iron, tin, and cobalt are commonly used as mordants. Since the mordant affects the electron distribution and density within the dye, the colour of the dyed fabric tends to change.

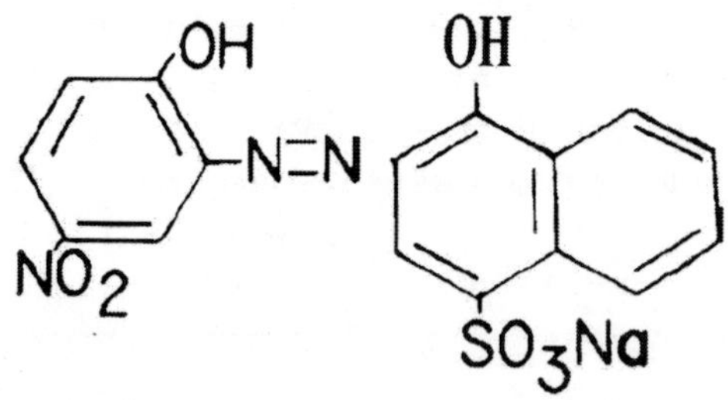

MORDANT BROWN 35

Reactive Dyes

Reactive dyes are dyes which usually have the basic structure of acid, direct, or mordant dyes but which in addition have a reactive group capable of covalent bond formation with the fibre. Since the fibre must have reasonable reactivity towards the dye reactive group, application of these dyes has been limited to cellulosic, protein, and nylon fibres for the most part.

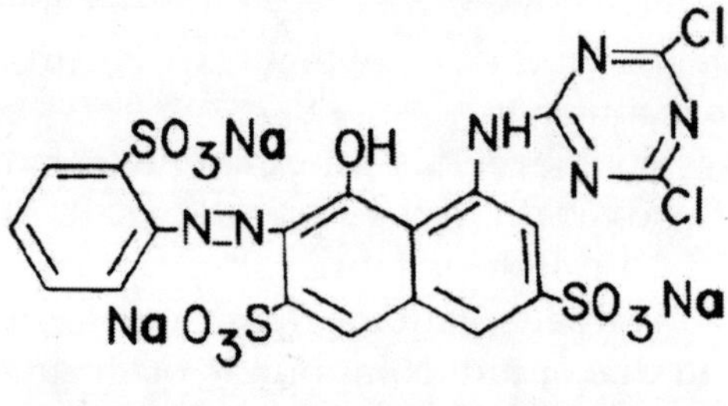

REACTIVE RED

The fastness of reactive dyes covalently bound to the fibre is excellent. Reactive functional groups have been selected for incorporation into reactive dyes which will react readily with the fibre after diffusion into the structure but which will not hydrolyse in the water solvent used in dye application.

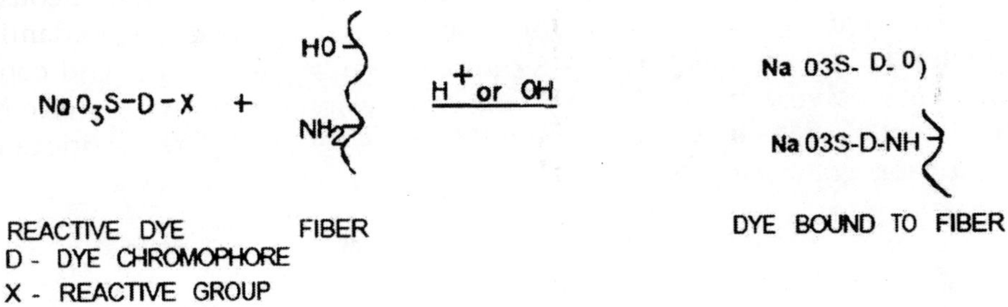

Acidic or basic conditions are necessary for successful and rapid reaction of the reactive dye with the fibre, so dye application is carried out at either slightly acid or basic pH. Procion dyes are the best known of the reactive dyes.

Dyes Containing Cationic Groups

Basic or cationic dyes are coloured cationic salts of amine derivatives. Basic dye cations will migrate towards negative charges inside the fibre. The dyes may be applied to cellulosic, protein, nylon, acrylic, and specially modified synthetic fibres. Although the dyes generally are of striking brilliance and intensity, the colourfastness of the dyes on cellulosic, protein, and nylon fibres is generally poor. Colourfastness can be improved through mordanting with tannins or other complexing agents. Since the insoluble parent amine is regenerated from basic dyes at basic pH, the basic dyes are applied from mildly acid or neutral solutions. The dyes are also important in "one-shot dyeing" of paper products.

Dyes Requiring Chemical Reaction before Application

Both vat and sulfur dyes must be chemically reduced before application to a fibre, whereas azoic or naphthol dyes are formed through reaction of two separate dye components after application to the fibre. These dyes tend to penetrate the fibre less than other dyes, and care must be exercised in application to get reasonable fastness properties.

Vat Dyes

Vat dyes are usually water-insoluble dyes that can be chemically reduced in the presence of base to form a water-soluble and colourless leuco form of the dye, which is then applied to the fibre. Vat dyes can be readily applied to cellulosic fibres and most synthetic fibres, but care must be taken in applying the dyes to protein fibres due to the high passivity of the leuco dye solution which can damage protein fibres.

The dyes are usually indigoids or anthraquinone derivatives and applied at low temperatures. After application of the leuco form of the vat dye, the dye is reoxidised on the fabric by oxygen in the air or through treatment of the dyed fabric with a mild oxidising agent. The vat dyes are reasonably colourfast if poorly held surface dye has been removed:

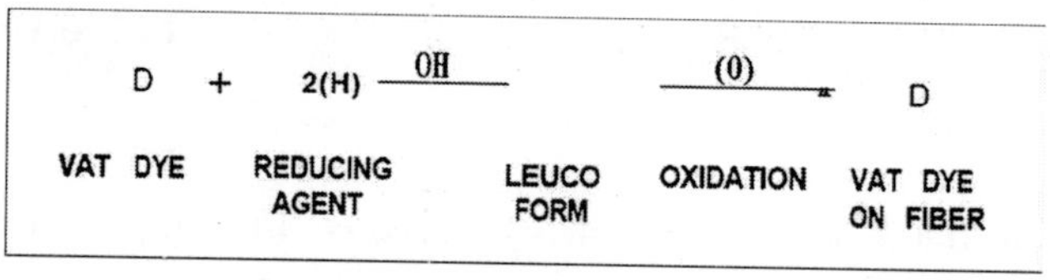

Sulfur Dyes

Sulfur dyes are inexpensive complex reaction mixtures of selected aromatic compounds with sodium polysulfide. The sulfur dyes are chemically reduced in the presence of base prior to application to the fibre, and are reoxidised after dyeing on the fibre by oxygen in the air or by application of a mild oxidising agent such as hydrogen peroxide.

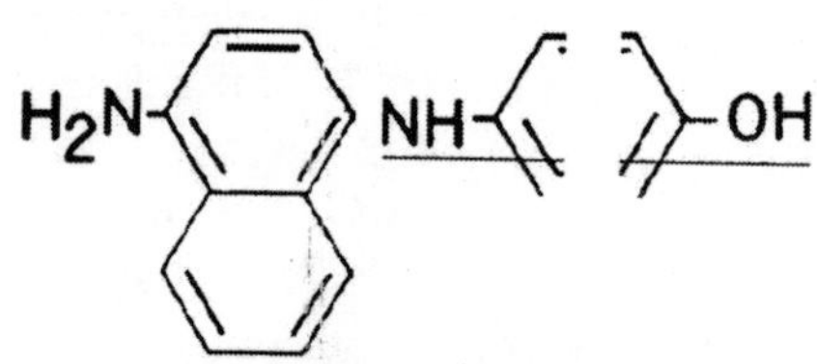

SULFUR GREEN 6

The sulfur dyes are similar in application and fibre affinity to vat dyes, and also are available in a solubilised leuco form:

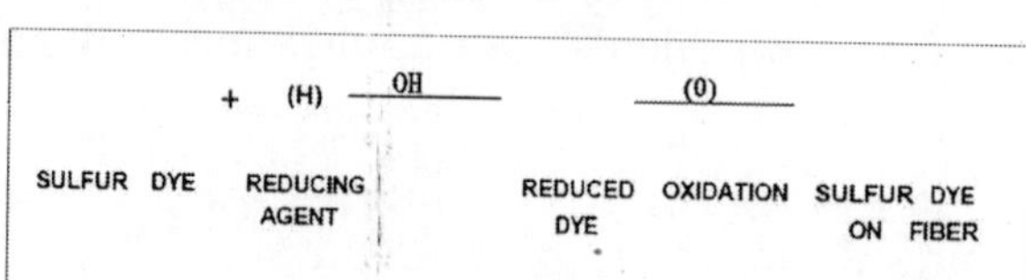

Azoic Dyes

Azoic or naphthol dyes are formed in situ on the fabric through a coupling reaction of an aromatic alcohol or amine such as naphthol. The dye formed contains an azo group:

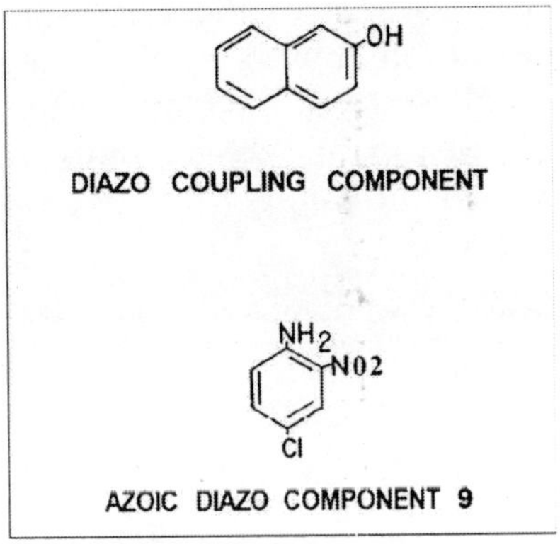

The fabric is usually impregnated first with the aromatic coupling component followed by immersion of the fabric in a solution containing the diazo component, with the azoic dye being formed instantaneously. Owing to the instability of the components, the dyeings are carried out near room temperature.

Special Colourant Classes

Several types of dyes or colourants do not "fit" logically into the other classifications and have been included in this special classification. Disperse dyes are small polar dye molecules which can be used to dye thermoplastic fibres such as triacetate, nylon, polyester, and other synthetic fibres. Solvent dyes are dyes which are specially formulated so that they can be applied from solvents other than water. Pigments are not dyes at all, but rather colourants that must be incorporated in the fibre during spinning or fixed on the surface of the fibre by use of a polymer adhesive. Natural dyes are complex mixtures derived from natural sources which can be placed in a number of the above classifications.

Disperse Dyes

Disperse dyes were formulated and introduced to permit dyeing of hydrophobic thermoplastic fibres including acetate, triacetate, nylon, polyester, acrylic, and other synthetics. The disperse dyes are small polar molecules, usually containing anthraquinone or azo groups, which do not have charged cationic or anionic groups within the structure. The disperse dyes are sparingly soluble in water and must be dispersed with aid of a surfactant in the dyebath.

As the small amount of dissolved disperse dye diffuses into the fibre, additional dye dispersed in solution is dissolved, until the disperse dye is nearly completely exhausted onto the fibre. A special class of reactive disperse dyes has been introduced that can react with fibres like acetate and nylon after diffusion into the fibre.

The light and wash fastness of these dyes is generally good, but difficulty has been encountered with fume fading with certain of the disperse dyes. Many disperse dyes have appreciable vapor pressures at elevated temperatures and can be "dyed" onto thermoplastic fibres by sublimation, which involves diffusion of the dye vapors into the fibre.

Solvent Dyes

Solvent dyes often resemble dyes in other classes, except that these dyes contain groups that improve their solubility in solvents such as alcohols and chlorinated hydrocarbons. It is often possible with solvent dyes to dye certain fibres which would be poorly dyeable from aqueous solution.

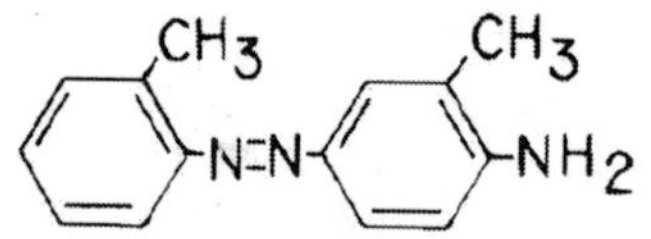

SOLVENT YELLOW 3

Pigments

Pigments as a class are coloured materials that are insoluble in their medium of application. As a result, they cannot penetrate or become readily fixed to a fibre and must be "locked" onto the fibre surface by use of a polymeric adhesive binder that encapsulates and holds the pigment onto the fibres. Pigments include inorganic salts, insoluble azo or vat dyes, toners, lakes, metallic complexes, and organometallic complexes. Some binders are preformed water-insoluble polymers applied from solvents or as emulsions, whereas others are water-soluble or emulsifiable polymers which can be chemically crosslinked and insolubilised after application by drying and heating. The pigment-binder systems tend to stiffen textiles, and have moderate to poor fastness, since they are surface treatments.

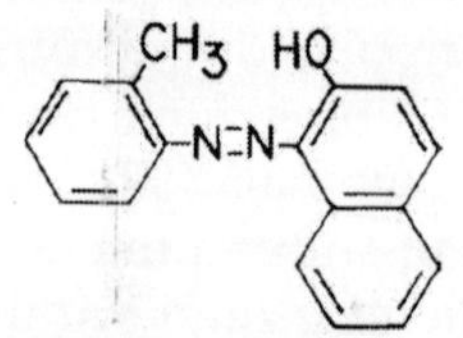

PIGMENT ORANGE 3

Natural Dyes

Natural dyes and pigments are derived from mineral, animal, or plant sources and generally are complex mixtures of materials. A number of natural dye s can be classified as acid or vat dyes and can be readily mordanted. In general, the natural dyes give more muted tones than synthetic dyes and are useful only on natural or regenerated fibres.

Dyeing of Blends

Textile structures are often blends of more than one fibre type. Blends containing similar fibres are easy to dye with dyes of similar structure and application characteristics. Care must be taken in dyeing blends containing fibres of highly different dye affinities, if the dyeing is carried out in the same dyebath.

The dyes and their auxiliaries must be compatible with one another. When fibres in a blend are dyed the same colour, the dyeing is referred to as "union dyeing," whereas dyeing fibres in a blend of different colours is referred to as "cross dyeing." In blends, interesting tone-on-tone, tone-on-white, and differential dyeings are possible by selection of appropriate dyes and dyeing conditions.

DISPERSE DYEING

For dyeing polyester fibres, in practical terms only disperse dyes are suitable. Through their hydrophobic properties, these dyes are capable of penetrating into the similarly hydrophobic polyester fibre. This class of dyes has only extremely poor solubility in water; for this reason, dispersing agent is added to the dyebath to maintain dispersion stability, especially in the case of high temperature dyeings.

BASIC PRINCIPLE

The inclusion of dispersing agent in the dyebath is a crucial factor in the application of disperse dyes. Once such a compound is added to water, its dual character results in the formation of micells, but low, concentration. The hydrophobic tails of the dispersing agent molecules are inside the micelle which, as a consequence, is able to solubilise the disperse dye molecules, so conferring a higher apparent solubility on the dye. The dye transfer to the fibre from the micelles. As micelles empty their dye, they re-from and dissolve more dye from the solid particles. Much of the evidence that is available on the subject suggests that in dyed polyester fibres the disperse dyes are present chiefly in the monomolecular state.

At the end of the dyeing process, the dye that has been absorbed by the fibre is in a state of dynamic equilibrium with the dye that remains in the bath, and the fraction of the latter that is in aqueous solution must be present in the same state of aggregation as the dye in the fibre. It is reasonable to infer that the transfer of the dye to the fibre takes place from a monomolecular aqueous solution, the concentration of which is maintained during the first phase of the dyeing process by the progressive dissolution of solid dye from the particles in dispersion in the bath. In the presence of dispersing agents the following equilibrium situation is set up.

The four stages of the process mechanism are as follows:

1. Some of the dyes dissolve in the water of the dyebath.
2. Molecules of dye are transferred from solution to the surface of the fibre.
3. The solution in the dyebath is replenished by the dissolution of more solid material from the dispersion.
4. The adsorbed dye diffuses monomolecularly into the fibre.

The process of transfer from the aqueous solution to the fibre is comparable with the extraction of a solute from one solvent by a second, immiscible solvent and similar laws of partition are applicable. Distribution coefficients that are related to the solubilities of the dyes in the aqueous and fibre phases can be determined for different processing temperatures, although they may be affected by the simultaneous equilibrium between the aqueous and solid phases of the dye. The rates of the first and second stages of the process mechanism are governed by these solubilities.

It was established that the disperse dyeing system was truly reversible and that the results conformed to a rectilinear isotherm. Typical results show linear relationship in distribution of dye between polyester and water. It is well established that dyeing with disperse dyes is the transfer of dye molecules from a molecular dispersion into the fibre and because of the linearity of the isotherms obtained, the amount of dye adsorbed [D]ad relative to the concentration in the bath [D]s can be expressed by a partition coefficient K, i.e. $\frac{[D]_{ad}}{[D]_s} = K$

As more dye is introduced into the system a point will be reached at which the amount of dye in the dyebath at equilibrium exceeds the solubility of dye. In the ideal case further additions of dye will produce no further change in the concentration of dye in solution, and hence no change in the concentration of dye on the fibre. At this point, therefore, if the abscissa denotes total dye in the bath rather than dye in solution, then the isotherm will become horizontal.

Dye molecules that have been adsorbed on the fibre surface diffuse into the interior of the fibre by a relatively simple mechanism, which appears to obey Fick's equation. That is to say, the rate of diffusion of dye through unit area at any point in the fibre is directly proportional to the concentration gradient of the dye at that point. As would be expected, the amount of dye taken up by polyester fibres from a bath of constant concentration is found to be proportional to the square root of the dyeing time, until a saturation value is approached.

Very similar results are observed during the earlier stages of the process in dyebaths of normal composition and concentrations, such as are employed in commercial 'exhaustdyeing' processes. It is found that the rate of dyeing is quite independent of the concentration of the dyebath, practically up to the point at which equilibrium is established. For dyeings carried out at a constant temperature, a plot of the instantaneous fractional 'dye uptake' against time of dyeing gives a steeply-rising asymptotic curve, which appears to fit a law based on the hyperbola or, possibly, on the hyperbolic tangent.

An important difference between the dyeing behaviour of polyester fibres and that of other fibres such as nylon and secondary acetate, which also accept disperse dyes, is in their rates of dyeing. Polyester fibres dye very slowly at temperatures much below 100°C. Disperse dyes can be applied to cellulose secondary acetate readily over approximately 1 hour at 80°C. Higher temperatures are avoided as otherwise acetate groups on the cellulosic fibre can be hydrolysed to hydroxyl groups, which can spoil the surface of the fibres and reduce their substantivity towards the disperse dyes.

Cellulose triacetate is more difficult to penetrate with disperse dyes because of its more compact molecular structure, but it can be dyed at the boil. Nylon fibres can be dyed under conditions similar to those used for cellulose acetate fibres. In case of acrylic fibres, the presence of anionic groups such as $–SO_3H$ and –COOH permit only pale shades to be obtained under normal conditions with disperse dyes.

THE EFFECTS OF VARIATIONS IN DISPERSE DYEING

Several factors affect the dyeing of polyester fibre with disperse dye such as crystal form of the dye, dispersing agents, particle size of the dye, pH of the dyebath, temperature of dyeing and heat setting, and fibre fineness.

Crystal form of the Disperse Dyes

The possible different crystal forms of disperse dyes have been suggested to influence the saturation values achieved on polyester, due to differences in the vapour pressure and solubility of the different forms of dye in both water and fibre.

Dispersing Agent

Disperse dyes are sparingly soluble in water and often crystalline with varying particle size. These characteristics are inadequate for dispersing the dyes in water and cause unlevel dyeing. In order to achieve the required particle size and distribution, the disperse dye is milled, usually in the presence of a dispersing agent. Generally, the dispersing agents are anionic, ligninsulphonates or polycondensates of arylsulphonic acids with formaldehyde which facilitate milling by preventing agglomer-ation of the dye particles.

Particle Size in Dispersion of the Dyes

The aqueous solubility of disperse dye particles in a dispersion increases with decreasing particle size. Thus an increase in the severity of milling that accompanies a reduction in the particle size of the dye enhances the solubility and adsorption of disperse dye.

pH of Dyebath

Generally, in the commercial dyeing of polyester fibres with disperse dyes, dyeing is carried out within the pH range 5.5 to 6.5. Strongly alkaline or acidic conditions, such as higher than pH 9 and lower than pH 4, induce hydrolysis of the fibre as well as decomposition of azo disperse dyes. In the case of high temperature dyeing, this degradation of polyester fibre and dye is accelerated.

Substantivity of Disperse Dyes

The substantivity of disperse dyes towards polyester fibres is one of the most critical factors in determining dyeing behaviour and there have been many studies carried out to evaluate the substantivity of disperse dyes towards hydrophobic fibres, including polyester, in order to select suitable dyes. These attempts include the 'Solubility Parameter Concept' and 'IOR (Inorganic/ Organic) values'.

Temperature

The adsorption and diffusion of disperse dyes on polyester are greatly influenced by temperature as an increase in temperature increases the mobility of the polymer chains in the amorphous regions of the fibre. Polyester fibres dye very slowly at temperatures much below 100°C. At 85°C, the temperature normally used for the dyeing of secondary cellulose acetate, it was found that polyester fibre dyed at rates between 700 and 1000 times slower than those measured for the same dyes on secondary cellulose acetate and nylon.

When, however, sufficient time was allowed for the polyester fibre to come nearly to equilibrium with the dyebath, it was found that it had taken up approximately the same amount of dye as had secondary acetate and in most cases about twice as much as nylon. For the dye-hydrophobic fibre system, the affinity of the disperse dye decreases with increase in dyeing temperature while the saturation value of the dye in the fibre increases with increasing temperature.

Heat setting changes the morphology of the polyester fibres. When fabrics of polyester are heat set in air under conditions of free shrinkage, the dye exhaustion first decreases and then increase with increasing setting temperature. The minimum exhaustion occurs after seeing at around 160-

190°C. If applied tension prevents fabric shrinkage during heat setting, the dye uptake/temperature profile is similar to that under conditions of free shrinkage, but with higher uptake values.

Fibre Fineness

Much attention has been given recently to dyeing microfibres. In a broad sense, especially in Europe, the term microfibre means fine fibres of less than 1.0 denier. However, in South Korea and Japan, where fine-fibre technology is more advanced, fine fibres of 0.04–0.4 denier class are generally used in this filament area. A useful preliminary relationship between the percentages of dye on weight of goods needed to achieve a particular depth of shade on polyester fibres of two different fineness was suggested by Fothergill:

$$\frac{C_2}{C_1} = \sqrt{\frac{D_1}{D_2}}$$

It takes much more dye to dye the microfibre to the same apparent depth as the regular fibre. Therefore, such marked denier difference can affect dyers in a number of ways.

RECENT REQUIREMENTS IN DISPERSE DYEING TECHNOLOGY

Environmental issues have been gaining importance in all aspects of industrial production and various legislative requirements have emerged with increasing regularity to reduce the impact of dyeing processes on the environment. In response, the industry has been forced to become increasingly environmentally friendly than existing ones. Therefore, innovation and developments in colour chemistry and dyeing will allow the colourist to meet ever-increasing environmental restrictions, produce novel effects, and reduce processing costs.

The demand for environmentally friendly dyes with high wet fastness on polyester is increasing, and the so-called alkali-clearable disperse dyes suggest a promising new direction. These alkali-clearable disperse dyes obviate the need for sodium hydrosulphite and significantly reduce the cost of effluent treatment. Recently, these types of dye have become technically important for the colouration of polyester and its cellulosic blends. They perform well on international standard and commercial wash fastness test.

To achieve acceptable levels of wet fastness after post-heat treatment, the development of modern disperse dyes must be directed towards satisfying a number of needs. Firstly, new dyes need to be tailored towards satisfying shorter, more easily reproducible and more economical dyeing processes. Secondly, with the increasing use of polyester and polyester blends in sports and leisurewear, there is a clear demand for dyes of higher wet fastness.

Indeed this requirement has become even more important with the introduction of polyester microfibres, where higher depths of shade have to be dyed in order to obtain the same visual yield as with conventional polyester fibre. Finally, the development of new disperse dyes must take into account the effect that effluent from the dyeing process will have on the environment, and aim to minimize such pollution. These objectives are not mutually exclusive but interrelated; they must all be taken into account in any dye development programme.

MAIN METHODS OF DISPERSE DYEING

Disperse dyes are the most important class of dye used in dyeing polyester fibres and provide a wide range of hues with good build-up and fastness properties adequate for most purposes. The rate of dyeing may be raised to the level of commercial acceptability, either by raising the working temperature to the region of 130°C, or by dyeing at the boil in the presence of an accelerating agent or 'carrier'. Disperse dyes can also be transferred to polyester fibres under dry conditions by impregnating the goods with a suitable dispersion, drying and then baking at temperatures in the range 190-220°C.

CARRIER DYEING

The term 'carrier' is originated from the idea that the compound and the dye formed a complex which could 'carry' the dye into the fibre, thus causing more rapid dyeing. It is now known that the carrier is adsorbed by the fibre and operates by modifying the structure of the amorphous regions. A carrier dyeing of even deep shades at the boil within a reasonable dyeing time. Common polyester dyeing carriers include butyl benzoate, methylnaphthalene, dichlorobenzene, diphenyl and o-phyenylphenol, the latter two being the most popular.

The actual mechanism by which a carrier accelerates dyeing has been widely debated and probably depends on the carrier used. The polyester fibres absorb the carrier and swell. This swelling can impede liquor flow in packages causing unlevelness. The overall effect seems to be a lowering of the polymer glass transition temperature, thus promoting polymer chain movements and creating free volume. This speeds up the diffusion of the dye into the fibre. A typical carrier dyeing procedure involves running the goods in the bath 60°C and adding dilute dispersing agent, emulsified carrier and lastly the disperse dyes. The temperature is then gradually raised to the boil and dyeing continued at this temperature.

The sorped carriers must be removed from the polyester after dyeing, usually by hot-air drying the goods from 150-180°C. Residual carriers can adversely affect lightfastness if left on the goods. The benefits of carriers were overwhelming in the early days of polyester dyeing because polyester fabrics could be dyed in unpressurised becks with no more dyeing problems than with direct dyes. However, carrier dyeing has steadily declined since the development of suitable machines for dyeing polyester under pressure at temperature around 130°C. Carriers are still used in some garment and small commission dyehouses where high temperature pressurised dyeing machines are not available.

HIGH TEMPERATURE DYEING

High temperature dyeing is the most widespread method of batch colouration. The temperatures require pressurised equipment and impart increased diffusion of the dyestuff by reducing cohesion between polymer chains and increasing the kinetic energy of the dye molecules.

Adsorption Phase

The heating or adsorption phase is the most critical in determining the levelness of the dyed fibre and it is essential therefore that the heating rate is appropriate to allow controlled adsorption of the dye. Although in the dyeing of polyester, levelling can occur through migration at top dyeing temperature, in rapid dyeing cycles the time at top temperature is minimal and it is even more critical to ensure dye is applied in a uniform manner during the adsorption phase. The adsorption behaviour is strongly influenced by a number of factors, the most important of which are concentration of dye, temperature gradient, fibre type and auxiliary system is an organic compound, dissolved or emulsified in the dyebath. Carriers allow rate at which the temperature is raised. At some temperature between 80°C and 120°C the dyeing rate for that dye reaches a maximum. The temperature range over which the dyeing rate is at this maximum is known as the 'critical dyeing temperature' (CDT). Slow-diffusing high-energy dyes have a high CDT, whereas more rapidly-diffusing dyes have a lower CDT. Specific values of CDT depend on the rate of temperature rise, dye concentration, liquor flow rate, liquor ratio and the substrate to be dyed. Rapid-dyeing procedures depend on adding the disperse dyes at a temperature just below the CDT and then raising the temperature slowly in the vicinity of the CDT to ensure that the exhaustion rate that just permits level dyeing is not exceeded. The temperature is then raised from just above the CDT to the top dyeing temperature at the maximum rate.

Diffusion Phase

The dyeing of polyester is often described as a diffusion-controlled process. Including convective transfer through the liquor adsorption and molecular diffusion into the fibre, is the rate-determining step. Where the time needed for the adsorption phase is largely influenced by the machine conditions, in the diffusion phase the time required at top temperature is directly related to the diffusion characteristics of individual dyes and dyeing depth, but generally, the standard time is 10-20 minutes for dyeing up to pale shades, 20-30 minutes for medium shades and 30-35 minutes for deep shades.

In the high temperature phase of the dyeing process, another important property of dyes is migration, or their tendency to level out. This phenomenon can be very important, particularly if dyes have been adsorbed in a non- uniform manner, perhaps due to inadequate liquor circulation or too rapid a heating rate. While the migration properties of disperse dyes may become a key factor if dyes are applied unevenly during the adsorption phase, the key parameter in the diffusion phase is the diffusion rate of the disperse dye.

Clearing Phase

Because disperse dyes have such limited solubility in water, some particulate disperse dye may still be occluded on fibre surfaces after the dyeing phase is complete. If not removed, this surface contamination can undermine the brightness of shade as well as the wash, sublimation and crock fastness results. Commonly, the dyed polyester is cleared of surface-deposited dye as well as auxiliaries by means of treatment with detergent or reductive or oxidative treatments, in order to secure optimum fastness of the dyeing and also to improve the brightness of shade. The usual treatment carried out, especially in heavy depth, is reduction- clearing, where the dyed fibre is treated in a strong reducing bath, usually made up of sodium dithionite and caustic soda is an organic compound, dissolved or emulsified in the dye bath. Carriers allow to clear the fibre surface, but the ease of removal varies from chromophore to chromophore and dye to dye. This treatment acts to destroy loose azo disperse dye through chemical reduction of the azo link. Anthraquinone disperse dyes are not fully destroyed by such a treatment but a degree of removal of surface dye is achieved through temporary solubilisation of the disperse dye to the alkali-leuco form.. Research indicates that the polyester dyer will typically reduction-clear in the range of 30- 50 per cent of production shades and sometimes an even higher proportion in blend dyeing.

Minimizing the need for reduction-clearing can lead to substantial productivity improvements and water and chemical savings as well as a reduction on the effluent load and should be a key objective in implementation of a rapid dyeing approach for polyester. In the cases of pale and medium- depth dyeings or for those dyes which cannot withstand reduction-clearing, the dye fibre can be given an alkaline scour; residues of anthraquinone dyes which may remain after reduction-clearing, may be removed using an oxidative treatment.

THERMOSOL PROCESS

Thermosol dyeing process is important continuous process for dyeing polyester and polyester/cellulose fibre mixture with disperse dyes, which is used mainly for wovens and knitted materials. A dispersion of the disperse dye is padded onto the polyester fabric. The material is then dried using a hot flue air dryer or by infrared radiation, the latter usually giving much less migration of the dye. Final drying of the padded material takes place using heated cylinders and the dry fabric is then heated in air, or by contact with a hot metal surface, to a temperature in the range of 190-220°C for 1-2min. In hot air, as the fabric approaches the maximum temperature, the disperse dyes begin to sublime and the polyester fibres absorb their vapours.

Dyes of lower molar mass tend to sublime more readily, but they also suffer from low fastness and poor resistance to heat treatments. Dyes of higher molar mass have better fastness properties but are more difficult to apply. After thermofixation, scouring or even a reduction-clearing treatment is necessary to remove any dye remaining on the fibre surfaces. PET seatbelt webbing is typically dyed with disperse dyes using thermosol dyeing processes in which the webbing is dipped continuously into a dye solution and passed through a hot chamber for approximately 2–3 min.

The dyestuffs can penetrate the molecular chains of the fibres during their exposure to the hot chamber. This method has some advantages that could avoid a batchwise process, which is regarded as time-consuming and tedious, and would speed up the dyeing process.

❒

4

Textile Fabric Computing

Fabric computing or unified computing involves the creation of a computing fabric consisting of interconnected nodes that look like a 'weave' or a 'fabric' when viewed collectively from a distance. Usually this refers to a consolidated high-performance computing system consisting of loosely coupled storage, networking and parallel processing functions linked by high bandwidth interconnects (such as 10 Gigabit Ethernet and InfiniBand) but the term has also been used to describe platforms like the Azure Services Platform and grid computing in general (where the common theme is interconnected nodes that appear as a single logical unit).

The fundamental components of fabrics are "nodes" (processor(s), memory, and/or peripherals) and "links" (functional connection between nodes). While the term "fabric" has also been used in association with storage area networks and switched fabric networking, the introduction of compute resources provides a complete "unified" computing system.

Other terms used to describe such fabrics include "unified fabric", "data centre fabric" and "unified data centre fabric". According to Ian Foster, director of the Computation Institute at the Argonne National Laboratory and University of Chicago, "grid computing 'fabrics' are now poised to become the underpinning for next-generation enterprise IT architectures and be used by a much greater part of many organizations." IBM, TIBCO, Brocade, Cisco, HP, Egenera, Avaya and Xsigo Systems currently manufacture computing fabric equipment.

History

While the term has been in use since the mid to late 1990s the growth of cloud computing and Cisco's evangelism of unified data centre fabrics followed by unified computing (an evolutionarydata centre architecture whereby blade servers are integrated or unified with supporting network and storage infrastructure) starting March 2009 has renewed interest in the technology. Other companies offering unified or fabric computing systems include Liquid Computing Corporation and Egenera. There have been mixed reactions to Cisco's architecture, particularly from rivals who claim that these proprietary systems will lock out other vendors. Analysts claim that this "ambitious new direction" is "a big risk" as companies like IBM and HP who have previously partnered with Cisco on data centre projects (accounting for $2–3bn of Cisco's annual revenue) are now competing with them.

Key Characteristics

The main advantages of fabrics are that a massive concurrent processing combined with a huge, tightly-coupled address space makes it possible to solve huge computing problems (such as those presented by delivery of cloud computing services) and that they are both scalable and able to be dynamically reconfigured. Challenges include a non-linearly degrading performance curve, whereby adding resources does not linearly increase performance which is a common problem with parallel computing and maintaining security.

TEXTILE FABRICS

However, a knowledge of the characteristics of each kind of fibre helps a good deal, as every fibre has certain inherent qualities, which cannot be wholly reproduced in any imitation fibre. For example, wool has its own features and no other fibre has identical ones.

The look and even the touch of pure wool flannel may be copied in the cotton flannelette and an inexperienced purchaser may find it difficult to distinguish the wool from the cotton. Fabrics made with newer blends, synthetic fibres are also not easy to judge merely by the appearance or touch. To identify such fabrics, the help of other tests, even of chemical tests is needed.

FEATURES OF FIBRES

Natural Fibres

Man-made Fibres: These fibres do not take place in fibre form but have been turned into it by man, by breaking down from their original form and reassembled into various sort of structure, e.g., rayons.

Cellulose-Fibres

These fibres have as their origin cellulose which is the chief matter of the plant cells. Cellulose is a complex compound made up of carbon, hydrogen and oxygen with the molecular formula of $(C_6H_{10}O_6)n$.

Fig.4.1: Cellulose Fibre

Cotton comprises about 91 per cent and hemp rame and flax contain similarly large amounts of cellulose. Cellulose is very sensitive to the action of mineral acids, and oxidising agents. However, it is very resistant to alkalies, including strong caustic alkalies at high temperature and pressure. Cellulosic fibres are low in resiliency so the fabrics wrinkle easily. Due to the high absorbency of the fibre they are comfortable for summer wear.

Animal-Fibres

Wool and silk are obtained from animals and are, therefore, known as animal fibres. They have protein as one of the chief constituents and are made up of carbon, hydrogen and nitrogen. Wool contains sulphur besides the above elements. Both are destroyed by concentrated mineral acids but the specific action of the dilute acids is not very harmful on either. Thus, dilute acids are the basis of dyeing and finishing processes for the materials made from these fibres. Wool as well as silk burn with the special odour of burning proteins like burning of hair, dals or milk.

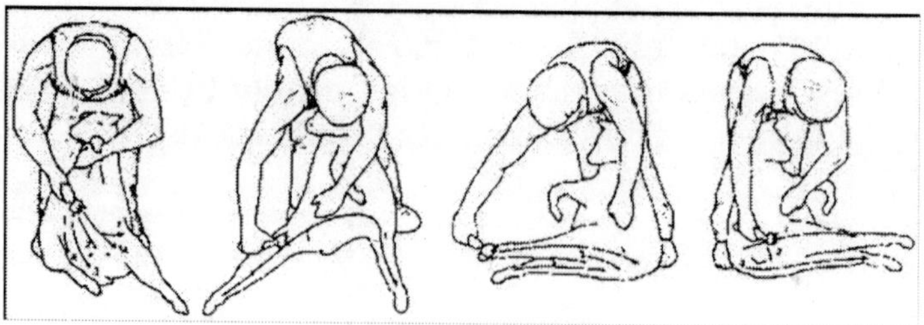

Fig.4.2: Animal-Fibres

Alkalies have a harmful effect on both. Animal fibres are very resilient and the wrinkles go out between wearings. However, they are bad conductors of heat and build up static electricity in cold and dry weather. Wool loses about 40 per cent of its strength when wet and silk, 15 per cent. Wool has a natural crimp which supports to increase its elasticity and strength. It has a springiness or resilience which no other natural fibre possesses. commonly speaking, woollen fabrics are soft to the touch and present a fuzzy appearance.

Worsteds are an exception, as their yarns are tightly twisted and firm. Wool, mixed with cotton, produces in the fabric a distinct hardness and heaviness about the material, which further tends to soil readily, fade and to wrinkle. Silk has a luxurious soft texture, and a deep lustre. The sheen is not loud or bright as in man-made fabrics.

This fibre is strong and retains most of its strength even when wet. It possesses elasticity and does not wear out soon. It is the lightest of all the fibres. Man-made fabrics may similiar to pure silk in appearance but are not so light. Silks weighted with metallic salts are still heavier and produce a sharp crease on the line of the fold. There are two kinds of man-made fibres: thermo- plastic and non-thermo-plastic.

Thermo-plastic Fibres

These are those that soften with heat and thus become liable or if the heat is sufficient high, will melt. These fibres are resistant to friction and wrinkling.

Fig.4.3: Thermo-plastic Fibres

They have low moisture content which makes them an easy to care fabric, however, they are not easy to dye. Due to this property they build up static electricity in cold and dry weather like animal fibres.

Non-Thermo-plastic Fibres

Which neither soften or melt with the application of heat but will scorch or burn if the temperature is very high. As a group they are soft, absorbent, pliable and comfortable to wear. They do not accumulate static electricity. They, except for mineral fibres, may be cared much as the natural fibres.

Fibres of Mineral Nature

These are inorganic and used for fireproof fabrics. Asbestos is practically the only natural mineral fibre. It is utilised in fabrics intended for make dress, fire-proof curtains and screens, and for man uses. It is also used for floor and table mats. Mineral fibres are really drawn threads from metals, e.g., gold, silver in tissues and brocades, and even baser metals are utilised in fabrics like tinsel. Thus, their origin is inorganic matter. They have an unusually bright sheen. Cotton is limp and has a dull surface because of to its fibre structure.

It lacks the lustre and the natural creaminess of linen. It is quite inflammable, and soils and crushes easily. It is heavier than comparable fabrics of other fibre content. It is brittle and is elastic when dry; but, when moist, its strength and elasticity increases. Mercerized cotton is stronger, smoother and lustrous, hence it soils less readily than cotton. Linen is smooth and cool to the touch as compared to cotton. Fine linen has a lustre almost equal to that of silk. It has crispness and is strong enough for hard wear. Moisture soaks through and spreads over linen fabrics much more quickly than in the case of cotton fabrics.

Linen, when torn, has straight, glossy fibre-ends of unequal length. The fibre-ends of torn cotton curl and are lustreless. Linen yarn when not twisted, a more or less parallel arrangement of glossy, individual fibre. Rayon is produced to replace pure silk and so has a similar appearance, but with a better luster generally; though sometimes dull rayons are also produced. The rayon fibre if subtly examined, will be found to be coarser and heavier than a silk fibre. Rayon realised stiffer to the touch and is less elastic. It breaks more easily than silk, thus showing less strength. It loses strength when wet and regains it when dry.

FIBRE CLASSIFICATION

Textile fibres are normally broken down into two main classes, natural and man-made fibres. All fibres which come from natural sources (animals, plants, etc.) and do not require fibre formation or reformation are classed as natural fibres. Natural fibres include the protein fibres such as wool and silk, the cellulose fibres such as cotton and linen, and the mineral fibre asbestos. Man-made fibres are fibres in which either the basic chemical units have been formed by chemical synthesis followed by fibre formation or the polymers from natural sources have been dissolved and regenerated after passage through a spinneret to form fibres.

Those fibres made by chemical synthesis are often called synthetic fibres, while fibres regenerated from natural polymer sources are called regenerated fibres or natural polymer fibres. In other words, all synthetic fibres and regenerated fibres are man-made fibres, since man is involved in the actual fibre formation process.

In contrast, fibres from natural sources are provided by nature in ready- made form. The synthetic man-made fibres include the polyamides (nylon), polyesters, acrylics, polyolefins, vinyls, and elastomeric fibres, while the regenerated fibres include rayon, the cellulose acetates, the regenerated proteins, glass and rubber fibres.

Another method of classifying fibres would be according to chemical structure without regard of the origin of the fibre and its starting materials. In this manner all fibres of similar chemical structure would be classed together. The natural man-made fibre classification given in figure does this to a certain extent. In this way, all fibres having the basic cellulosic unit in their structures would be grouped together rather than separated into natural and man-made fibres.

This book essentially presents the fibres in groups of similar basic chemical structure, with two exceptions. In one case the elastomeric fibres have been grouped together due to their exceptional physical property, high extensibility and recovery.

FIBRE PROPERTIES

There are several primary properties necessary for a polymeric material to make an adequate fibre:

- Fibre length to width ratio,
- Fibre uniformity,
- Fibre strength and flexibility,
- Fibre extensibility and elasticity, and
- Fibre cohesiveness.

Certain other fibre properties increase its value and desirability in its intended end-use but are not necessary properties essential to make a fibre.

Such secondary properties include moisture absorption characteristics, fibre resiliency, abrasion resistance, density, luster, chemical resistance, thermal characteristics, and flammability.

FIBRE LENGTH TO WIDTH RATIO

Fibrous materials must have sufficient length so that they can be made into twisted yarns. In addition, the width of the fibre (the diameter of the cross section) must be much less than the overall length of the fibre, and usually the fibre diameter should be 1/100 of the length of the fibre. The fibre may be "infinitely" long, as found with continuous filament fibres, or as short as 0.5 inches (1.3 em), as found in staple fibres. Most natural fibres are staple fibres, whereas man-made fibres come in either staple or filament form depending on processing prior to yarn formation.

FIBRE UNIFORMITY

Fibres suitable for processing into yarns and fabrics must be fairly uniform in shape and size. Without sufficient uniformity of dimensions and properties in a given set of fibres to be twisted into yarn. The actual formation of the yarn may be impossible or the resulting yarn may be weak, rough, and irregular in size and shape and unsuitable for textile usage. Natural fibres must be sorted and graded to assure fibre uniformity, whereas synthetic fibres may be "tailored" by cutting into appropriate uniform 1engths to give a proper degree of fibre uniformity.

FIBRE STRENGTH AND FLEXIBILITY

A fibre or yarn made from the fibre must possess sufficient strength to be processed into a textile fabric or other textile article. The resulting textile must have sufficient strength to provide adequate durability during end-use. Many experts consider single fibre strength of 5 grams per denier to be necessary for a fibre suitable in most textile applications, although certain fibres with strengths as low as 1.0 gram per denier have been found suitable for some applications.

The strength of a single fibre is called the tenacity, defined as the force per unit linear density necessary to break a known unit of that fibre. The breaking tenacity of a fibre may be expressed in grams per denier (g/d) or grams per tex (g/tex). Both denier and tex are units of 1inear density (mass per unit of fibre length) and are defined as the number of grams of fibre measuring 9000 meters and 1000 meters, respectively. As a result, the denier of a fibre or yarn will always be 9 times the tex of the same fibre. Since tenacities of fibres or yarns are obtained by dividing the force by denier or tex, the tenacity of a fibre in grams per denier will be 1/9 that of the fibre tenacity in grams per tex. As a result of the adaption of the International System of Units. The appropriate length unit for breaking tenacity becomes kilometer (km) of breaking length or Newtons per tex (N/tex) and will be equivalent in value to g/tex. The strength of a fibre yarn or fabric can be expressed in terms of force per unit area, and when expressed in this way the term is tensile strength.

FIBRE EXTENSIBILITY AND ELASTICITY

An individual fibre must be able to undergo slight extensions in length (less than 5 per cent) without breakage of the fibre. At the same time the fibre must be able to almost completely recover following slight fibre deformation. In other words, the extension deformation of the fibre must be nearly elastic. These properties are important because the individual fibres in textiles are often subjected to sudden stresses, and the textile must be able to give and recover without significant overall deformation of the textile.

FIBRE COHESIVENESS

Fibres must be capable of adhering to one another when spun into a yarn. The cohesiveness of the fibre may be due to the shape and contour of the individual fibre s or the nature of the surface of the fibres.

In addition, long-filament fibres by virtue of their length can be twisted together to give stability without true cohesion between fibres. Often the term "spinning quality" is used to state the overall attractiveness of fibres for one another.

MOISTURE ABSORPTION AND DESORPTION

Most fibres tend to absorb moisture (water vapor) when in contact with the atmosphere. The amount of water absorbed by the textile fibre will depend on the chemical and physical structure and properties of the fibre, as well as the temperature and humidity of the surroundings.

The percentage absorption of water vapor by a fibre is often expressed as its moisture regain. The regain is determined by weighing a dry fibre, then placing it in a room set to standard temperature and humidity (21° ± 1° C and 65 per cent relative humidity [RH] are commonly used). From these measurements, the percentage moisture regain of the fibre is determined:

$$\text{Percentage Regain} = \frac{\textit{Conditioned weight} - \textit{Dry Weight}}{\textit{Dry Weight}} \times 100\%$$

Percentage moisture content of a fibre is the percentage of the total weight of the fibre which is due to the moisture present, and is obtained from the following formula:

Percentage moisture content Conditioned weight

$$= \frac{\textit{Dry weight}}{\textit{Conditioned weight}} \times 100\%$$

The percentage moisture content will always be the smaller of the two values. Fibres vary greatly in their regain, with hydrophobic (water-repelling) fibres having regains near zero and hydrophilic (water-seeking) fibres like cotton, rayon, and wool having regains as high as 15 per cent at 21°C and 65 per cent RH. The ability of fibres to absorb high regains of water affects the basic properties of the fibre in end-use. Absorbent fibres are able to absorb large amounts of water before they feel wet, an important factor where absorption of perspiration is necessary. Fibres with high regains will be easier to process, finish, and dye in aqueous solutions, but will dry more slowly.

The low regain found for many man-made fibres makes them quick drying, a distinct advantage in certain applications. Fibres with high regains are often desirable because they provide a "breathable" fabric which can conduct moisture from the body to the outside atmosphere readily, due to their favourable moisture absorption-desorption properties. The tensile properties of fibres as well as their dimensional properties are known to be affected by moisture.

FIBRE RESILIENCY AND ABRASION RESISTANCE

The ability of a fibre to absorb shock and recover from deformation and to be generally resistant to abrasion forces is important to its end-use and wear characteristics. In consumer use, fibres in fabrics are often placed under stress through compression, bending, and twisting (torsion) forces under a variety of temperature and humidity conditions. If the fibres within the fabric possess good elastic recovery properties from such deformative actions, the fibre has good resiliency and better overall appearance in end-use. For example, cotton and wool show poor wrinkle recovery under hot moist conditions, whereas polyester exhibits good recovery from deformation as a result of its high resiliency.

Resistance of a fibre to damage when mobile forces or stresses come in contact with fibre structures is referred to as abrasion resistance. If a fibre is able to effectively absorb and dissipate these forces without damage, the fibre will show good abrasion resistance. The toughness and hardness of the fibre is related to its chemical and physical structure and morphology of the fibre and will influence the abrasion of the fibre. A rigid, brittle fibre such as glass, which is unable to dissipate the forces of abrasive action, results in fibre damage and breakage, whereas a tough but more plastic fibre such as polyester shows better resistance to abrasion forces. Finishes can affect fibre properties including resiliency and abrasion resistance.

Luster

Luster refers to the degree of light that is reflected from the surface of a fibre or the degree of gloss or sheen that the fibre possesses. The inherent chemical and physical structure and shape of the possesses. The inherent chemical and physical structure and shape of the fibre can affect the relative luster of the fibre. With natural fibres the luster of the fibre is dependent on the morphological form that nature gives the fibre, although the relative luster can be changed by chemical and/or physical treatment of the fibre as found in processes such as mercerisation of cotton.

Man-made fibres can vary in luster from bright to dull depending on the amount of delusterant added to the fibre. Oelusterants such as titanium dioxide tend to scatter and absorb 1ight, thereby making the fibre appear duller. The desirability of luster for a given fibre application will vary and is often dependent on the intended end-use of the fibre in a fabric or garment form and on current fashion trends.

RESISTANCE TO CHEMICALS IN THE ENVIRONMENT

A textile fibre to be useful must have reasonable resistance to chemicals it comes in contact with in its environment during use and maintenance. It should have resistance to oxidation by oxygen and other gases in the air, particularly in the presence of light, and be resistant to attack by microorganisms and other biological agents. Many fibres undergo light-induced reactions, and fibres from natural sources are susceptible to biological attack, but such deficiencies can be minimized by treatment with appropriate finishes. Textile fibres come in contact with a large range of chemical agents on laundering and dry cleaning and must be resistant from attack under such conditions.

Density

The density of a fibre is related to its inherent chemical structure and the packing of the molecular chains within that structure. The density of a fibre will have a noticeable effect on its aesthetic appeal and its usefulness in given applications. For example, glass and silk fabrics of the same denier would have noticeable differences in weight due to their broad differences in density. Fishnets of polypropylene fibres are of great utility because their density is less than that of water. Oensities are usually expressed in units of grams per cubic centimeter, but in 51 units will be expressed as kilograms per cubic meter, which gives a value 1000 times larger.

THERMAL AND FLAMMABILITY CHARACTERISTICS

Fibres used in textiles must be resistant to wet and dry heat, must not ignite readily when coming in contact with a flame, and ideally should self-extinguish when the flame is removed. Heat stability is particularly important to a fibre during dyeing and finishing of the textile and during cleaning and general maintenance by the consumer. Textile fibres for the most part are made up of organic polymeric materials containing carbon and burn on ignition from a flame or other propagating source. The chemical structure of a fibre establishes its overall flammability characteristics, and appropriate textile finishes can reduce the degree of flammability. A number of Federal, state, and local statutes eliminate the most dangerous flammable fabrics from the marketplace.

PRIMARY FIBRE PROPERTIES FROM AN ENGINEERING PERSPECTIVE

The textile and polymer engineer must consider a number of criteria essential for formation, fabrication, and assembly of fibres into textile substrates. Often the criteria used will be similar to those set forth above concerning end-use properties.

Ideally a textile fibre should have the following properties:

- A melting and/or decomposition point above 220°C.
- Elongation at break above 10 per cent with reversible elongation up to 5 per cent strain.
- Resistance to attack, swelling, or solution in solvents, acids, and bases.
- Self-extinguishing when removed from a flame.

FIBRE FORMATION AND MORPHOLOGY

Fibre morphology refers to the form and structure of a fibre, including the molecular arrangement of individual molecules and groups of molecules within the fibre. Most fibres are organic materials derived from carbon combined with other atoms such as oxygen, nitrogen, and halogens. The basic building blocks that organic materials form as covalently-bonded organic compounds are called monomers.

Covalent bonds involve the sharing of electrons between adjacent atoms within the monomer, and the structure tons between adjacent atoms within the monomer, and the structure of the monomer is determined by the type, location, and nature of bonding of atoms within the monomer and by the nature of covalent bonding between atoms. Monomers react or condense to form long-chain molecules called polymers made up of a given number (n) of monomer units which are the basic building unit of fibres. On formation into fibres and orientation by natural or mechanical means the polymeric molecules possess ordered crystalline and non-ordered amorphous areas, depending on the nature of the polymer and the relative packing of molecules within the fibre. For a monomer A the sequence of events to fibre formation and orientation would appear as shown in figure.

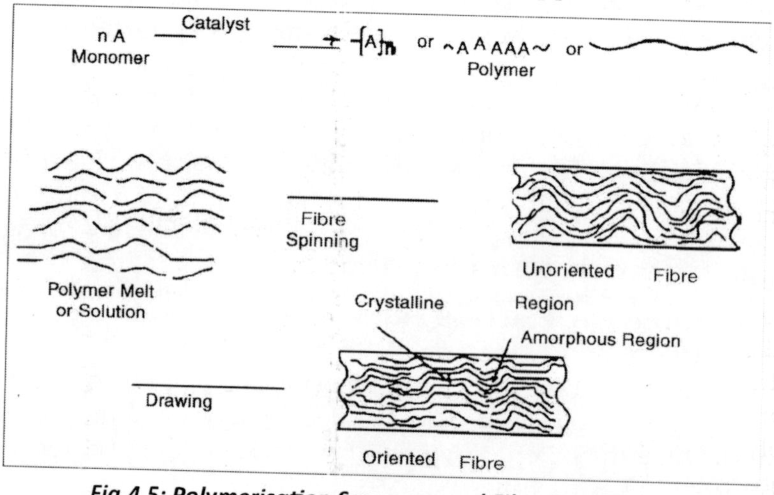

Fig.4.5: Polymerisation Sequence and Fibre Formation.

Polymers with repeating units of the same monomer (An) would be referred to as homopolymers. If a second unit B is introduced into the basic structure, structures which are copolymers are formed with structures as outlined in figure.

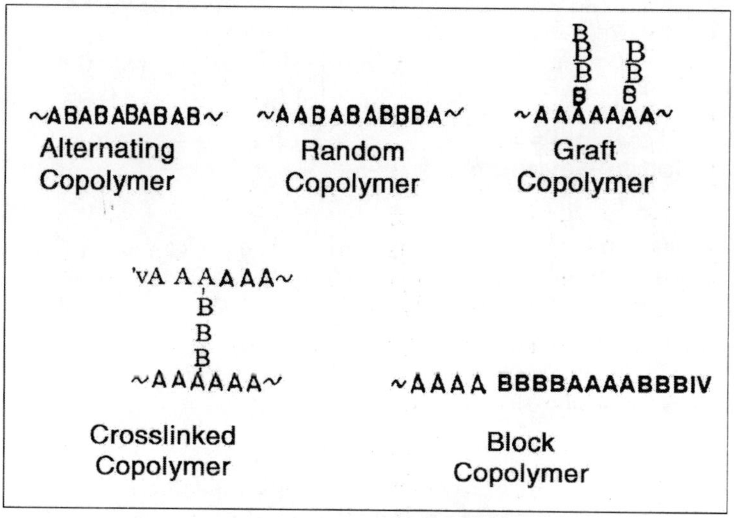

Fig.4.6: Copolymer Structures.

POLYMER FORMATION

Synthetic polymers used to form fibres are often classified on the basis of their mechanism of polymerisation—step growth (condensation) or chain growth (addition) polymerisation. Step growth polymerisation involves multifunctional monomers which undergo successive condensation with a second monomer or with itself to form a dimer, which in turn condenses with another dimer to form a tetramer, etc., usually with loss of a small molecule such as water. Chain growth involves the instantaneous growth of a long molecular chain from unsaturated monomer units, followed by initiation of a second chain, etc.

The average number of monomer repeating units in a polymer chain (n) is often referred to also as the degree of polymerisation, DP. The DP must exceed an average 20 units in most cases to give a polymer of sufficient molecular size to have desirable fibre-forming properties. The overall breadth of distribution of molecular chain lengths in the polymer will affect the ultimate properties of the fibres, with wide polymer size distributions leading to an overall reduction of fibre properties. Although the polymers from natural fibres and regenerated natural fibres do not undergo polymerisation by the mechanisms found for synthetic fibres, most natural polymers have characteristic repeating units and high degrees of polymerisation and are related to step growth polymers. Basic polymeric structures for the major fibres are given in figure.

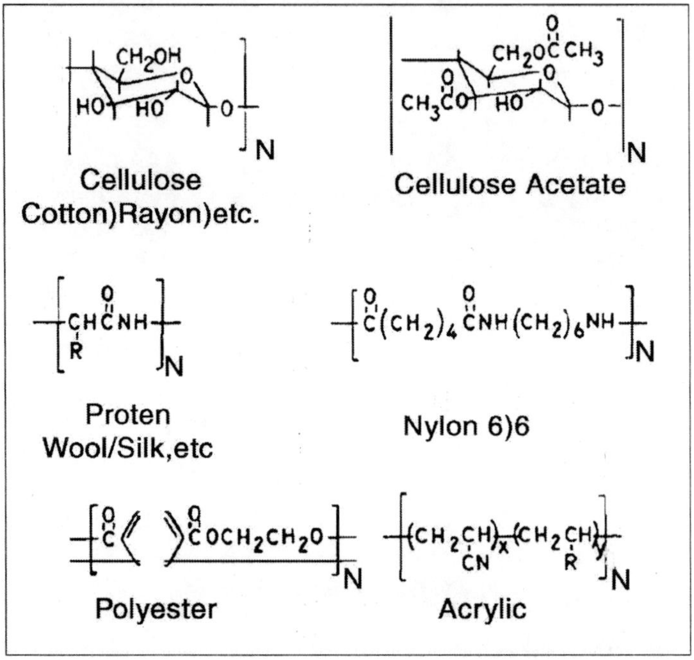

Fig.4.7: Basic Polymeric Structures for Major Fibres.

FIBRE SPINNING

Although natural fibres come in a morphological form determined by nature, regenerated and synthetic man-made fibres can be "tailor-made" depending on the shape and dimensions of the orifice (spinning jet) that the polymer is forced through to form the fibre. There are several methods used to spin a fibre from its polymer, including melt, dry, wet, emulsion, and suspension spinning. Melt spinning is the least complex of the methods. The polymer from which the fibre is made is melted and then forced through a spinneret and into air to cause solidification and fibre formation. Dry and wet spinning processes involve dissolving the fibre-forming polymer in an appropriate solvent, followed by passing a concentrated solution (20 per cent- 50 per cent polymer) through the spinneret and into dry air to evaporate the solvent in the case of dry spinning or into a coagulating bath to cause precipitation or regeneration of the polymer in fibre form in the case of wet spinning.

There is a net contraction of the spinning solution on loss of solvent. If a skin of polymer is formed on the fibre followed by diffusion of the remainder of the solvent from the core of the forming fibre, the cross-section of the fibre as it contracts may collapse to form an irregular popcorn like cross section. Emulsion spinning is used only for those fibre-forming polymers that are insoluble. Polymer is mixed with a surface-active agent (detergent) and possibly a solvent and then mixed at high speeds with water to form an emulsion of the polymer. The polymer is passed through the spinneret and into a coagulating bath to form the fibre. In suspension spinning, the polymer is swollen and suspended in a swelling solvent. The swollen suspended polymer is forced through the spinneret into dry hot air to drive off solvent or into a wet non-solvent bath to cause the fibre to form through coagulation.

The spinning process can be divided into two steps:

1. Flow of spinning fluid within and through the spinneret under high stress and sheer.
2. Exit of fluid from the spinneret with relief of stress and an increase in volume (ballooning of flow).

Common cross sections of man-made fibres include:

- Round,
- Trilobal,
- Dog-bone, and
- Crescent shapes.

When two polymers are used in fibre formation as in bicomponent or biconstituent fibres, the two components can be arranged in a matrix, side-by-side, or sheath-core configuration. Round cross sections are also found where skin formation has caused fibre contraction and puckering (as with rayons) has occurred or where the spinneret shape has provided a hollow fibre. Complex fibre cross-sectional shapes with special properties are also used.

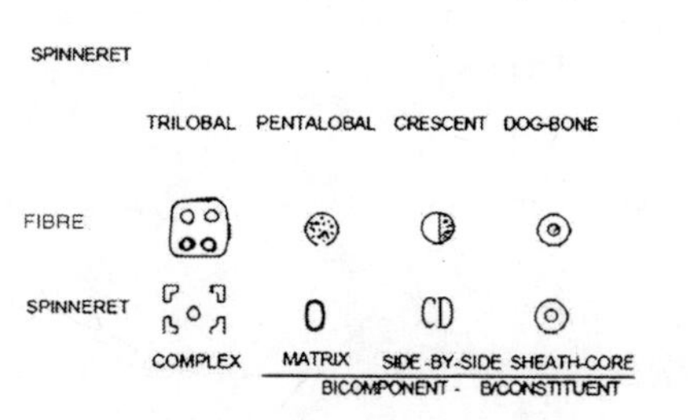

Fig.4.8: Fibre Cross Sections.

FIBRE DRAWING AND MORPHOLOGY

On drawing and orientation the man-made fibres become smaller in diameter and more crystalline, and imperfections in the fibre morphology are improved somewhat. Side-by-side bi component or bi constituent fibres on drawing become wavy and bulky. In natural fibres the orientation of the molecules within the fibre is determined by the biological source during the growth and maturity process of the fibre. The form and structure of polymer molecules with relation to each other within the fibre will depend on the relative alignment of the molecules in relationship to one another. Those areas where the polymer chains are closely aligned and packed close together are crystalline areas within the fibre, whereas those areas where there is essentially no molecular alignment are referred to as amorphous areas. Dyes and finishes can penetrate the amorphous portion of the fibre, but not the ordered crystalline portion.

CROSS-SECTION

A number of theories exist concerning the arrangement of crystalline and amorphous areas within a fibre. Individual crystal 1ine areas in a fibre are often referred to as microfibrils. Microfibrils can associate into larger crystalline groups, which are called fibrils or micelles. Microfibrils are 30-100 Å in length, whereas fibrils and micelles are usually 200-600 Å in length. This compares to the individual molecular chains, which vary from 300 to 1500 Å in length and which are usually part of both crystal line and amorphous areas of the polymer and therefore give continuity and association of the various crystal line and amorphous areas within the fibre.

A number of theories have been developed to explain the interconnection of crystal line and amorphous areas in the fibre and include such concepts as fringed micelles or fringed fibrils, molecular chain folding, and extended chain concepts. The amorphous areas within a fibre will be relatively loosely packed and associated with each other, and spaces or voids will appear due to discontinuities within the structure. Figure outlines the various aspects of internal fibre morphology with regard to polymer chains.

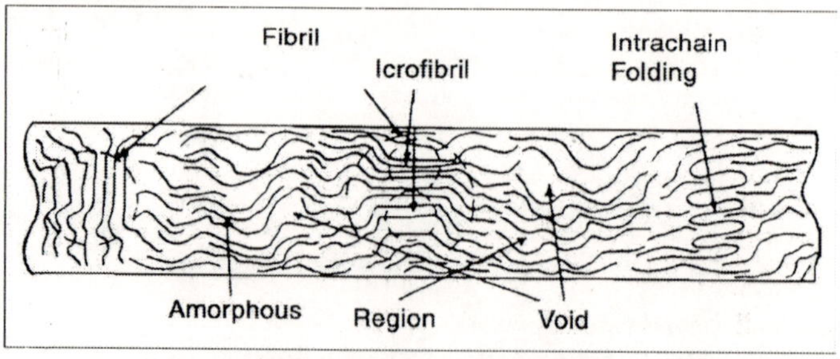

Fig.4.9: Aspects of Internal Fibre Morphology.

The force s that keep crystalline areas together within a fibre include chemical bonds (covalent, ionic) as well as secondary bonds. Cova lent bonds result from sharing of electrons between atoms, such as found in carboncarbon, carbon-oxygen, and carbon-nitrogen bonding, within organic compounds. Covalent bonds joining adjacent polymer chains are referred to as crosslinks. Ionic bonding occurs when molecules donate or accept electrons from each other, a s when a metal salt reacts with acid side chains on a po1ymer within a fibre. Chemical bonds a re much stronger than secondary bonds formed between polymer chains, but the total associative force between polymer chains can be large, since a very large number of such bonds may occur between adjacent polymer chains.

Hydrogen bonds are the strongest of the secondary bonds and occur between electropositive hydrogen atoms and electronegative atoms such as oxygen, nitrogen, and halogen s on opposing polymer chains. Nylon, protein, and cellulosic fibres are capable of extensive hydrogen bonding. Van der Waals interactions between polymer chains occur when clouds of electrons from each chain come in close proximity, thereby promoting a small attractive force between chains. The more extended the cloud of electrons, the stronger the van der Waals interaction will be. Covalent bonded materials will show some uneven distribution of electron density over the molecule due to the differing electronegativity of the atoms and electron distribution over the molecule to form dipoles. Dipoles on adjacent polymer chains of opposite charge and close proximity are attracted to each other and promote secondary bonding. When a synthetic fibre is stretched or drawn, the molecules in mo s t cases will orient themselves in crystalline areas parallel to the fibre axis, although crystalline areas in some chain-folded polymers such as polypropylene can be aligned vertical to the fibre axis. The degree of crystallinity will be affected by the total forces available for chain interaction, the distance between parallel chains, and the similarity and uniformity of adjacent chains. The structure and arrangement of individual polymer chains also affects the morphology of the fibre.

BULKING, TEXTURISING, AND STAPLE FORMATION

Thermoplastic man-made fibre s can be permanently heat-set after drawing and or ientation. The fibre will possess structural integrity and will not shrink up to that setting temperature.

Also, thermoplastic fibres or yarns from this fibre s can be texturised to give two dimensional loft and bulkiness:

1. Through fibre deformation and setting at or near their softening temperature,
2. Through air entanglement, or

Table.4.1: Texturising Methods

Heat-setting Techniques	Air Entanglement	Differential Setting
False Twist Knife edge Stuffer box Gear crimping Autowist Knit-de-knit	Air Jet	Bicomoponent-biconstituent Fibre orientation Heat shrinkage of thermoplastic fibres in a blend

Schematic representations of these methods are given in figure.

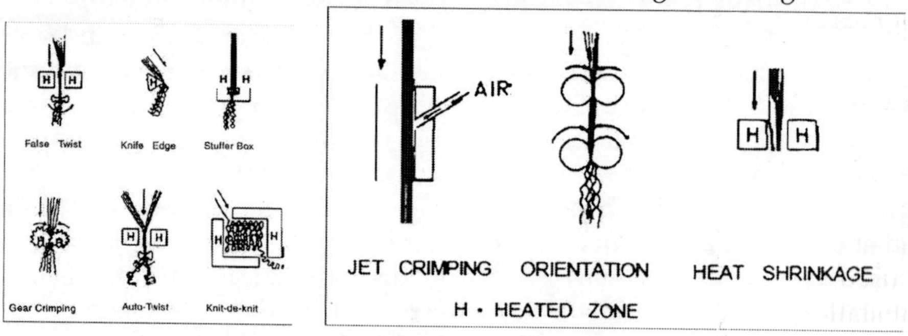

Fig.4.10: Texturising Methods.

Heat-Setting Techniques

The false twist heat-setting technique is extremely rapid, inexpensive, and most widely used. The filament fibre tow is brought in contact with a high- speed spindle running vertical to the moving tow. This action results in a high twist in the tow up to the spindle. The twisted tow is heated near its softening point before passing the spindle and then cooled and untwisted to give a wavy bulky yarn.

In knife edge texturising, filament tows or yarns are passed over a heated knife edge under tension. The fibres near the knife edge are changed in overall orientation in relation to the unheated yarns or portion of the filaments away from the knife edge, thereby causing bulking of the yarn. In stuffer box texturising, the filament tow is fed into a heated box, causing the tow to double up against itself. On removal, the cooled tow retains the zigzag configuration caused by the process. In gear crimping, the tow is passed between heated intermeshing gears. On cooling the fibres retain the shape induced by the heated gears. In auto-twisting, two tows or yarns are twisted together and then heat set. On untwisting the yarns have equal but opposite twists, which causes a spiral bulking of the yarn. In the knit-de-knit process a yarn is fill knitted, heat set, cooled, and deknitted to give a bulked yarn retaining the shape and curvature of the knit.

Air Entanglement

In air entanglement texturising, a fibre tow is loosely fed into and through a restricted space and a high-speed air jet is impinged on the fibres at a 45° angle. The loose fibres within the tow are looped to give a texturised effect.

Differential Setting

Heat shrinkage techniques cause a bulking of fibre tows containing different fibres through heating one component of the blend sufficiently to cause heat shrinkage of the fibre and compaction, contraction, and bulking. Side-by-side bicomponent and biconstituent fibres recover different degrees on each side from fibre stretching and causing a waving, crimping, or bulking of the fibre.

STAPLE FORMATION

Continuous filaments can be cut into staple by wet or dry cutting techniques. In wet cutting, the wet spun fibre is cut to uniform lengths right after spinning, while dry cutting involves partial cutting, debonding, and shuffling of the dry tow to form a sliver. Before the filament or staple is used in yarn spinning, spin finishes are added to give lubricity and antistatic characteristics to the fibres and to provide a greater degree of fibre cohesiveness. Such finishes are usually mixtures including such materials as fatty acid esters, mineral oils, synthetic esters, silicones, cationic amines, phosphate esters, emulsifiers, and/or non-ionic surfactants. Spin finishes are formulated to be oxidation resistant, to be easily removed by scouring, to give a controlled viscosity, to be stable to corrosion, to resist odour and colour formation, and to be non-volatile and readily emulsifiable.

STRUCTURE-PROPERTY RELATIONSHIPS

The basic chemical and morphological structure of polymers in a fibre determine the fundamental properties of a fabric made from that fibre. Although physical and chemical treatments and changes in yarn and fabric formation parameters can alter the fabric properties to some degree, the basic properties of the fabric result from physical and chemical properties inherent to the structure of the polymer making up the fibre. To that end, in the following stages as suggested, describe the various textile fibres in terms of their basic structural properties, followed by physical and chemical properties, and finally the end-use characteristics inherent to constructions made from the fibre. Initially the name and general information for a given fibre is set forth followed by an outline of the structural properties, including information about chemical structure of the polymer, degree of polymerisation, and arrangement of molecular chains within the fibre.

Physical properties include mechanical (tensile) and environmental properties of the fibre, whereas the effect of common chemicals and chemically induced processes on the fibre is listed under chemical properties. The end- use properties are then listed and include properties coming inherently from the structural, physical, and chemical properties of the fibre as well as end- use properties that involve evaluation of performance, subjective aspects, and aesthetics of the fabrics. Where possible, the interrelationships of these properties are presented.

TECHNICAL TECHNOLOGY USES IN FIBRES AND TEXTILES

A number of definitions have been used to describe the term 'technical textiles' with respect to their intended use, functional ability and their non- aesthetic or decorative requirements. However, none of these carefully chosen words include the fundamental fibre elements, technical or otherwise, which make up the technical textile structures. The omission of the word 'fibre' may indeed be deliberate as most technical textile products are made from conventional fibres that are already well established. In fact over 90% of all fibres used in the technical sector are of the conventional type.

Historically, utilisation of fibres in technical capacities dates back to the early Egyptians and Chinese who used papyrus mats to reinforce and consolidate the foundations respectively of the pyramids and the Buddhist temples. However, their serious use in modern civil engineering projects only began after the floods of 1953 in The Netherlands in which many people lost their lives. The event initiated the famous Delta works project in which for the first time synthetic fibres were written into the vast construction programme. Since then, geotextiles in particular have matured into important and indispensable multifunctional materials. Use of silk in semitechnical applications also goes back a long way to the lightweight warriors of the Mongolian armies, who did not only wear silk next to their skin for comfort but also to reduce penetration of incoming arrows and enable their subsequent removal with minimal injury.

In light of extensive utilization of conventional fibres in the technical sector, this chapter initially attempts to discuss fibres under this category highlighting their importance and the scope of their versatility. The discussion covers concisely an outline of fibre backgrounds, chemical compositions and their salient characteristics. It then introduces other fibres which have been specially developed to perform under extreme stress and/or temperature; ultrafine and novel fibres are also discussed. Finally, the chapter concludes by identifying areas of application and the roles that selected fibres play in fulfilling their intended purpose. The complete range of fibres available to the end-user and some of their mechanical properties.

HIGH MODULUS ORGANIC FIBRES

Keller's much-published contribution to the understanding of crystal growth in 1957 and confirmation of the tendency of polymers to form folded-chain crystals, provided the insight and inspiration for development of high strength, high modulus organic fibres that would surpass conventional fibres. During crystallisation, long chains of molecules fold back on themselves to form folded-chain crystals which only partly unfold during normal drawing. In the Netherlands in the 1970s DSM developed a super drawing technique known as gel spinning, which uses dilute solutions of ultra-high molecular weight polymers such as polyethylene to unfold the chains further and thus increase both tensile strength and fibre modulus. Ultra-high molecular weight polyethylene (UHMWPE) fibres, Dyneema or Spectra, are today the strongest fibres known, with tensile moduli in excess of 70 GN m~2. Weight for weight this fibre genus is claimed to be 15 times stronger than steel and twice as strong as aromatic polyamides such as Kevlar. It is also low in density, chemically inert and abrasion resistant. It, however, melts at around 150 °C and thermally degrades at 350°C which restrict its use to low temperature applications.

To achieve even better performance characteristics at higher temperatures, other means of fibre production were explored in the 1960s. One successful approach eventually led to the advent of liquid crystalline polymers. These are based on polymerisation of long stiff molecules such as para-phenylene terephthalamide achieving molecular weights averaging to around 20,000. The influence of the stiff aromatic rings, together with hydrogen-bonding crosslinks, combines the best features of both the polyamides and the polyesters in an extended-chain configuration.

Molecular orientation of these fibres is brought about by capillary shear along the flow of the polymer as it exits from the spinneret thus overriding the need for subsequent drawing. Kevlar by DuPont and Twaron by Akzo (now Acordis) were the first of such fibres to appear in the early 1970s. There now exists a series of first, second and third generations of para-aramids. Kevlar HT for instance, which has 20% higher tenacity and Kevlar HM which has 40% higher modulus than the original Kevlar 29 are largely utilised in the composite and the aerospace industries.

Para-aramids generally have high glass transition temperatures nearing 370 °C and do not melt or burn easily, but carbonise at and above 425 °C. All aramid fibres are however prone to photodegradation and need protection against the sun when used out of doors. These will be discussed later. Other high tenacity and high modulus fibres include the isotropically spun Technora (Teijin) and Supara, based upon para-aramid copolymers, with slightly lower maximum strength and modulus values than Kevlar. Several other melt spinnable liquid crystalline polymers are also available.

Combustion-resistant Organic Fibres

The fibres were developed following earlier observations that aromatic polymer backbones yielded improved tensile and heat resistance compared with conventional fibres. However, if the polymer chains have lower symmetry and order, then polymer tractability and textile fibre characteristics are improved. Solvent-spun Nomex and Conex were the first so-called meta- aramids made from poly(meta-phenylene isophthalamide) and were produced by DuPont in 1962 and by Teijin in 1972, respectively. The meta-phenylene isophthalamide molecule is identical in all but the position of its —NH— and—CO— groups to para-phenylene terephthalamide (or Kevlar) molecules. The different positioning of these groups in meta-aramids creates a zig-zag molecular structure that prevents it from full crystallisation thus accounting for its relatively poorer tensile properties. However, Nomex is particularly well known for its resistance to combustion, high decomposition temperature prior to melting and high limited oxygen index (LOI), the minimum amount of oxygen required to induce ignition.

Melt-spinnable aromatic fibres with chains containing paraphenylene rings, like polyether ether ketone (PEEK), polyether ketone (PEK) and poly(p- phenylene sulphide) (PPS), also have high melting points but, since their melting points occur prior to their decomposition temperature, they are unsuitable for fire-retardant applications. However, their good chemical resistance renders them suitable for low temperature filtration and other corrosive environments. The polyheterocyclic fibre, polybenzimidazole or PBI, produced by Hoechst-Celanese has an even higher LOI than the aramids.

It has excellent resistance to both heat and chemical agents but remains rather expensive. P84, initially produced by Lenzing and now produced by Inspec Fibres, USA, comprises polyimide groups that yield reasonably high resistance to fire and chemical attack. The acrylic copolymer-based fibre produced by Acordis known as Inidex (although now no longer produced) unlike many aramid fibres has high resistance to UV (ultraviolet) radiation and a fairly high LOI at the expense of much reduced tenacity and rather low long-term exposure resistance to heat.

Oxidised acrylic fibre, best known as Panox (SGL, UK) is another crosslinked, high combustion-resistant material produced by combined oxidation and pyrolysis of acrylic fibres at around 300°C. Although black in appearance, it is not classed as carbon fibre and preserves much of its original non-carbonaceous structure. In addition, it does not have the graphitic or turbostratic structure of carbon fibres. It retains a sufficiently high extension- at-break to be subjected to quite normal textile processes for yarn and fabric formation. Panox has a very high LOI of 0.55. Fully carbonised, or carbon fibres with even higher tensile properties, are achieved by full carbonisation of these oxidised precursor fibres or by the melt spinning of liquid crystalline mesophase pitch followed by their oxidation and pyrolysis.

Ultra-fine and Novelty Fibres

Ultra-fine or microfibres were developed partly because of improved precision in engineering techniques and better production controls, and partly because of the need for lightweight, soft waterproof fabrics that eliminate the more conventional coating or lamination processes. As yet there are no universal definitions of microfibres. Textile Terms and Definitions simply describes them as fibres or filaments with linear densities of approximately 1.0dtex or less. Others have used such terms as fine, extra-fine and micro-fine corresponding to linear densities ranging from 3.0dtex to less than 0.1dtex. They are usually made from polyester and nylon polymers, but other polymers are now being made into microfibres. The Japanese first introduced microfibres in an attempt to reproduce silk-like properties with the addition of enhanced durability. They are produced by at least three established methods including island-in-sea, split process and melt spinning techniques and appear under brand names such as Mitrelle, Setila, Micrell, Tactel and so on. Once in woven fabric form their fine diameter and tight weave allows up to 30000 filaments cm2, making them impermeable to water droplets whilst allowing air and moisture vapour circulation.

They can be further processed to enhance other characteristics such as peach-skin and leather-like appearances. The split technique of production imparts sharp-angled edges within the fibre surface, which act as gentle abraders when made into wiping cloths that are used in the optical and precision microelectronic industries. Microfibres are also used to make bacteria barrier fabrics in the medical industries. Their combined effect of low diameter and compact packing also allows efficient and more economical dyeing and finishing. Finally, constant pressure to achieve and develop even more novel applications of fibres has led to a number of other and, as yet, niche fibrous products. In principle, the new ideas usually strive to combine basic functional properties of a textile material with special needs or attractive effects.

For example, Solar-Aloha, developed by Descente and Unitika in Japan, absorbs light of less than 2|jm wavelength and converts it to heat owing to its zirconium carbide content. Winter sports equipment made from these materials use the cold winter sun to capture more than 90% of this incident energy to keep the wearer warm. Another interesting material gives rise to thermochromic fabrics made by Toray which have a uniform coating of microcapsules containing heat-sensitive dyes that change colour at 5 °C intervals over a temperature range of -40 °C to 80 °C creating 'fun' and special effects.

Cripy 65 is a scented fibre produced by Mitsubishi Rayon (R) who have enclosed a fragrant essence in isolated cavities along the length of hollow polyester fibres. The scent is gradually released to give a consistent and pleasant aroma. Pillows and bed linen made from these materials are claimed to improve sleep and sleeping disorders. The effect can also be achieved by printing or padding microcapsules containing perfumes into fabrics which subsequently burst and release the perfume. With careful handling, garments made from these materials are said to maintain this property for up to two years. Infrared-emitting and bacteria-repelling fibres are some of the other emerging novel fibres.

High Performance Inorganic Fibres

Any fibre that consists of organic chemical units, where carbon is linked to hydrogen and possibly also to other elements, will decompose below about 500°C and cease to have long-term stability at considerably lower temperatures. For use at high temperatures it is therefore necessary to turn to inorganic fibres and fibres that consist essentially of carbon. Glass, asbestos and more recently carbon are three well-known inorganic fibres that have been extensively used for many of their unique characteristics.

Use of glass as a fibre apparently dates back to the ancient Syrian and Egyptian civilisations which used them for making clothes and dresses. However, the very high modulus or stiffness displayed by these fibres means that they are quite brittle and can easily be damaged by surface marks and defects. They are, therefore, best utilised by embedding in matrix forms where the fibres are fully protected.

Epoxy resins, polyester and other polymers, as well as cement, have commonly been used both to protect and to make use of their contributory strength. Glass-reinforced boat hulls and car bodies, to name but two application areas of such composites, reduce overall weight and cost of fabrication as well as eliminating the traditional problems of rotting wood and rusting metals associated with traditional materials. Their good resistance to heat and very high melting points have also enabled them to be used as effective insulating materials.

Asbestos is a generic name for a variety of crystalline silicates that occur naturally in some rocks. The fibres that are extracted have all the textile-like properties of fineness, strength, flexibility and more importantly, unlike conventional fibres, good resistance to heat with high decomposition temperatures of around 550 °C. Their use as a reinforcement material has been found in clay-rich prehistoric cooking pots discovered in Finland.

In more recent times they have been extensively used to reinforce brittle matrices such as cement sheeting, pipes, plastics and also as heat insulators. However, with the discovery of their carcinogenic hazards, their use has gradually declined and alternative fibres have been developed to replace them totally.

High purity, pyrolysed acrylic-based fibres are classified as carbon fibres. The removal of impurities enhances carbon content and prevents the nucleation and growth of graphite crystals which are responsible for loss of strength in these fibres. Carbon fibres with different structures are also made from mesophase pitch. The graphite planes in PAN-based fibres are arranged parallel to the fibre axis rather than perpendicular as is the case with pitch- based carbon fibres. Their high strength and modulus combined with relatively low extensibility means that they are best utilised in association with epoxy or melt-spinnable aromatic resins as composites.

Increasing demand in the defence and aerospace industries for even better performance under extreme conditions led, within the last quarter of the 20th century, to yet another range of new and rather expensive metal oxides, boron and silicon-based fibres. These are often referred to as ceramic fibres and will now be briefly discussed. Aluminosilicate compounds are mixtures of aluminium oxide (Al_2O) and silicon oxide (SiO_2); their resistance to temperature depends on the mixing ratio of the two oxides. High aluminium oxide content increases their temperature tolerance from a low of 1250°C to a maximum of 1400°C.

However, despite their high temperature resistance, these fibres are not used in high stress applications owing to their tendency to creep at high temperatures. Their prime applications are in insulation of furnaces and replacement of asbestos fibres in friction materials, gaskets and packings. Both aluminium oxide or alumina fibres and silicon oxide or silica fibres are also produced. Pure boron fibres are too brittle to handle but they can be coated on tungsten or carbon cores.

Their complex manufacturing process makes them rather expensive. Their prime application is in lightweight, high strength and high modulus composites such as racket frames and aircraft parts. Boron fibre use is limited by their thickness, their relatively poor stability in metal matrices and their gradual loss of strength with increasing temperature. Boron nitrides (BN) are primarily used in the electronic industry where they perform both as electrical insulators and thermal conductors.

The most outstanding property of silicon carbide (SiC) is the ability to function in oxidizing conditions up to 1800 °C with little loss of mechanical properties. Silicon carbide exceeds carbon fibre in its greater resistance to oxidation at high temperatures, its higher compressive strength and better electrical resistance.

Finally, many of the inorganic fibres so far referred to are now also produced in microcrystalline or whisker form and not in the more normal textile-fibre form. Whiskers have extremely good mechanical properties and their tensile strength is usually three to four times those of most reinforcing fibres. They are, however, costly to produce and their inclusion into composite structures is both difficult and cumbersome.

CONVENTIONAL AND NATURAL FIBRES

Cotton accounts for half of the world's consumption of fibres and is likely to remain so owing to many of its innate properties and for economical reasons that will not be discussed here. Cotton is made of long chains of natural cellulose containing carbon, hydrogen and oxygen otherwise known as polysaccharides. The length of the chains determines the ultimate strength of the fibre. An average of 10000 cel-lulosic repeat or monomeric units make up the individual cellulose chains which are about 2 | jm in length. The linear molecules combine into microfibrils and are held together by strong intermolecular forces to form the cotton fibre. The unique physical and aesthetic properties of the fibre, combined with its natural generation and biodegradability, are reasons for its universal appeal and popularity. Chemical treatments such as Proban and Pyrovatex are two examples of the type of durable finishes that can be applied to make cotton fire retardant. High moisture absorbency, high wet modulus and good handle are some of the more important properties of cotton fibre.

Wool, despite its limited availability and high cost, is the second most important natural fibre. It is made of protein: a mixture of chemically linked amino acids which are also the natural constituents of all living organisms. Keratin or the protein in the wool fibre has a helical rather than folded chain structure with strong inter- and intrachain hydrogen bonding which are believed to be responsible for many of its unique characteristics. Geographical location, the breeding habits of the animals, and climatic conditions are some of the additional variables responsible for its properties.

The overall high extensibility of wool, its natural waviness and ability to trap air has a coordinated effect of comfort and warmth, which also make it an ideal insulating material. The sophisticated dual morphology of wool produces the characteristic crimp which has also been an inspiration for the development of some highly technical synthetic fibres. Wool is inherently fire retardant, but further improvements can be achieved by a number of fire- retardant treatments. Zirconium- and titanium-treated wool is one such example which is now universally referred to as Zirpro (IWS) wool.

Flax, jute, hemp and ramie, to name but a few of the best fibres, have traditionally taken a secondary role in terms of consumption and functional requirements. They are relatively coarse and durable, and flax has traditionally been used for linen making. Jute, ramie and to a lesser extent other fibres have received attention within the geotextile sector of the fibre markets which seeks to combine the need for temporary to short-term usage with biodegradability, taking into account the regional availability of the fibres.

Silk is another protein-based fibre produced naturally by the silkworm, Bombyx Mori or other varieties of moth. Silk is structurally similar to wool with a slightly different combination of amino acids which make up the protein or the fibroin, as it is more appropriately known. Silk is the only naturally and commercially produced continuous filament fibre which has high tenacity, high lustre and good dimensional stability. Silk has been and will remain a luxury quality fibre with a special place in the fibre market. However, its properties of biocompatibility and gradual disintegration, as in sutures, have long been recognised in medical textiles.

Synthetic Fibres

All synthetic fibres originate from coal or oil. The first synthetic fibre that appeared on the world market in 1939 was nylon 6.6. It was produced by DuPont and gained rapid public approval. A series of nylons commonly referred to as polyamides now exists in which the amide linkage is the common factor. Nylon 6.6 and nylon 6 are most popular in fibre form. They are melt extruded in a variety of cross-sectional shapes and drawn to achieve the desired tenacity. They are well known for their high extensibility, good recovery, dimensional stability and relatively low moisture absorbency. Nylon 6.6 in particular soon became a popular household carpet fibre and was developed into fibres commonly known as Antron manufactured by DuPont. Antron fibres of various generations use additives, varied cross-sectional shapes and modified surface characteristics to enhance the aesthetic and visual appeal of carpets as well as improving their resilience and dissipating static charges.

Nylon was later surpassed by the even more popular fibre known as polyester, first introduced as Dacron by DuPont in 1951. Polyester is today the second most used fibre after cotton and far ahead of other synthetics both in terms of production and consumption. Polyethylene terephthalate or polyester is made by condensation polymerisation of ethylene glycol and terephthalic acid followed by melt extrusion and drawing. It can be used in either continuous form or as short staple of varying lengths.

The popularity of polyester largely stems from its easycare characteristics, durability and compatibility with cotton in blends. Its very low moisture absorbency, resilience and good dimensional stability are additional qualities. Many manufacturers across the world produce polyester under different commercial names with almost tailor-made properties. A high glass transition temperature of around 70 °C with good resistance to heat and chemical degradation also qualifies this polymer for most technical textile applications. These will be discussed in greater detail later. Flame-retardant Trevira CS and Trevira high tenacity, both polyesters developed and marketed by Trevira GmbH in Germany, are examples of the many varieties available today.

Wool-like properties are shown by polyacrylic fibres which are produced by the polymerisation of acrylonitrile using the addition route into polyacrylonitrile. They can then be spun into fibres by dry or wet spinning methods. Orlon was produced by DuPont. It had a distinctive dumbbell shaped cross-section and was extruded by the dry process in which the solvent is evaporated off. Acrilan produced by Mon-santo and Courtelle produced by Acordis are spun by the wet extrusion technique and have near circular cross- sections. Acrylic fibres now also appear in bicomponent form with wool-like characteristics.

Chemically modified acrylics, principally the modacrylics, include chlorine atoms in their molecular structure which are responsible for their low burning behaviour and, unlike acrylics, have the ability to self-extinguish once the source of ignition has been removed. A selected fibre in terms of fibre chemistry is Oasis, a superabsorbent fibre made by the collaborative efforts of Acordis and Allied Colloids, based on crosslinking copolymers of acrylic acid. This fibre is claimed to absorb moisture many times its own weight and holds it even under pressure. Its application in hygiene and medical care in different forms is being pursued. Polyolefin fibres include both polyethylene and polypropylene made by addition polymerisation of ethylene and propylene and subsequent melt extrusion, respectively.

Polyethylene has moderate physical properties with a low melting temperature of about 110 °C for its low density form and about 140 °C for its high density form which severely restricts its application in low temperature applications. Polypropylene has better mechanical properties and can withstand temperatures of up to 140 °C before melting at about 170 °C. Both polymers have a density less than that of water which allows them to float as ropes, nets and other similar applications. The availability, low cost and good resistance to acid and alkaline environments of polypropylene has greatly influenced its growth and substantial use in geotextile applications.

Finally, elastane fibres are synthetic-based elastomeric polymers with at least 85% segmented polyurethane in their structure. They have rubber-like properties, which means they can be extended up to six or more times their original length. They are used in combination with most natural and synthetic fibres in knitted and woven materials. They were initially produced by DuPont in 1959 under the now well-known trademark of Lycra.

Regenerated Fibres

Viscose rayon was the result of the human race's first attempts to mimic nature in producing silk-like continuous fibres through an orifice. Cellulose from wood pulp is the main constituent of this novel system, started commercially in the early 1920s. Thin sheets of cellulose are treated with sodium hydroxide and aged to allow molecular chain breakage.

Further treatment with carbon disulphide, dissolution in dilute sodium hydroxide and ageing produces a viscous liquid, the viscose dope, which is then extruded into an acid bath. he continuous filaments that finally emerge are washed, dried and can be cut to staple lengths. The shorter cellulose molecules in viscose and their partial crystallisation accounts for its rather inferior physical properties relative to cotton. Further development and refinement of the manufacturing technique have created a whole range of fibres with improved properties.

High tenacity and high wet modulus viscose compare in all but appearance to cotton in both dry and wet conditions. Chemically altered regenerated cellulose di- and triacetates do not burn like cotton and viscose to leave a fluffy black ash, but melt and drip instead. This characteristic enables them to be shaped or textured to enhance their visual and aesthetic appeal. Hollow viscose modifications give enhanced bulk and moisture absorbency and have an improved cotton-like feel. Fire-retardant (FR) viscose was first introduced in the 1960s. A major example is produced by Lenzing in Austria by incorporating organophosphorous compounds into the spinning dope prior to extrusion. The additive is reasonably stable and has no chemical interaction with the cellulose molecules. It is also unaffected by bleaching, washing, dry cleaning, dyeing and finishing processes.

Early in the 1990s Kemira (now Sateri Fibres) of Finland introduced an alternative version of FR viscose known as Visil in which polysilicic acid is present. The fibre chars upon heating leaving a silica residue. Lyocell, is the latest addition to this series of fibres, commercially known as Tencel

(Acordis), has all the conventional properties of viscose in addition to its much praised environmentally friendly production method. The solvent used is based on non-toxic JV-methyl morpholine oxide used in a recyclable closed loop system, which unlike the viscose process avoids discharge of waste. Highly absorbent derivatives of Tencel, known as Hydrocell are establishing a foothold in wound dressing and other medical-related areas of textiles.

CIVIL AND AGRICULTURAL ENGINEERING

Natural fibres such as flax, jute and ramie can be used for most temporary applications where, for instance, soil erosion is the problem. The geotextiles made from these natural polymers help to prevent the erosion of soils by allowing vegetative growth and their subsequent root establishment. Once the purpose is served, the geotextile material gradually disintegrates into the soil. In most medium to long term applications however, where physical and chemical durability and dimensional stabilities are of prime concern, synthetic fibres are preferred.

There are currently at least six synthetic polymers considered suitable for this purpose; they include:

- Polypropylene
- Polyester
- Polyethylene
- Polyvinyl chloride
- Polyamide
- Aramids.

Polypropylene is by far the most utilised geotextile, followed by polyester, the other three trailing behind with polyamide as the least used synthetic polymer. Para-aramids are only used where very high creep resistance and tolerance to prolonged heating are required.

Generally, geosynthetics must have lifetimes which are defined and relate to their function. Durability, therefore, is mainly determined by the resistance offered by the component fibre and its assembled structure to the degrading species that causes a reduction in the tensile and mechanical properties. At least three main degrading mechanisms have been identified that ultimately determine the durability and life of the contending polymer; they include:

- Physical degradation
- Chemical degradation
- Biological degradation.

Physical degradation is usually sustained during transport or installation in one form or another. Initiation of cracks is normally followed by their subsequent propagation under environmental or normal stress. In the first instance, polymer susceptibility to physical degradation depends on such factors as the weight of the geotextile; generally lightweight or thin geotextiles suffer larger strength losses than thick and heavy materials. Secondly, woven geotextiles suffer slightly larger strength losses than nonwovens, owing to their greater stiffness and, finally, the generic nature of the polymer itself plays an important role.

Polyester, for instance, suffers greater strength losses than polyolefin fibres owing to its high glass transition temperature of around 70°C. Under normal soil conditions, the polymer is relatively brittle and therefore susceptible to physical damage. Polypropylene with its glass transition averaging at about 10°C is much more pliable under these conditions but suffers from the rather critical phenomenon of extension with time or creep.

Chemical degradation is the next mechanism by which chemical agencies, often in combination with ultraviolet light or/and heat, attack the polymer whilst in use or being stored. The presence of energy starts off a self-destructing chain of events that ultimately renders the polymer ineffective. Ultraviolet radiation normally attacks the surface of the polymer and initiates chain breakage or scission which leads to embrittlement and eventual failure of the polymer.

Generally, chemical degradation is a function of polymer type, thickness and availability of stabilizers. The type, quantity, and distribution of stabilizers also controls the degree of resistance to degradation. Polyolefins are particularly susceptible to ultraviolet degradation and need protection using light-stabilising additives. Oxidation due to heat operates similarly by weakening the polymer thus causing rapid degradation. A range of antioxidants are often included in the polymer during manufacture and processing to minimise this harmful effect.

Biological degradation can result from at least three types of microbiological attack: direct enzymatic attack, chemical production by microorganisms which may react destructively with the polymer, and attack on the additives within the polymer. High molecular weight polymers are much more immune to biological attack than low molecular weight polymers because microorganisms cannot easily locate the molecular chain endings. However, some microorganisms can permeate less digestible polymers in order to gain access to food.

Automotive and Aeronautics

Mechanical functionality has increasingly become an almost secondary requirement for travel safety, weight efficiency, comfort and material durability of the transporting medium. From bicycles to spacecraft, fibres in one form or another fulfil these important requirements. Carbon fibre reinforcement of the frame of a bicycle ridden in the 1992 Olympics was the first of its kind to allow a comfortable win ahead of its competitors. The one-piece, light, fibre- reinforced composite structure and design of the bike have since become an earmark of this industry.

In the simplest terms, composites utilise unique fibre properties such as strength, stiffness and elasticity whilst incorporating the compression resistance, and torsion and bending characteristics of the matrix used. Glass fibres have been traditionally used for the manufacture of boat hulls and car bodies. UHMWPE, aramids and carbon-reinforced composites in a variety of matrix materials are now routinely produced and utilised in low to very high temperature applications. Reinforcement of tyres is another area where the transport industry has benefited from fibres and where rapid temperature change and changing weather conditions demand effective response and durability.

High tenacity viscose and polyester yarns built into the internal structure of tyres now address these needs adequately. In addition to all the obvious upholstery materials used in the interior of cars, trains and aeroplanes, fibres are now used in one form or another in such parts as the engine components, fan belts, brake pads, door panels, seat skeletons, seat belts and air bags. Fire- retardant additives or inherently fire-retardant fibres are today standard requirements in the public sector use of all transport in order to improve safety.

Protection and Defence

In textile terms, protection and defence can be a passive response in which the textile product receives and absorbs the impending impact or energy in order to protect the underlying structure. Ballistic garments are obvious examples, where the assembled fibrous material is deliberately designed to slow down and reduce the penetration of an incoming projectile. But they may also have a more active role, where the fibres show positive response by generating char or protective gases, shrinking or expanding to prevent penetration of moisture or vapour and so on. In each scenario, the protection of the underlying structure is the common objective.

In the early days, leather and metal mesh garments were used to protect the body against sword and spear attacks, but with the passage of time development of new materials occurred and, for example, early in the 1940s, nylon-based flack jackets were introduced. They were a considerable improvement on the leather and metal garments but were still rather heavy and uncomfortable to wear. With the advent of para-aramids in the early 1970s, advanced fibres were for the first time used to make much more acceptable protective gear. In these garments, Kevlar or Twaron continuous filament yarns are woven into tight structures and assembled in a multilayer form to provide combined with high thermal stability enables these garments to receive and neutralise a range of projectiles from low calibre handguns, that is 0.22 to 0.44 inch (5.6-11.2mm) to military bullets within the 5.56-7.62mm range. In the latter case, the fabric will require facing with ceramic tiles or other hard materials to blunt the tips of metal-jacket spitzer-pointed bullets.

To strike a better balance between garment weight, comfort and protection an even stronger and lighter fibre based on ultra-high molecular weight polyethylene was developed and used in the early 1990s, which immediately reduced average garment weight by 15%. UHMWPE, commercially known as Dyneema (DSM) and in composite form as Spectra Shield by Allied Signal, is now used to make cut-resistant gloves and helmets, as well as a wide range of protective garments. However, unlike Kevlar, with a fairly low melting temperature of 150 °C, it is best suited to low temperature applications.

Fire is another means by which fatal and non-fatal injuries can be sustained. No textile-based material can withstand the power and ferocity of a fire for sustained periods of greater than 10min or so. However, if the fire ignition point could be increased or the organic structure converted to a carbonaceous char replica and its spreading rate delayed, then there may just be enough time gained to save an otherwise lost life. This is in essence the nature and objective of all fire-retardant compounds. Such treatments give fibres the positive role of forming char, reducing the emission of combustible volatile gases and effectively starving the fire of oxygen or providing a barrier to underlying surfaces.

In contrast, water-repellent fabrics may shed water by preventing water droplets from physically passing through them owing to their fine fibre dimensions and tight weaves, as is the case with ventile fabrics or perforated barrier inlays such as Goretex, whose tiny holes allow water vapour to pass through them but not water droplets. Wax and chemically treated fabrics reduce water/fabric surface tension by allowing water to roll off but do not allow permeation of moisture and air, so compromising comfort.

FABRICS OF PLAIN WEAVE NATURE

Wool

Homespun, flannel crepe.

Silk

Crepe de chine, chiffon, shantung, crepe georgette, taffetta and voile.

Cotton

Calico, cambric, canvas, cheese cloth, chintz, cretonne, crepe, cotton, flannelette, long cloth, gingham, muslin, organdy, seersucker and voile.

Linen

Cambric,.dress linen, handkerchief linen and towelling.

Rayon

Chifton,.crepe, geogette, seersucker, organdy, taffetta and voile.

Variation of Plain Weave

Basket Weave

Basket weave is a balanced weave. The fabrics with basket weave have flenth and if the count is not very highlite fabric is even porous and pliable.

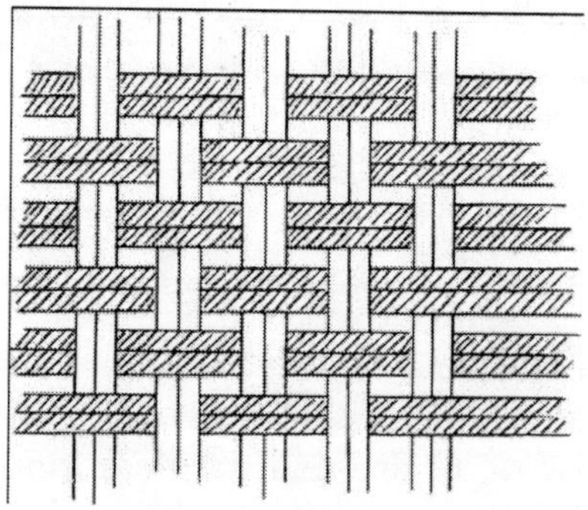

Fig.4.11 Basket Weave

However, fabrics with arrangements like 3x3, 4x4, 6x6 snag easily. In this two or more yarns in both warp and filling are treated as one, and interlaced as in plain weave. This weave is utilised in materials for sport. Basket weave. coats and suits. This is a relatively loose weave and therefore, the fabrics are more likely to shrink.

Rib Weave

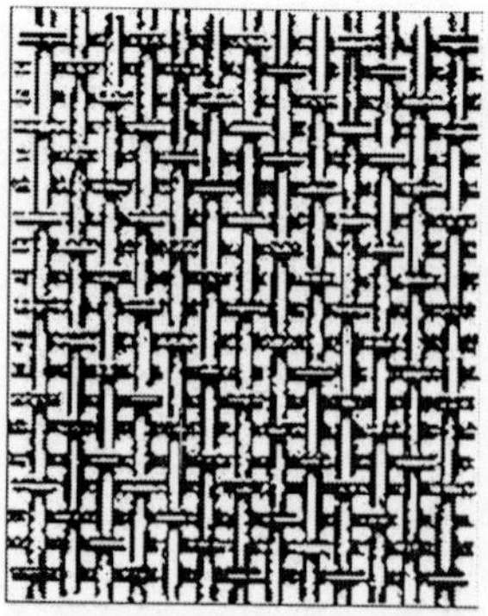

Fig.4.12: Rib Weave

Their high tenacity and good energy absorption warp than those in the weft, and this produces a ribbed effect. Sometimes, the order is reversed and the heavier yarn is used in the weft. Ego eve, faille gross grain bengalene, ottoman, broad cloths poplin and iabralco are some of the instances.

Twill Weave

Fig.4.13: Twill Weave

The simplest form of the twill weave is made by throwing the filling yarn over two warp yarns, then under one, over two, under one and so 'on, with a progression of one. This weave needs at least three shifts of the loom to complete the unit of the design and three harnesses. In this weave, either the warp or the filling may be utilised to form the face of the cloth. The progression, which produces the diagonal effect of the twill may be to the right or to the left. It may be plain or varied which makes the cloth decorative. The common variation in the twill weave is herring bone. In this, the diagonal effect runs in one direction a few rows and them in the opposite direction.

The whole pattern is thus repeated. Another variation is made for a giamon Q pattern. Varifions are also introduced by using yarns of various sizes, qualities and colours. It will weave has fewer points of interlacings than plain weave. So it allows closer picking of warp yarns to produce heavier fabrics which results in longer wear. Twill weave produces strong material because of the tightly twisted yarns which are utilised to bring out the diagonal effect, and the compactness of its construction.

Twill weave fabrics are very precious because of their elaborate construction, but they are strong and stand hard and long wear. This weave is generally used in wool and cotton fabrics where durability is prime need. Twill weave fabrics do not-shew dirt or dust as much as the fabric woven in plain weaves do, and are, therefore, more appropriate for dresses, men's shirts and suits and children's garments. The side on which the diagonal effect is more prominent is the right side of the cloth. Bet when twill weave fabrics are finished by 'napping', the napped side is the right-side.

Fabrics of Twill Weave Nature

Wool

Covert cloth, broad cloth, cashmere; flannel, gabardine, tweed, serge, worsted

Cotton

Covert cloth denim, drill, gabardine,.Jean, khaki serge.

Linen

Table linen, towels, drills and ticking.

Silk

Twill, serge, Surat.

Sateen and Satin

Satin Weaveing

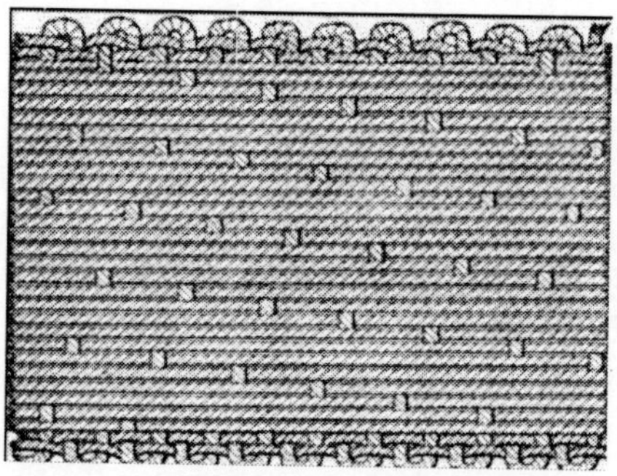

Fig.4.14: Satin Weaveing

This weave differs from the twin weave as in this the interlacing of the warp and filling yarns not regular. The filling yarn is passed over several warp threads. The floasts in sateen are generally shorter than those in the stin weave. Other variations may be introduced by throwing long or short floats or by throwing long or short floats upon the surface. Then again, a combination of satin and sateen weaves may be utilised to produce elaborate or figured designs.

The satin and sateen weaves need more shafts in weaving them are needed in the stain or twill weaves and, therefor fabrics of the former weaves are very expensive. The Satin or, Sateen weave fabrics are more decorative than serviceable. These are durable only if they are not subjected to excessive or hard use. Stain or Sateens with short floats are more durable. To differentiate between satin and sateen weaves fingers are passed over the cloth to condition the direction of the floats. If the fingers run-smoohtly and smoothly along the length olthe fabric, thus indicating the presence of the warp floats, the weave is satin. This weave is most commonly utilised in the silks and rayons. Satins are extremely lustrous and smooth the sateen weave will have floats running on the cross side of the fabric. This weave is utilised in a few mercerised cotton fabrics. These, fabrics are not as lustrous or smooth as satin.

Sateen and Satin Fabrics

Dress satin, slipper satin, satin crepe, satin georgettee, satin canton, satin twill, sateen, venetian sateen.

Weaves of Novelty Nature

Figure Weaving

Several fabrics have various kinds of designs woven into them. There are two methods of making these figure weaves —Jacquard and Dobby. A Jacquard loom is essential for more elaborate patterns buti Dobby attachment is sutpcient for simple and small geometrical designs.

Dobby Weave

Only a few geometrical designs are possible in this weave, such as the diamond patterns. The Dobby attachment consists of a chain of parochial strips of wood hung on the top of the loom.

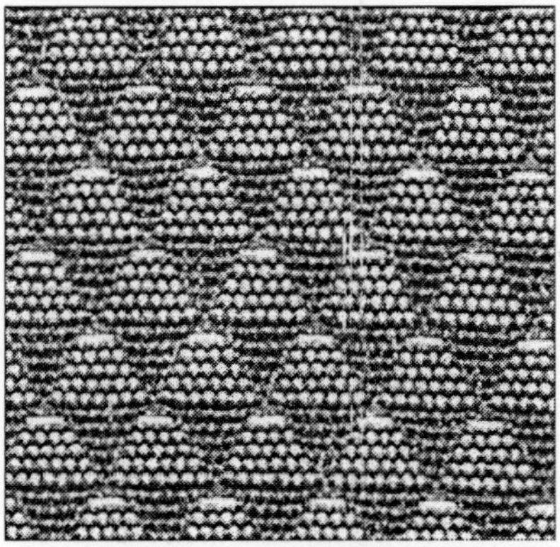

Fig.4.15: Dobby Weave

Pegs are inserted in each of the strips to connote the pattern. These strips of wood control the movements of the harness to form a shed. Another chain of strips of wood controls the shuttle, and thus the designs are woven in the fabric. The Dobby attachment can control no more than twenty-five harness. This is the reason, for the limited number of designs. Instances of Dobby weave are the "Birds eye" used in diapers and sharkskin suiting Huckaback or huck towtling of small diamond designs are also made in the Dobby weave

Jacquard Loom Weaveing

The Jacquard loom was invented by a French man, Joseph Jacquard, in 1801. The intricate arrangement of this loom weaves the most beautiful and exhaustive designs in the fabrics. In this loom every individual warp is controlled independently and not in series as in ordinary looms. In the place of harnesses, a series. of oblong punched cards called 'Jacquard card' control the raising of the warps. As several cards as there are picks are used in the design. The designs are first worked out on a graph paper in points. Then these points of the designs are punched on the cards in the same order and are rotated over a cylinder on the top of the loom.

Each of the steel wires has an eye through which a warp yarn is threaded. In working the loom, the needles press forward against a Jacquard Card. The needles which go through the punched holes in the card pull some cords which in their turn pull the steel wires and so the warps are-faised to form a shed simultaneousdly. The shuttle passes through throwing in the filling yarn. The cylinder Which holds the cards, turns slightly and another card israised. This again forms a contact with the needles, a new shred is formed, and the filling yarn is passed through. This process is continued till all the cards have been used once. The pattern is thus completed. The process is then repeated till the whole length of the cloth is woven.

The Jacquard weave fabrics are fairly expensive because of:

- The elaborate process used for this weave,
- The time and skill required for preparing the cards. The actual weave is a combination of two or more kinds of fundamental weaves or a variation of such combinations.

For instance, in damask the design is woven in sateen weave with filling floats, and the ground of the cloth is in satin weave with warp floats. In brocades, the design may be in the twill weave and the background in satin weave. The face and back of the fabrics in figured weaves may display the same design (as in the case of huckaback) or in the reverse as in damask, the design may be totally different on either side as in brocades. The durability of the figured fabrics relies on the length of the floats, and the type of the yarn. Long floats increase the sheen and softness of the fabric but affect its wearing quality.

TREATING FABRICS WITH CHEMICAL REAGENTS

These comprise a process of treating the fabrics with chemical reagents which change either the appearance or the,intrinsic properties of the cloth, e.g.. mercerising changes their appearance of the cloth, whereas crease resistant finishes or. fire proofing changes its properties.

Process of Mercerising

This process provides a high degree of lustre tottons through the chemical action of caustic soda. John Mercer, a calico printer in England, first discovered in 1844, that the application of a strong solution of caustic soda made cotton cloth transparent. The process comprises of impregnating the yarn or the fabric with cold caustic soda solution, applied under tension to reduce shrinkage, and to increase the lustre. The process removes the twist in the fibre and thus led to the fibre to become smooth and cylindrical which produces a silky effect. Mercerised cotton absorbs dyes very soon.

Process of Fire-Proof Finish

A simple method which comprises treatment with boric acid and borax. This, however, dissolves in water. Another method is the treatment of the fabric with chlorinated compounds, like Vinyle Chloride or chlorinated rubber and antimony oxide. This solution covers the fabric with a thin, non- inflammable film which renders the fabric fire-proof.

The Process of Crease Resistant Finish

The process is used mostly for cotton because cotton, owing to its natural inelasticity, wrinkles badly. In this process the fabrics are impregnated with a solution of synthetic resin, live:

- Phenol formaldehyde,
- Urea formaldehyde
- Acrylic resins, and dried by a very high temperature in a moist atmosphere.

This forms a clear insoluble resin in the fibre; which improves the resilience of the fabric. Urea formaldehyde is colourless and can be utilised for white and light coloured fabrics but phenol formaldehyde being dark coloured is used for dark coloured fabrics only.

Process of Creping

Creping by the chemical process is the treatment of fabrics with caustic soda. The soda paste is used to fabrics in a definite design of stripes or figures. The parts to which the paste is applied shrink leaving the other parts unshrunk; thus the effect of a puckered or creped material will be produced. Another method is to apply a paste of a substance which opposed the effect of caustic soda to the fabric in a definite design, and then place the fabric in a solution of caustic soda. The untreated places will shrink and produce the crepe effect. This method is more lasting than the mechanical one. The crepe produced in weaving is of course very different to the crepe effect produced by these finishes.

Process of Dyeing

Dyeing may also be called a finishing process as it colours the fabric and so adds to its eauty. Dyeing is a very ancient Indian art which the other countries learnt from the Indians. In the earliest stages, the fabrics were coloured with the juices of flowers, fruits, stems, leaves and barks of plants and trees. Later on, dye stuffs from vegetable and mineral sources came into utilisation. The chemical dyes are the discovery of relatively recent times.

Process of Raw Stock-dyeing

Fibres of wool, cotton, linen and waste silk are dyed. The stock of fibres are rotated in the dye bath, then removed and dried.

Process of Piece-dyeing

This is the process utilised for dyeing materity woven from any fibre. The penetration of colour is not quite so thorough as in the preceding forms of dying. The fabrics art wrapped around rollers which are placed in the dye bath and left there until they are saturated with the colour. Cotton fabrics require to be held under tension while passing through the dye. The other fabrics are not held taut.

Process of Stuh-dyeing

This method is brought into use in dyeing wool fibres after these have been combed. The skeins of wool slivers are hung on rods. The rods are then placed on the top of the dye bath. The rods are made to rotate, so that the slubbings keep constantly moving through the dye bath. These are then rinsed and dried.

Process of Skein-dyeing

Yarns of almost all fibres are dyed. Cotton and linen are generally dyed at the yarn stage. But the penetration of colour in skein-dyeing is much better. Skeins of yarns are hung on rods, which are placed in a dye bath. These rods rotate causing the skeins to 'circulate through the dye bath. This method is known as skein-dyeing.

Cross Dyeing

Fabrics woven with mixed yarns, like cotton, wool, or acetate rayon and viscose rayon, are dyed by this method. The affinity of dye-stuffs differs according to the two sorts of yarns mixed in weaving. thus, the fabrics are to be dyed in two successive dyebaths. In one, the dye suitable for one kind of yarn is used and in the other is utilised the dye suitable for the other yarn. Sometimes, a mixed fabric is dyed in one and the same dye bath and so each one of the yarn takes its own particular and. Various shade of cot our, or one takes the colour and the other remains colourless.

Process Tie and Dye

This is a kind of resist dying, which was practised as far back as the sixteenth century in India or probably even earlier. It is a simple method and yet man, fascinating and intricate designs are produced in the fabric, as for instance in the famous 'Patola' of Gujarat. By this method either the yarn is dyed before the fabric is woven as in 'Paldani' or the woven material is dyed as in 'Bandani' saris of Gujarat, Kathiawar and Rajasthan.

The parts of the fabric on the yarn which are to oppose the dye are tied with strings or narrow strips of cloth. The strings or the sirips are waxed to enhance the dye-resistance and so get better results. The skeins of the yarn or the material is then dipped in the dye bath. Then these are rinsed, dried and the strings removed. This method of dying produces beautiful patterns. Work of 'Bandani' this is used by women in India to dye their saris and scarves or 'dupattas' at home.

Process of Batik

This is another form to resist dyeing which produces patterns like those in prints. This also was first practised in India. The Javanese then took this art to their country, and now 'Batik' dyeing is a big industry in Java. The method is as follows: A full sized design is drawn or traced on the material. Hot, melted wax is applied on the lines of the design with a paint brush. The size of the brush depends on the thickness of the lines of the design.

After coating the lipes with wax, the fabric is immersed in cold water to harden the wax and to wet the fabric. The dye bath is then prepared. Cold water dye or dyes which car be utilised at low temperature are used for"Batik' dyeing. If the dye bath is hot, the wax applied on the design will melt and the process will be a failure. The dye-bath vessel must be lane enough to permit the entire fabric to be moved freely without any pressure or friction which might cause the wax lines to crack and thus spoil the design.

The material is kept in the dye bath long sufficient for the cloth to be thoroughly impregnated with the dye. The cloth is then rinsed and dried and the waf is removed. A 'Batik' in which more than one colour and an intricate design is used needs very great care and more than one operation is necessary as in the case of multi-coloured print.

Practice of Printing

Printing also was practised in India thousands of years before the Christian Era. The designs were either drawn by a brush or were stamped on the material by wooden blocks carved or cut in relief. A simple method of printing utilised at first comprised dipping the carved block in a paste of colour and then stamping the fabrics with it in a definite pattern. This method is still utilised extensively. Later, a screen made of fine wires (wire-cloth) or silk bolting cloth came into use. In machine printing engraved copper rollers, or cylinders are utilised. The dyes used in printing are the same as those used for dyeing but these are utilised in the form of pastes. If mordants are necessary, the fabrics are treated with mordant solution before being printed.

Practice of Block Printing

This is follows is in India even today to get beautiful patterns. Blocks are made of wood or wood and lino. The design is carved on lino which is generally cut to a thickness of ¼ inch. This cut piece of lino is stuck on to a wooden piece of the same size. In India, several printers use only wood blocks on which the design has been carved. The paste of colour is poured on trays lined with cloth. The material to be printed is spread on a padded table and held taut and smooth. Then the block carrying pate of one colour is stamped on the material and allowed to dry. Then another block carrying paste of various colour is stamped over it to form the multi-coloured patterns. The process is repeated over the entire fabric-surface which is to be printed.

Process of Screen Printing

Silk bolting cloth or wire cloth is stretched over a wooden frame. Over this, a line is drawn of such portions of the design as are to take one colour. The sphere of the screen which are to be utilised to prevent the spreading over of the colour are filled with water proof varnish, enamel or some other insoluble filter The fabric to be printed is then stretched on a table which is padded and covered with oil-cloth.

The wooden frame with the screen is then placed in the material, and the paste of colour is brushed over its surface and then lightly pressed. The colour is permitted to dry. Then another frame carrying a several colour and different outline is utilised and the process continues till the design is complete. A separate screen is required for the application of each colour in the design. The size of the screen used is generally 4 ft. by 6 ft.

Machine Printing

A printing machine comprises several copper cylinders or rollers which are engraved. The actual printing of the design on the cloth by this method takes very little time but the engraving of the design on the rollers means hard and careful work lasting many days. The roller is as wide as the cloth. The number of rollers needed depend on the number of colours utilised in the design as one roller can print only one colour.

MANUFACTURE OF THE INDIVIDUAL FIBERS

A considerable lag always exists between the marketing of a new product and the publication of specific details about its manufacture. Of the five fibers under consideration, excellent accounts of the production steps are available for nylon 66 only, a product which has been on the market for almost twenty years. For the other fibers, all of very recent origin, broad pictures of the process of production, but not the details of the individual steps, can be obtained.

Therefore, the nature of the technical literature on the subject should be made clear. The published accounts employed are surveys, based on the patent literature and the literature of chemistry, of alternative approaches to each general process step. Since only the general steps are important for the identification of the locationally strategic inputs, no pretense is made that the accounts which follow are of any firm's actual manufacturing operation.

Production of Nylon 66

The monomer from which nylon 66 is made is hexamethylene diammonium adipate, commonly called nylon salt. If fiber manufacture is separate from chemical intermediate manufacture, the salt is made into a water solution to facilitate handling and shipment to yarn plants. In conversion into nylon 66 fiber the salt is first run from storage tanks into evaporator kettles where it is concentrated. Acetic acid is added as a viscosity stabilizer in polymer formation. From the evaporator kettles a 60 per cent solution of the salt is run into autoclaves where polymerization takes place. If a delustered yarn is wanted, an aqueous suspension of titanium dioxide is added to the reaction mass soon after it begins to boil. When polymerization is completed, nitrogen pressure is applied to force the polymer, a sirupy material, to flow out through a slot in the bottom of the autoclave. Nylon 66 is spun by the melt-spinning process. Several steps are required to prepare the polymer for melt spinning.

From the autoclave a ribbon of the polymer flows onto a casting wheel, where it is hardened by sprays of water and cooled with streams of air. Then a mechanical cutter reduces the ribbons of polymer to small flakes; these flakes are conveyed to a blender and then transferred to supply hoppers which ride (via an overhead rail) over the spinning machines. Specially designed spinning machines, consisting of batteries of spinnerets, are used to extrude the polymer. From an overhead supply hopper the flaked polymer is fed into funnel-shaped, nitrogen-filled melt chambers which, in turn, feed one or more spinnerets. In the melt chamber a heated grid melts the polymer, which can then be pumped directly to the spinnerets. The holes of the spinnerets vary in size and number according to the size of the filaments and yarn desired. From the lower face of the spinneret the viscous filaments pass down through the orifices into a cooling chimney and are subjected there to an air blast to aid in solidification.

A converging guide gathers the filaments into a bundle of yarn. To prevent elongation and to keep the yarn from loosening and slipping in a subsequent winding operation, it is passed through a chamber and humidified with steam. After the steam treatment, the yarn is passed over glass finish rollers which apply an oil emulsion as a lubricant for other operations. At the bottom of the spinning unit the yarn is wound up in undrawn and untwisted form on bobbins. At this point the remaining process steps depend on the form in which the yarn is to be sold.

Continuous Filament

To make continuous-filament fiber, bobbins of yarn are conveyed to the textile area of the plant. Most nylon 66 filament is sold as low-twist yarn. In preparing the untreated yarn the filaments are twisted together—on conventional textile machinery-with about one or two twists per inch. Then the yarn is rewound on bobbins for a cold-drawing process on machines which stretch it to about four times the original length by passing it through sets of rollers moving at different speeds. From the viewpoint of chemistry the molecules of the undrawn filaments have random orientation only. After drawing, the linear molecules are aligned parallel to the fiber axis, a change which gives the yarn its particular physical properties. After the yarn has been drawn, it is wound on bobbins, the typical put-up, and is inspected and packaged for shipment.

Staple and Tow

For the manufacture of nylon 66 staple thousands of continuous filament fibers are combined into a rope or tow. The tow is drawn and then crimped by mechanical means to give the yarn the loftiness associated with natural fibers such as wool. The crimped ropes of yarn are set with steam and then cut into the desired length by staple cutters. At the end of this operation the staple is dried and baled for shipment. If tow is to be sold, it is packaged after being drawn.

Production of Orlon

Orlon is made from monomeric acrylonitrile, and Morgan suggests that for a large-scale operation polymerization can best be carried out as a continuous process. A water-soluble catalyst, such as ammonium persulphate, and a reduction agent, such as sodium bisulphite or sodium thiosulphate, can be used. In the suggested continuous process streams of acrylonitrile and aqueous solutions of the catalyst and reducing agent are fed into a reactor.

Low rates of conversion of the monomer to polyacrylo-nitrile make it necessary, after filtration of the slurry issuing from the reactor, to recover unconverted acrylonitrile by fractional distillation so that it may be recycled. As the polyacrylonitrile is formed, it precipitates in fine granular form which can be readily filtered.

Lessing, in writing on the development of Orlon, notes that in the experimental production of filaments both the wet- and dryspinning processes were employed but that the latter method proved best. In either event a spinning solution must be prepared by dissolving the dry polymer in an organic solvent. For Orlon manufacture polyacrylonitrile is dissolved in dimethyl formamide. If a delustered yarn is desired, an agent such as titanium dioxide is introduced into the spinning solution, or dope. Once prepared, the solution for dry spinning must be carefully filtered for the removal of foreign matter and gels of undissolved material. Each batch of polymer solution can be processed through conventional filter presses.

In a typical dry-spinning process sketched by Fremon the filtered dope is stored in tanks which feed the cells of the spinning units. Spinning dope is pumped into the top of each cell by metering pumps. As the polymer is forced through the spinneret, filaments are formed and solidified as the solvent in the solution is evaporated by hot air. The volatized solvent can be drawn off from an aperture in the cell by air flows and conveyed to a solvent recovery unit, a vital operation in the economics of the process. As the new filaments are gathered together in each cell by wind-up devices at the bottom, they are passed over a roller which applies a protective lubricant and wound up on spools for further processing.

Fibers produced by the dry-spinning process are hot-stretched rather than cold-drawn as in the case of nylon. The stretching operation may be preceded by a washing treatment in which the yarn is passed through a bath to remove solvent residue. Frey and Sippel point out three alternative hot-stretching methods.

First, the yarn may be drawn between two or more sets of rollers, moving at different velocities, through a hot bath consisting of a nonsolvent for the fiber or of hot air. In the second approach hot drawing is made possible by passing the yarn through heated rollers or over hot plates. Finally, they note that for polyacrylonitrile fibers the yarn may be stretched in special steam tubes. To stabilize the molecular arrangement brought about by stretching and to relieve the strains in the drawn fibers, the yarn may be "relaxed" by a heat treatment in an annealing oven.

Continuous-filament Orlon is sold with low twist or none at all, so that the final operation is to wind the yarn on bobbins or to give it a low twist and then put it up. In describing the production of Orlon staple Mauersberger cites a seven-step operation. Filaments are gathered together to form a tow which is drawn and then passed through mechanical devices which put a crimp in the fiber. A relaxing step follows, and the yarn is cut into staple fiber. The cut staple is dried and put up into bales for use by the textile industry.

Dynel Output

Dynel, the vinyl fiber of the Union Carbide and Carbon Corp., is made of a copolymer of vinyl chloride (60 per cent) and acrylonitrile (40 per cent). Harris describes an emulsion polymerization procedure for the preparation of constant composition copolymers of vinyl chloride-acrylonitrile containing the monomers in the proportion 60/40. The step is carried out by mixing vinyl chloride and acrylonitrile in water containing a water-soluble catalyst and an emulsifier. At the end of the reaction the polymer is a resin in powder form.

The published literature shows that dynel is made by the wetspinning process. Although none of the wet-spinning methods used in the production of vinyl fibers has been described in detail, the general nature of the operation is known from viscose rayon production. Just as in the case of dry spinning, a solution is prepared by dissolving resinous polymer in a suitable solvent. For dynel production acetone is used.

The solvent, the resin powder, and a viscosity stabilizer are mechanically mixed to form the spinning dope. To prepare it for use in spinning, the solution is filtered. In the wet process the spinning apparatus lies horizontal, submerged in a liquid-bath medium. The spinning solution is extruded into the liquid, and filaments are formed by coagulation. As indicated in the introduction, dynel is manufactured in the form of staple and tow only. Fremon has described a wet-spinning process for making synthetic staple which provides a glimpse of the general steps which follow filament formation. After the fiber in tow form emerges from the coagulating medium it can be taken to a second bath where it is washed and stretched.

In the next step the tow is dried in an oven and is also annealed to stabilize the molecular structure brought about by stretching. From the annealing oven the tow is passed through a mechanical crimper and then can be cut into staple form and baled. In an alternative approach the tow can first be dried to low moisture content, cut, and then passed through a device known as a tunnel dryer. The air temperature of the dryer is maintained as high as possible without injury to the yarn, and the fiber shrinks unevenly, taking on a crimp.

Acrilan Manufacture

Few details have been released by the Chemstrand Corp. on the manufacture of Acrilan, its vinyl fiber. Production so far has consisted of staple and tow only. Like dynel, the fiber is a copolymer. Acrilan is made principally of acrylonitrile (85 to 90 per cent), and the other component has been most frequently identified in the technical accounts as vinyl acetate or vinyl pyridine.

Morgan notes that copolymers of acrylonitrile containing small amounts of a second monomer, such as vinyl pyridine, can be manufactured in a manner similar to the process described in the Orlon section for the polymerization of acrylonitrile. The second monomer can be mixed in with the acrylonitrile stream. In the most recently published account Mauersberger has described the general steps for the manufacture of Acrilan. He reports that the spinning process employed is the wet method. Whatever solvent is used to prepare the spinning solution of the powdered copolymer has not been specifically identified.

Dacron Production

Dacron, Du Pont's polyester fiber, is the condensation product of dimethyl terephthalate and ethylene glycol. A commercial route used in the production of the polymer, polyethylene terephthalate, has been described by Reynolds. Ester interchange between dimethyl terephthalate and excess ethylene glycol yields a condensate which is heated in a vacuum to effect removal of the excess glycol and to give a polymer of high molecular weight. Ester interchange requires a catalyst such as magnesium or zinc borate. As the temperature of the reaction mixture is raised, methanol forms and is removed by distillation. Pressure filtration can be used to purify the initial condensate product before it is transferred to a polymerization reactor. In the polymerization step excess ethylene glycol is evolved which presumably can be recycled.

The molten polymer is released from a heated extrusion valve at the base of the vessel by the application of nitrogen pressure.Dacron is melt-spun, and the manufacturing steps are reported to be very similar to the general procedure followed in the production of nylon. The molten polymer emerges from the polymerization reactor as a solid ribbon, which is run onto a casting wheel, cooled by water sprays, and cut into flakes for the spinning operation. Again, if a delustered yarn is desired, titanium oxide is used and it can be added to the condensate mixture as a dispersion in the ethylene glycol. The fiber is produced as continuous-filament yarn without twist and as staple and tow. Since the remaining steps in a fiber plant with a melt-spinning process were described for nylon, the details are assumed to apply in an approximate way for Dacron.

LOCATION THEORY AND THE SYNTHETIC-FIBER INDUSTRY

An empirical location study must turn to location theory for a systematic coverage of all factors which might possibly influence the location of an industry and, in general, the geographical distribution of its plants. In this location study of the synthetic-fiber industry an attempt has been made to apply the general substitution approach to the locational equilibrium of the firm. Underlying the location pattern of an industry are decisions made by business firms. The general area of economic theory which embraces this type of decision-making activity is a branch of microeconomics, the theory of the firm, and, in particular, the locational equilibrium of the firm. Traditionally, the theory of the firm has been made synonymous with price theory, the postulates of which are inferred through the implications of profit-maximizing behabiour of the firm in three roles: first, in the process of production, i.e., the transformation of inputs into outputs; second, as a buyer of inputs; and third, as the seller of a product.

Given the familiar data of the problem, including the structure of markets faced by the firm (defined in terms of numbers of buyers and sellers and homogeneity of product), profit-maximizing levels of output can be deduced. Price theory ignores the location problem because buying, production, and selling are looked upon as single-dimension activities, i.e., as occurring at a point.

This assumption is abandoned in the theory of the location equilibrium of the firm. As a buyer of inputs, the firm incurs costs in assembling them over space and is also confronted with regional differences in their availability; the impact of site on the technical possibilities of production is recognized; and the selling activity embraces a market area in which transportation costs are also incurred in delivering the product. Thus the attributes of plant-location theory stem from firm behabiour in a fourth role as well: that of selecting from an array of geographical possibilities, minimum-cost production, and selling sites; and cost minimization is focused on variations which result from the factor of space.

The Weberian Framework

In his pioneering work Weber's signal contribution was the development of the principal categories of industrial location, largely on the basis of technical empirical knowledge. To Weber, the transportation network of a nation is the basic magnetic field of economic attraction which, through its lines of force, determines the position of industrial particles. He regarded transportation orientation as the basic principle of industrial location.

Conceptually, competing magnetic fields are sometimes capable of causing particles to be drawn away from the transportation lines of force to their own. In short, all other types of orientation, such as power or labor, are deviations from minimum-cost transportation sites. Weber also singled out the importance of agglomeration economies in industrial location. Although his types of location are suggestive for empirical studies, Weber's geometrical approach to the locational equilibrium of the firm, which, for example, requires the solution of location triangles, offers only a rough methodological guide.

The General Substitution Approach

That the Weberian location categories could be derived by means of the familiar substitution principle of price theory was suggested by Predohl in 1928, but it was not until 1949 that an operational framework was established for the general substitution approach to location theory by Isard. In his work Isard has extended the bounds of traditional production theory to include the locational equilibrium of the firm. Since cost minimization has a spatial dimension, it is specifically recognized by way of transport inputs. Within the enlarged framework the problem of production is that of choosing the right combination of capital, labor, land, and transport inputs.

From the most significant cost difference which occurs through variation over space the orientation of an industry can be determined. Isard distinguishes two types of substitution. The exploration of alternative outlays from the use of transport inputs can determine whether costs for a transport-oriented industry are minimized at market or at raw-material sites; and the traditional outlay substitutions of production theory between capital, labor, and land can be used to deduce other types of industrial location such as labor or power orientation.

APPLIED GENERAL SUBSTITUTION ANALYSIS AND THE SYNTHETIC-FIBER INDUSTRY

The general substitution approach to the locational equilibrium of the firm provides an effective operational tool for empirical analysis. This approach can be put in simple terms in the case in which a given market, or set of markets, is to be served by a plant with given physical inputs per unit of output and is able to draw raw materials from alternative supply areas. As this plant is moved from region to region, the effect on its costs and revenue via the substitution of inputs and of diverse outlays can be determined. Consider, for example, the alternative in the synthetic fiber industry of producing the chemicals for fiber synthesis at sites in chemical raw-material regions or of manufacturing them in fiber-market regions in the textile area of the United States.

Output at a raw-material site requires little outlay on movement of raw materials, but outlays are incurred on the transportation of the finished product and on utilities, labor, etc. At a market site a transportation cost on raw materials is substituted for the cost of moving the finished product, and the market-site utility, labor costs, etc., are substituted for those at the raw-material site. In addition, market-site agglomeration economies are substituted for those at the raw-material site. Substitutions such as these can be used to generate regional cost differences so that the most favorable region for plant location can be uncovered.

The Hypothesis

It is clear that the successful use of the general substitution approach in an empirical location study depends in a large measure upon the extent to which production functions, the physical relationship between various inputs (including transportation inputs) and output, can be obtained or estimated. If, for instance, the location of an ammonia plant is in question, it is necessary to know the raw-material inputs per unit of output, the utility and labor inputs, the manner in which these inputs vary with the size of plant, the manner in which the capital investment varies with size of plant, etc.

The hypothesis in this study of the synthetic-fiber industry is that:

- From an examination of the industry's production functions and market areas a spatial framework of regions which are suitable for plant location can be established.
- General substitution analysis can be used to convert the data of the production functions into production and distribution cost differences at selected sites.

In this manner basic regional advantages and disadvantages for plant location can be ascertained. The computation of regional differences in production and distribution costs will also point out the basic type of location orientation for each stage of the synthetic-fiber industry as well as the minimum-cost regions among all those tested.

COSTS AND LOCATION ANALYSIS

Although in the location analysis of the synthetic-fiber industry it might be desirable to employ all the costs which the chemical engineer or the cost accountant would include, from the standpoint of location theory the estimation of costs, hence the estimation of production functions, can be simplified. All inputs which have a locational significance must be identified, but the cost items which do not vary significantly from region to region can be set aside. Thus the application of the general substitution approach to the synthetic-fiber industry begins with prior determination of relevant cost categories to guide the estimation of production functions. The basic cost categories in the theory of the firm are variable and fixed costs, and these are applicable in location analysis. With respect to the locational equilibrium of the firm, variable and fixed costs may vary spatially because of interregional differences in achievable agglomeration economies.

Cost Variation Plants of Equal Size

An examination of specific items in fixed production costs in both the chemical-intermediate and the fiber-producing stages of the synthetic-fiber industry leads to the conclusion that for any given predetermined size of plant regional uniformity in fixed charges can be assumed without doing violence to reality.

The chemical intermediates from which synthetic fibers are produced can be manufactured by more than one process, but the technology of petrochemical production is assumed in almost all cases in this study, since this particular route promises the most locational mobility for the future. In their study of the petrochemical industry Isard and Schooler found the assumption of regional uniformity of fixed costs for plants of given size to be a realistic one, after considering plant construction costs, interest charges, depreciation, plant maintenance, insurance costs, taxes, and land costs. In general, the analysis of the components of fixed charges also applies to the synthetic-fiber stage, even though fiber output is a combined chemical-textile operation.

In the past chemical-plant construction costs in warm-weather regions, such as Texas or California, have tended to be lower than in regions of the North by 10 or 12 per cent because certain structural parts unnecessary in the "outdoor" type of plant were thought to be indispensable in the "indoor" design for northern regions. However, Isard and Schooler note that the recent technical literature of chemical-plant construction points to the feasibility of the cheaper outdoor design for all regions. Plant construction cost inequalities which originate in labor-cost and material-cost variations cannot be systematically forecast and are not considered vital to the location problem in question.

For the large firms engaged in the development of synthetic fibers and their chemical intermediates ready access to the nation's capital market excludes the possibility of interest-cost disparities at different sites; therefore, the United States can be regarded as an area characterized by homogeneous capital availability for the location analysis. In considering the possibility of plant location in Puerto Rico, branch plants of American firms are assumed so that capital-cost uniformity applies to the island as well.

Since depreciation allowances are determined principally by tax legislation at the Federal level, there is little room for regional differences in this item of fixed costs. Plant maintenance has a regional variation and could be expected to be higher for cold weather regions, but the practice of performing major maintenance work in good weather limits the magnitude of the cost difference.

Insurance costs are significant in chemical production because of the risk hazard. Manufacture in a raw-material region with plants concentrated at specific sites raises plant insurance costs over areas in which chemical production is dispersed. Since the insurance cost differences are small and cannot be predicted in their variation with space, they are neglected in the cost analysis.

To account for regional variations in the burden of taxes which enter into fixed charges is a difficult matter. Property taxes are important but are set by legislative bodies and are not amenable to location analysis. Some states offer property-tax exemptions, usually for a five-year period, as an inducement to the location of new industry. The practice is so widespread, however, that its impact on location decisions tends in the long run to become neutralized regionally, although it may be a factor in the selection of a site within a region. For the cost analysis land outlays are assumed to be equal in all regions. The problem of minimizing land outlays in factory construction is not one of choosing the right region but the proper site within a region.

Although interregional equality in fixed charges may be justifiably assumed, in both stages of the synthetic-fiber industry regional differences in variable costs do exist. Computation of the amounts of these differences requires first an estimation of the most important variable physical inputs per unit of output.

Agglomeration Economies

For the synthetic-fiber industry the major agglomeration economies are:

- Large-scale production economies;
- Integration economies from the output of several chemical products in a multiunit plant—savings are realized, for example, by the utilization of the by-product of one unit as a raw material for another;
- localization economies from the geographical concentration of chemical plants in a given area—a single large-scale chlorine plant may serve the needs of several users and make it unnecessary for each to construct a small-scale unit;
- External economies from the purchase of raw materials from large-scale producers-in Texas, for instance, large-scale oil refineries make available to chemical manufacturers huge streams of waste gas at low prices.

It may be valid to assume that for some products plants of the same predetermined size could be built in any region. In many cases this assumption would imply that agglomeration economies are uniform from region to region. However, if plants of the same predetermined size cannot be built in all regions, then location analysis must evaluate regional differences in variable and fixed costs caused by differences in the extent to which large-scale production and other agglomeration economies can be achieved.

All four of the above-mentioned types of agglomeration economy may be significant in the location of plants in the first stage of synthetic-fiber production, the manufacture of chemical intermediates. Since many of the intermediates have markets in other end uses, there may be regional differences in market potential.

A site suitable for fiber manufacture may not draw the chemical stage unless it can serve a market for the excess production over the fiber requirement, for otherwise the chemical unit would suffer a large-scale production economy disadvantage. The other three types of agglomeration economy generally favor raw-material over market regions or, among market regions, those with the most highly developed chemical industries.

In this study agglomeration economies are evaluated for the chemical—intermediate stage through the estimation of the influence of size on fixed and variable costs. The other agglomeration economies-integration, localization, and external—are given qualitative consideration only. In the second stage of the industry, the manufacture of synthetic fibers, the main agglomeration consideration is large-scale production economies. The market for each synthetic fiber is spread out geographically over the entire textile area so that the output of a single plant is not sold entirely in a specific region.

For this reason plant size is largely a function of technological and cost considerations common to all fiber producers and is somewhat independent of the region chosen for the location of a plant. Since the technological and cost considerations permit plants of economic size to be built in any region, agglomeration economies can be eliminated as a factor in the location of synthetic-fiber plants.

Conclusions of Preliminary Cost Analysis

For the first stage of the industry, the output of chemial intermediates, the assumption is made from the foregoing analysis that the location problem can be solved by comparing regional differences in variable costs alone for products for which the assumption is valid that plants of the same predetermined size can be built in any region.

In most cases, however, the comparison of regional differences in variable costs must be augmented by the estimation of the effect on both fixed and variable costs of agglomeration economies. With respect to the second stage, the manufacture of synthetic fibers from chemical intermediates, the assumption is made that the location problem can be solved by comparing regional differences in variable costs for plants of equal size.

❑

5

Modernisation and Automation of Textile Industry

As a whole the textile industry has made major progress process modernization and automation over the last 5 to 10 years. The focus of these programs has been in one of many directions in various companies. Generally new technology has been utilized to reduce the number of process steps, but just as often to reduce the labour content of the process. This is especially evident in the reduction of low skill-high drudgery jobs, but it also applies to the reduction of human intrusion into textile processes, which inevitably is a quality argument.

Examples of these process improvements include the automation of opening rooms, the setting up of chute-feeds and high production cards, the automation, at least in part, of drawing, the introduction of open end spinning, the increasing use of shuttleless looms, the use of automatic systems for handling waste, and the nearly universal use of microprocessor-controlled monitoring and reporting of production variables. Activities in applying existing available technology to textile processes are being pursued in all of the major process categories.

Bale Storage

There is potential for the automatic analysis of incoming bales of fiber, especially if a robot or other automatic device could be involved in the analysis and then direct the bale to the appropriate storage area. Automated bale storage is a labour saving technology that leads to less handling as well as presenting the opportunity of coding each bale for future identification.

This is important due to the desirability of tracking the identity of the material in each textile process process from the initial bale through all of the process steps. This in turn permits one to know the accurate history of all material and all processes and allows the solution of quality control problems on a more rational basis. Cards can be loaded and unloaded automatically and their output can be conveyed automatically to draw frames.

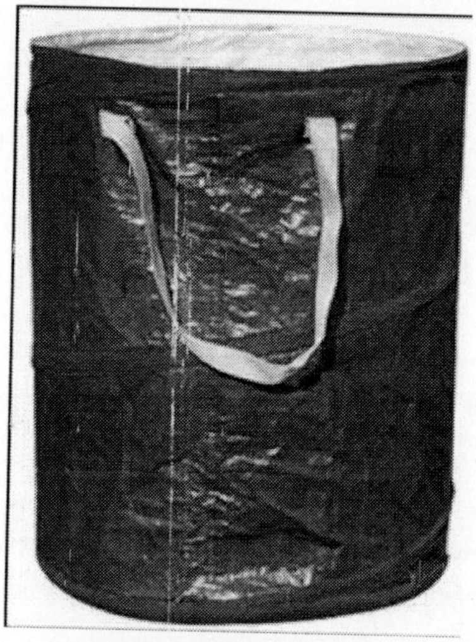

Fig.6.1: Bale Storage

However the requirement to mix the inputs to draw frames in such a way as to insure good blending is potent; these patterns also need to be capable of being changed from time to time.

Fig.6.2: Bale Storage Shed

Preparation of Yarn

The issues in yarn formation generally point toward reducing the number of steps wherever feasible. One view is that devising processes that can successfully do this is more potent than devising automated materials handling systems to move materials between currently popular process steps. Generally the ideal yarn manufacture process would take fiber from a bale, convert it to a sliver and move it to a spinning process, for example open end spinning, with automatic transfer of the yarn output either to a warper or to a loom.

Stress also must be placed on computer monitoring both of quality and of production rate, with the quality monitoring being tied to feedback and control mechanisms throughout the many processes. The monitoring technology is already available for drawing and the technology for monitoring either open-end yarn or other types of yarn is on the horizon. Another area of considerable importance with respect to monitoring is to be able to determine the need for machine maintenance by continuous monitoring of yarn from, for instance, open end rotors.

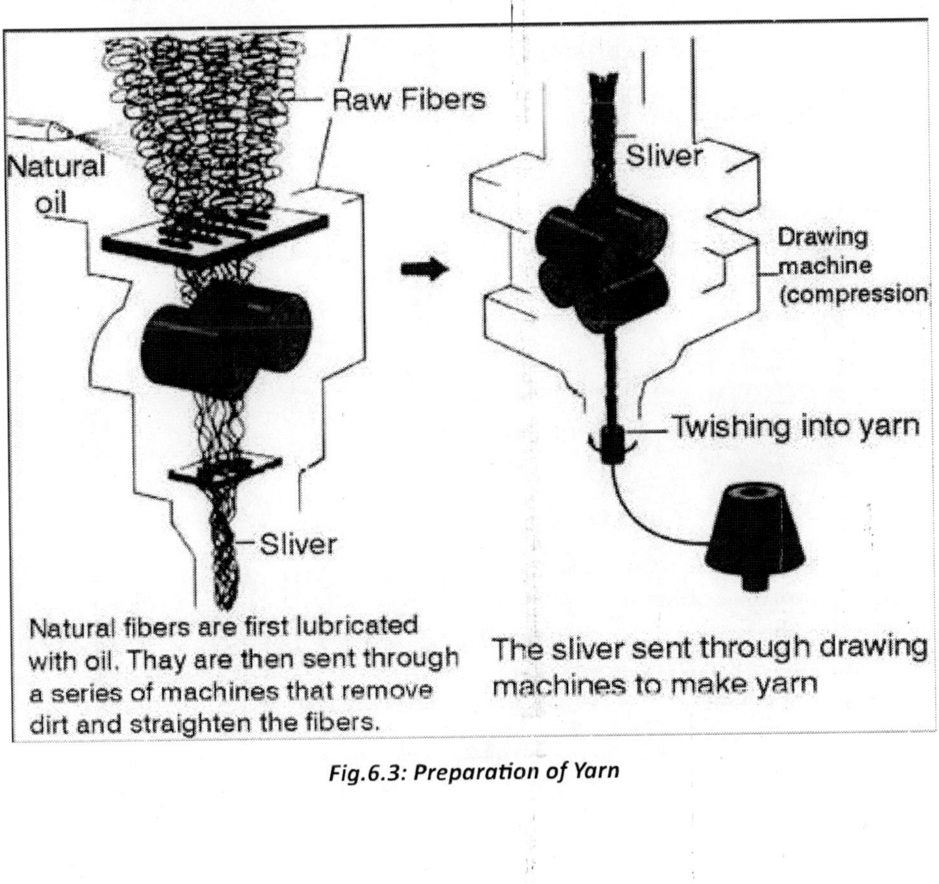

Fig.6.3: Preparation of Yarn

This needs that all ends be monitored regularly and that faulty positions be identified soon. The repair, when it is needed, could be made automatically or, alternatively, that end could be stopped and machine maintenance ordered. A useful system would also monitor and record for long-term gradual deterioration as opposed to short-term problems. In this whole system, the philosophy is to prevent defective material at its source. In general it is important to measure and to control quality on the spot at every step of the yarn formation process. The computer technology is already available; the real problem seems to be the development of appropriate sensing elements. There are a number of opportunities in present yarn processes for automated materials handling, including the use of robots.

This is especially true for systems that have reduced the number of process steps, i.e., open end or other systems, but it could also be utilised with ring spinning technology in which the automation of roving frames is a current need. Connecting winders to large spinning frames is a good idea, and it was demonstrated at the 1983 ITMA, but winders require to be designed to accommodate some flexibility of yarn count; this perhaps could be accomplished by designing winders with space for extra positions. This linking technique permits less handling of yarn packages, which is a distinct advantage, and it also allows better package identification and control.

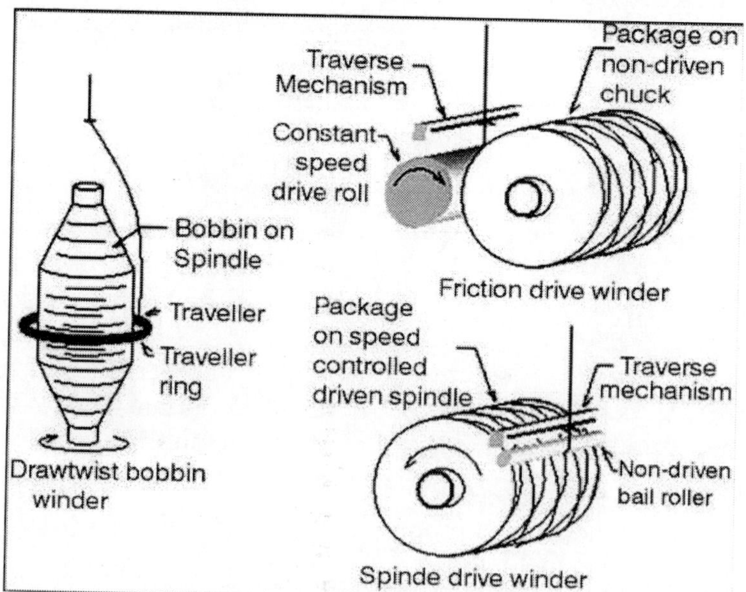

Fig.6.4: Different Stages of Yarn Processes

Since it is necessary to be able to identify abnormal parts of the process, the real issue is to condition where in a process faults occur, what their relations with other process steps will be, and the feedback loops in which to exercise control.

Preparation of Fabric

The issues in fabric preparation are almost all in the areas of monitoring and control, inspection, and material handling. Modern weaving and knitting machinery allows the choice of several options and a conscious decision of whether to stress productivity or flexibility. The important trend, outside of the design of fabric formation machinery, is the elimination of menial jobs that mostly are related to materials handling.

As an instance, fabric handling with driverless tractors is well-proven now, although this is an area in which potential savings other than labour savings are nat easy to identify; therefore this may remain fairly standard technology for the future. It also would be desirable to devise systems for automatic doffing of cloth and probably automatic cutting, in conjunction with automatic inspection and grading.

Inspection of fabric is thought by several to be a process which should be capable of elimination, if proper process monitoring and control systems can be invented. There is, however, a difference in philosophy depending on whether a greige mill or a dyeing and finishing plant is involved. In the former case it is perhaps more likely that inspection could be eliminated if it were to be carried out later on the finished fabric. Perhaps there will always be a need for some inspection, but it should be automated. In partical it should be capable of viewing the fabric with both the plant specifications and the customer's specifications in mind, changing the latter as the customer changes and changing the former as the fabric style changes from lot to lot. These issues become more significant as the textile industry as a whole moves to higher quality and output levels as then inspection speeds become the limiting process speeds.

Monitoring in weave rooms specially, but also in other fabric formation areas, is done today almost solely for the objective of generating management information. Although this is an important function of such systems, what is needed, besides, is diagnostic monitoring that will locate and diagnose loom malfunctions, preferably before they lead to producing off-quality material. Such systems would be part of a larger-monitoring system that deals with the flow of raw material into the fabric formation process as well as with fabric formation itself. The development of truly reliable monitoring and control systems is closely association with the development of automated inspection systems, since the latter rely on the assurance that defects are minimized in the process.

DYEING AND FINISHING

Discreate Process

In this area there is a common view that the number of discrete processes in dyeing and finishing needs to be reduced drastically, and as many as feasible should be combined. The goal would be to make dyeing and finishing a truly regular process rather than a series of batch processes, each with its own control and materials handling problems.

What this implies is the development of some rather sophisticated monitoring and control systems for dyeing and finishing processes generally. Among these systems, the more potent seem to be the ability to monitor and control the colour of wet fabric, as well as to monitor and control moisture content.

Fig.6.5: Dyeing Fabrics

The objective is to be able to predict accurately the colour of the final dry fabric by measuring its characteristics at the moment it is being dyed. Continuous dye ranges now have significant automation but are hampered by their inability to run very small lots efficiently. Systems need to be developed that will permit rapid change over from lot to lot on a continuous range system with a minimum fabric band between the changes. In addition to suitable monitoring and control functions, ways to rapidly alter dye baths in order to change colour fastly must be developed.

The aim is to produce systems with very rapid response times and this will require precision instrumentation for adding chemicals and controlling the parameters of the process. For similar reasons it is extremely important to have absolutely uniform desizing and bleaching. In this area there my well be applications also for computer-based monitoring, feedback, and control systems. There also are general needs for reducing the energy cost in dyeing by reducing either the setting or the drying needs. And for some products, it would be very useful to have dyeing the last of all finishing steps in order to improve order and warehouse versatility.

Process of Automation in Handling of Materials

From raw materials to the finished product there exist major opportunities for process automation in materials handling. Current applications of robotics are nearly all in this area, for the reason that it seems comparatively easy either to identify labour savings or to accomplish a reduction in menial and sometimes hard to fill jobs related to these processes. A significant concept that accompanies automated material handling is automated identification of the material which, if carried through in all parts of the process permitt the identification of quality control problems regarding their material source.

Much automated materials handling is, or will be, built into the process technology itself; but there remain materials handling problems that will need special technologies, the newest of which are driverless vehicles and robots. On the other hand, it can be considered that automated materials handling is really a second choice to the integration of processes; to the extent that some processes cannot be integrated, materials handling will remain a essential technology. There is much technology applications development to be accomplished, in the robotics area, which is not yet, in the view of some, suited for most textile applications. Particular issues comprise combining carding with breaker drawing with no intermediate materials handling, the doffing of ring spinning frames, the doffing of cloth at the loom, and the creeling of packages for dyeing, finishing, and warping.

Manufacturing Process of Apparel

It is easiest to approach this topic by beginning at the front end of an apparel manufacturing process, so the first topic should be computer-aided design. Unfortunately, in its apparel design context, this is a technology that is not quite ready for commercialization. It has the same goal as computer aided fabric design systems, namely, permitting the designer to quickly, and easily test his or her ideas at a computer console with an appropriate viewing mechanism to see the result of those ideas.

The problem in apparel design is inevitably that of converting easily and reliably between two-dimensional and three-dimensional information. Technically it would appear easier to take the two-dimensional information from a set of pieces (for instances, for a shirt) and change them to a three-dimensional image of the shirt's final appearance.

However, designers often operate in the reverse mode, that is, they make an illustration of a garment the way they realise it, and then the problem is to convert that picture to a series of two-dimensional pieces to outline the actual manufacturing process. Research progresses and so many theoretical reports are available in this area but, as far as commercialization of this technology goes, progress remains slow.

However, the situation is significantly better in the area of computer-aided marker-making, grading, and cut-order planning. There are many systems on the market that permit an experienced operator to take a standard pattern piece, generate other pieces from it on a graded size basis (i.e., grading) and then to pack all of the necessary pieces on a piece of fabric so as to give maximum fabric utilization. Maximizing fabric use is perhaps one of the greatest driving forces for this technology.

It is estimated that, for plain fabric, fabric wastage can be deducted to about 3 per cent with this technology compared with 5-6 per cent when human beings do the same job unaided. On the other hand, if instead of plain fabrics, one uses patterned fabrics in his process, then fabric wastage can be as high as 25 per cent and there is explicit room for improvement here. Although there is no current use of this idea, it appear logical that computer-aided pattern packing ought to be combined with fabric inspection information, performed at the textile manufacturer's plant.

Such a combination would allow the apparel maker to cut around any defects that might be present and guarantee that those pieces that were cut were defect free; this would effectively increase fabric utilization. Technologies for cutting fabric are increasingly being debated on a more philosophical basis. The issues are whether, in fact, the conventional bundle system of fabric cutting and material transport can be retained if other parts of the apparel manufacturing system are to be highly automated. The bundle system uses a spreading machine (which some say has not seen any major improvement in several years) to lay and then cut as several as 100 layers of fabric at once. Thus, this system produces 100 layers of shirt fronts, 100 layers of collars, and 100 sewing station.

This assumes that the person who does the cutting, if it is done manually, doesn't make a mistake. One mistake, of course, can ruin 100 shirt fronts. More importantly deducted, from an industrial engineering stand point, is that the bundle system inherently provides a buffer for each of the other steps in the process. If a sewing machine breaks down or if an operator is sick one day, the manufacturing process can still proceed because of the inherent build up of material available at all stations. The chief demerit of the bundle system is the long in-process time of the item being gathered. It is said that for some articles of clothing the in-plant time is as high as 20-30 days.

This represents an enormous inventory cost and is considered by some to be a major detriment to productivity enhancement. The bundle system also assumes that fabric is identical from one layer to another as the identity of several pieces effectively is lost in the system. To the extent that fabric is not uniform, then there are inevitable wastages because fabric pieces cannot be properly matched. The alternate system, used in some parts of the apparel industry where fabric is extremely expensive and a cutting mistake cannot be risked, is, for the sake of a better term, the one-layer system.

As the name means, each piece is cut individually in this system and then the problem is to route the pieces in the correct order to their assembly points. The merit of this system, other than the fact that the penalty for cutting errors is minimized, is that this process is actually more amenable to automation and control of the rest of the assembly process.

Besides, such a cutting system permits an enormous reduction of in-process time from 20-30 days to, in some cases, perhaps a few hours. It has obvious advantages. The major disadvantage of the one-layer system is that there is no inherent buffer capability. If a piece is missing or if an assembly station is inoperative, then the whole production process is held up.

On the other hand, it may be feasible to attack this problem by considering the "just in time" manufacturing philosophy that automobile makers use, in which a forward part of the manufacturing process calls to it material just as it is required and no sooner. There is no buffer concept in that philosophy, but it needs adequate material handling systems and reliable parts interchangeability. There are major innovations, some of them now quite old, in the area of cutting fabric.

Computer-controlled cutting, as exemplified by the Gerber cutter, is a technology that has been around for probably 10 years. It is precious machine and is utilized only by large companies that can justify having large cutting departments. In its present form, it takes information directly from the computer-aided marker-maker and cuts pieces from layers of fabric in a very fast and reproducible manner. There are more novel cutting techniques available, each of which has been downgraded in the past because of the demerit they have in working with the bundle system. Laser cutting is a technology that is used to cut out men's suits, for instance.

It can only work really well on one or a few layers of fabric at a time, and it works best on non-thermoplastic fabrics that otherwise would melt at the edges of the cut. (The problem in working with several layers of fabric is that the cut edges tend to fuse together during the cutting process and then they are very difficult to separate.) Water-jet cutting is a technology used in many other fields, such as the shoe industry, the automobile industry, and in a number of industries where complex shapes have to be cut rather rapidly.

Water jets don't work well with the bundle system either, as the power in the jet is severely retarded after the first few layers of fabric. Not with standing, if the one-layer system were to be adopted more uniformly, then either laser cutting or water-jet cutting systems would make considerable sense. Especially this is true as either of these technologies can be combined with robotic guidance of the cutting head. Joining techniques will continue, most people think, to emphasize sewn seams. Consumers hope certain aesthetic and mechanical attributes of sewn seams, and these are difficult to achieve with any other technology. Modern sewing machines operate mechanically much like the one that How invented, but they have advanced to the point where microprocessor control is an inherent part of several of them.

Microprocessors can control both the stitch pattern and the feeding and ejecting of material once it has been sewn. An emerging technology, not commercial yet, is three-dimensional sewing, in which a sewing head on a robot arm effectively operates in three dimensions on pieces of fabrics that have been placed on a form. There is a considerable amount of research going on in this area. In the sphere of non-sewn techniques, both adhesives and thermal bonding techniques are important.

Again, there seem to be applications for robot systems in this area, although the number of seams that can use these-technologies perhaps is limited. As in the textile industry, materials handling in the apparel industry is a major problem, which can be divided into many aspects. The first is materials presentation at the sewing machine itself. Some apparel companies ascribe as much as 80 per cent of their labour cost to the sewing part of their operations but closer inspection divnlges that actual sewing only contributes perhaps 20 per cent of this cost; the rest is materials handling. There are so many of devices already available to bring material in a more orderly fashion to the sewing machine operator. Two such are made by Gerber and by Eaton.

In each case, a rather complex overhead track system is loaded with pieces and partly assembled systems and moved by operator demand to the place where sewing is to take place.

These systems appear to be logical components of more automatic systems for the future. Several have investigated robots or robot-like systems as devices for materials handling, but the chief drawback is the classic limp fabric problem. It seems that it is nearly impossible to design a machine to pick up a piece of fabric, which may have only one of so many weights and stiffnesses, and to operate on it in a reliable and consistent manner. There exist devices which can handle certain classes of fabrics.

The Clupicker is definitely one of these, and there now exist robotic end effectors that are claimed to be able to operate with a wide variety of fabric types. One of these is comprised in the Draper project technology. Nevertheless, until the problems of reliable' materials flow, not only at sewing stations but between sewing stations, is solved, automation in any real sense apparel manufacturing will be severely handicapped. The manufacturing loop requires to be closed with sufficient management information, not only to track a process but also, at least in the ideal case, to determine when a process is reaching trouble.

There are a number of management information packages being sold into the apparel industry now which rely for the most part on operator input. Considering that a sewing machine operator has so many other things to do, one has to wonder just what the quality of the input data to these systems really is. Nevertheless, this represents a significant improvement from the traditional information gathering technology that has been prevalent.

Increasing Use of Automation

The general themes of all of these comments for all three industries are the increasing use of computer technologies, the requirement for the invention of suitable monitoring, feedback, and control loops and the increasing use of automation in materials handling. These trends arise because processes of the future in these industries will most desirably have minimum numbers of intermediate steps and minimum numbers of people involved in these steps.

Another general aim is to design processes with less dependence of unit cost on volume, which therefore would permit management more choice of flexibility or mass throughout for any special product at any particular time. In the fiber industry the will be on developing high-speed extrusion processes that can be fully automatic. Very large packages will be produced of at least 100 pounds, which will mean less inspection. These packages will be loaded directly onto a creel either for warping or directly for weaving or knitting. Boxes and other temporary storage devices will no longer be used. In staple fiber production the fiber instead of being processed into bales, may well be packed directly into a truck and on delivery, transferred to card chute feeds. In the textile industry, there are those who predict common automation of processes, especially materials transfer among carding, drawing, spinning, and fabric formation processes.

Special technology developments may include new spinning technologies that would either replace or refine current open end technology; these will become essential because cotton production is producing increasingly trashier material. Many respondents suggest that replacing the card is a necessary feature of future technologies, largely because cards don't permit for easy material transfer to the next step. An ideal system would send fiber directly to open-end spinning.

If cards are not replaced, provision for loading and unloading them automatically will require to be made and, in traditional systems, sliver cans will be transferred automatically to draw frames. The output from these can be transferred automatically to open end spinning frames and robots may become increasingly useful at this stage. In fabric production, an ideal situation will permit changing styles on looms much more rapidly than at present, and it will also include the rapid transfer of computer-generated fabric designs to looms for trial runs. Fabric grading will be largely automatic with the ability to distinguish not only sorts of defects, but also their placement within the fabric and to characterise those conditions with reference to either plant specifications or customer specifications.

Such systems will work on any style and any colour of fabric. Dyeing and finishing, but especially dyeing techniques, will be entirely automatic, capable of making nearly instantaneous changes from one shade to another and capable of reproducing shades absolutely. The implications for computer monitoring, feedback, and control of these systems are so many. Management information will be much more complete and easy to use than it is today. The information collecting used for managerial decision making will be part of the same process monitoring and control information gathering that will be essential to run an error-free process. There also will be a real requirement to be able to estimate cost, labour and material savings, and management time in the process of determining whether a new device or technology is worthwhile at a particular cost.

The emphasis, in general, in the textile industry as well as in the fiber industry will be on upstream quality improvement, which is more likely to produce a higher quality product than automated inspection systems. In the apparel industry, stress will be placed on more efficient materials use, and on speeding up material flow through the factory.

This may be more important in the long term than direct labour savings. However, the cost of inventory is so high that any technology that allowed a garment to pass through the system in a few hours as opposed to several days would be very cost-effective. There will be increasing emphasis on automation in sewing and other joining technologies and material transfer from station to station. This is the thrust of both of the widely publicized research programs in the automation of apparel manufacturing: the Draper Laboratories programme and the Japanese MITI programme.

Both of these programs use the concept of the "manufacturing cell", in which robots, hard automation, computer-aided design, and computer-driven information flow combine to define a self-contained manufacturing unit. The first is an American Project sponsored by the Tailored Clothing Technology Corporation, abbreviated (TC)2" but loosely called the "Draper" project after the Draper Laboratories where the work actually is being carried out. The philosophy of this project is that a manufacturing cell exists wherever a sewn seam must be accomplished, and that the significant problems are getting material into the system, performing some orientation and/or parts identification, probably folding the material, sewing it in a reliable fashion, and ejecting the material from the system.

The Draper prototype machine that was completed some time last year (reputed in its present form to cost around $50,000) consists of a number of novel devices to do these things. The important technology appears to many to be in the use of vision systems to identify and orient fabric parts, and in the claimed invention of a robot that can, in fact, reliably pick up single layers of fabric (although in this case it is for folding; i.e., moving one layer over another) and in a sewing head that travels to the place where the seam is to be made.

Each of these operations is microprocessor controlled and, at this time, the process has been designed to do only one thing, yo sew the sleeves of men's coats. The Draper project investigators claim that the technology is adaptable to a wide variety of apparel assembly processes and some of its aspects certainly are, especially the vision system and the materials handling technology. Some in the apparel industry criticize the' project, partly on the ground that it represents a very costly, very specialized machine, and partly on the basis that nothing has been done to change the sewing technology at all.

A project receiving almost equal publicity in this country is a Japanese project in which a group of Japanese companies under the auspices of the Japanese government (MITI) have banded together to form an organization known as Technology Research Association of Automated Sewing Systems, which has published a very elaborate programme for the entire automation of apparel manufacture—what really amounts to a completely automated factory.

Whereas the Draper project has cost on the order of $5 million so far, the Japanese project is reputed eventually to cost $50 or $60 million, and there are several who believe that it will cost much more than this before it is finished.

At this stage, planning and some fundamental work are being done in the areas of sewing preparation, sewing and assembly, fabric handling, and production control.

Thus, all of the apparel manufacturing process is being attacked, with the desired end result being an automated factory composed of so many individual work cells, into each of which material is fed as appropriate and taken out as appropriate, with the entire process operating very much as an integrated system. While the Draper project emphasis is partly on the reduction of labour content, the Japanese stress is almost completely on the elimination of labour content. Several explain this as the difficulty in Japan of obtaining apparel plant labour, and suggest that this really is an effort to preserve an industry for which a labour force has largely ceased to exist.

The Hereafter

Are we approaching the day when textiles and apparel will be assembled in an automated factory? This is the objective of several manufacturing industries. The traditional definition of the "factory of the future" is one that combines computer-aided design, hard automation, robotics, and computerized information systems to give a self-contained manufacturing cell that has as its input computer generated information and has as its output both computer generated information and a product that is uniformly manufactured to a specific quality standard. Whether or not this all can happen in the textile industries is dependent on other, nontechnical, aspects of these industries.

If any of these levels of automation are to take place, they almost certainly will take place according to company type and, as a result, several predict that the overall textile industry will become divided into two basic sorts of companies, those that are more manufacturing-oriented and those that are more marketing-oriented. The marketing-oriented companies will tend to be design-oriented, specialist companies who place foot market response above production efficiency.

They will react very quickly to the marketplace, they will manufacture high value-added products, and they will use less of the available technology than they might if they were manufacturing larger amounts of their product. However, some technologies will be potent to them, particularly in the area of computer-aided design and in management information systems.

They will tend to judge automation by its abilily to enhance the value that they consider most important, i.e., flexibility regarding market demands. On the other hand, manufacturing-oriented companies will be very large and they will make very large amounts of their product. They will be prime candidates for large scale automation and perhaps even for the automatic factory. At any rate, they will have to have the ability for great investment of capital and this; as much as anything, will condition whether a company can afford to be manufacturing-oriented or not. The primary thrusts of these companies will be productivity and quality and, with a view to realise these, they will effort very hard to lower their overall labour costs (not only their direct labour costs) and to lower their in-process time so as to escape the high cost of inventory.

TEXTILE INDUSTRY

In order to promote energy conservation in the textile industry, this manual analyses in detail the actual conditions of energy consumption in each field. Thus, it has been compiled to serve as reference material for the practical application of these techniques which are always kept available for the engineers. A step-by-step description is included as to how to implement the energy conservation measures, specifically in the area of the dyeing and finishing process, where many small- to medium-sized companies are operating. We strongly hope that this manual will be used as a guide to promote energy conservation in the textile industry and to rationalize the management.

CLOTHING MANUFACTURING

The energy consumption share of the clothing manufacturing division which consists of large numbers of small-sized companies and their employees in the overall textile industry is not necessarily low but the ratio of energy cost to the total cost is relatively low.

However, the energy cost forecast is inevitably a gradual increase under circumstances where the production of high value-added goods is required, along with the implementation of labour saving measures, as a result of the challenging market environment characterized by personalized and diversified consumer needs, high demand for quality goods, short product cycles, etc. Therefore, it is desirable that a comprehensive rationalization programme be investigated apart from reductions in energy consumption.

STRUCTURES OF TEXTILE MARKETS

In general, it is well known that the developmental process of a textile market moves from a product-oriented stage, where all goods produced are sold to a consumer-oriented stage where the desired goods are only those which will satisfy the consumer's demand, comprising his wants and purchasing power. This is via a mass-consumption stage which is supported by a mass-production system. The characteristics of textile products demanded in the markets in these different developmental stages may be classified into price-sensitive mass-production type basic clothing, which applies to the earlier stages, and multi-line, small-volume production type fashion clothing which pertains to the last stage and needs to satisfy each individual consumer's taste.

BASIC CLOTHING

Assuming the amount of fabric necessary for people to live a physically comfortable life in a given environment can be derived from the weight of clothes which is enough to keep a certain level of body temperature, given such factors as air temperature, humidity and wind velocity prevalent in the region, basic clothing can be regarded as a cumulative total of such clothes.

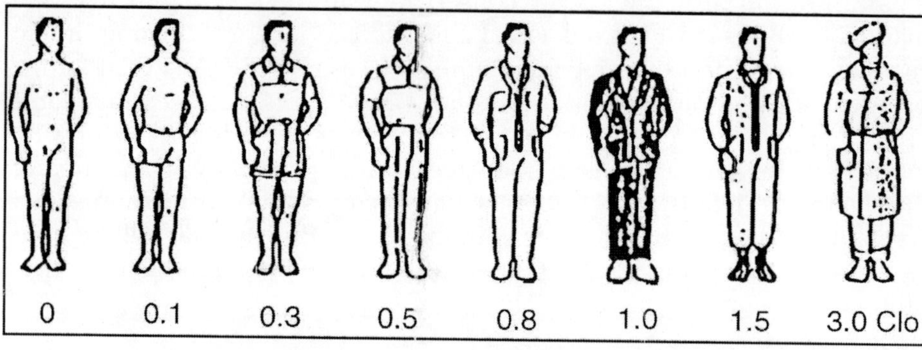

Fig. Typical Relationship between Clothing and Clo Value

Figure Summarizes the Relationship between Some Clo Values and Examples of the Corresponding Clothes. Table. shows the results of calculations to find the weight of clothes required under average climatic conditions in summer and winter in three Japanese cities.

Table. Example of Effect of Climatic Conditions on Clo Value and Weight of Clothing

Region	Season	Temperature (°C)	Humidity (%)	Wind Velocity (m/sec)	Clo Value	Required Weight of Clothing (g)
Sapporo	Jan	–4.9	74	2.3	4.1	4005
	Aug	21.3	79	2.7	1.2	1189
Tokyo	Jan	4.7	53	3.1	3.1	3034
	Aug	26.7	75	3.0	0.6	607
Fukuoka	Jan	5.7	67	3.7	3.0	2937
	Aug	27.3	76	2.9	0.6	607

Although the ultimately required quantity is difficult to determine, the per capita annual textile consumption (kg/person) can be estimated through multiplying the above weight by coefficient a (obtained from the service life of a textile product and its number of units demanded per annum).

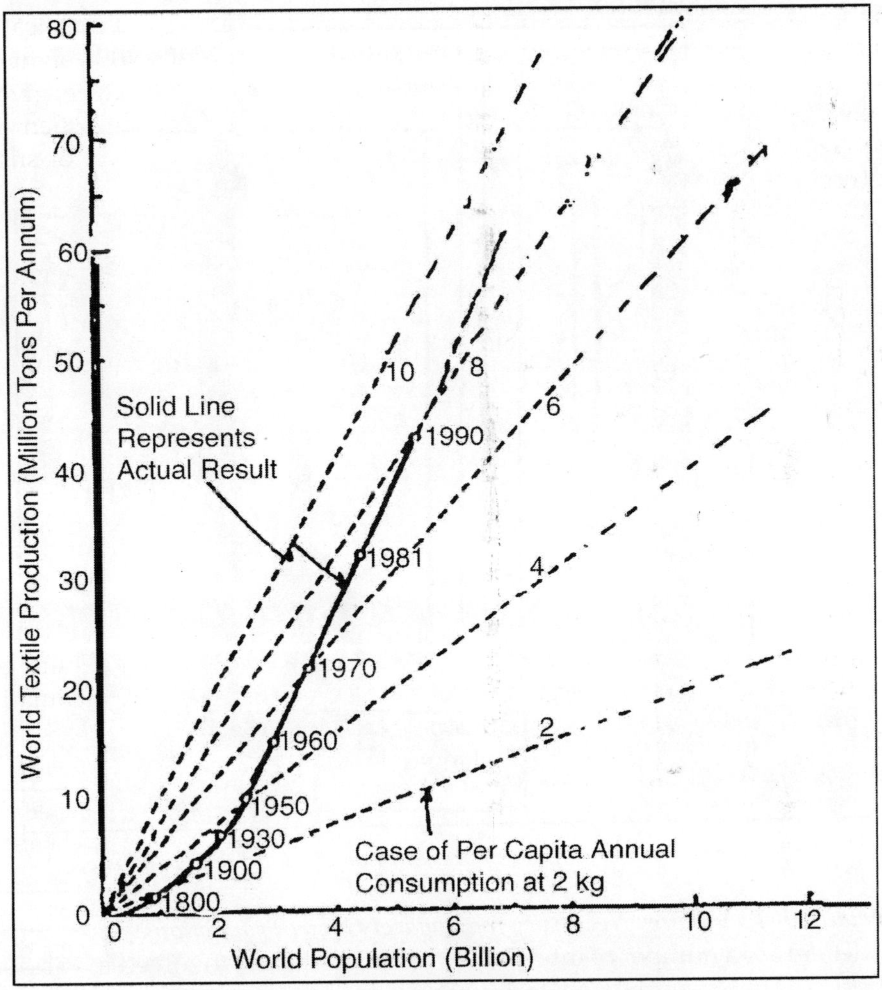

Fig.6.7: Relationship between World Population and World Textile Consumption and Production

The textile industry is traditionally regarded as a typical labour intensive industry developed on the basis of abundant labour supply and has a tendency to expand to overseas markets once the domestic demand is satisfied, as illustrated by examples of the established textile industries of many developed countries. For this reason, even when the textile industry of a specific country is to be examined, it is widely recognized that a business strategy taking into consideration the global textile industry setup is very important. Figure shows an example of the schematic representation of such a global setup of textile industries.

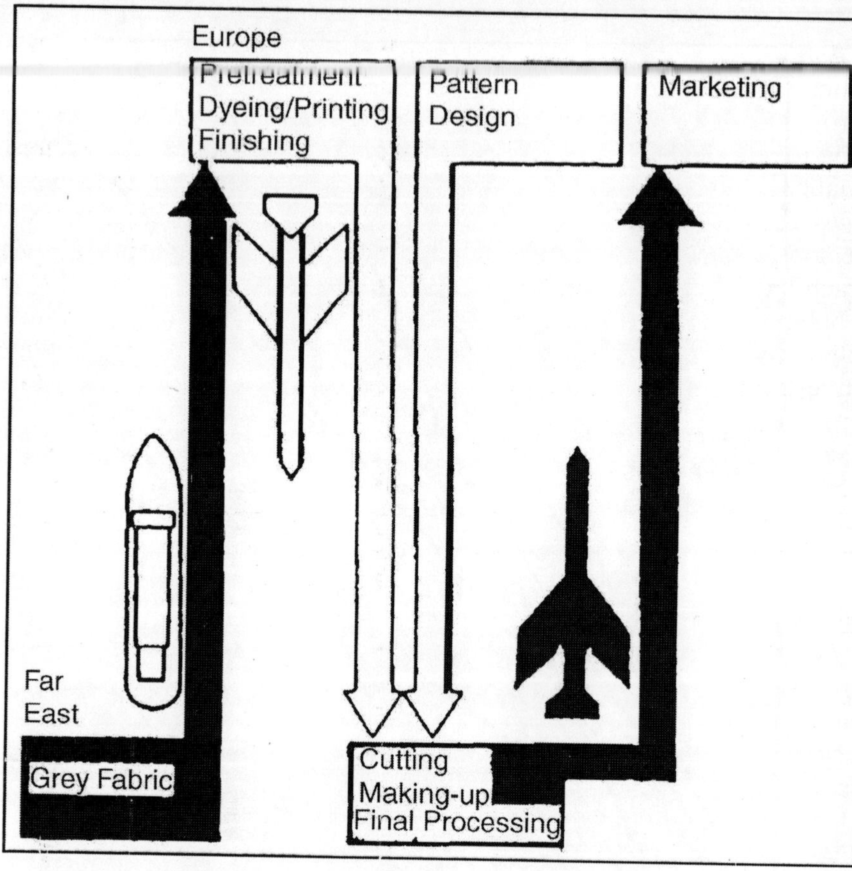

Fig.6.8: Example of Schematic Representation of World Textile Industry

Specialized Techniques Necessary for Apparel Goods Production

There are a number of intertwined technical factors involved in various subprocesses or specialized technical fields which make up the overall production process that fabricates and reshapes the raw fibre material into the final textile product to be used by the consumer.

Comparison of Characteristics of Specialized Technical Fields

In Fiscal Year 1989, the textile industry had a share of 4.4% in shipment value. 14.8% in the number of businesses (20%), and 10.4% in the number of employees (23.3%) in the overall Japanese manufacturing industries, characterized by a gradual decline in relative share, although in terms of absolute shipment value it has actually expanded to 1,053% of the Fiscal 1955 level.

As has been frequently pointed out throughout its development, the Japanese textile industry has a unique organizational structure consisting of groups of independent companies where all companies in a group belong to one of the specialized technical fields and operate in a horizontal specialization configuration. A comparison and summary of the major indices of these company groups, classifying them in accordance with their specialized technical fields. From these indices, common company characteristics for each group may emerge.

Namely, in terms of business size, the fibre production and spinning subdivisions are in contrast with the rest of the textile industry where relatively large numbers of small businesses coexist. In addition, these groups of small companies can only stay in business by relying on the supply of abundant cheap labour, exhibiting a legacy of the textile industry's past as a labour intensive industry, even on its path towards modernization. Table compares the energy consumption shares of various specialized technical fields and it can be seen that energy consumption is relatively high in the fields of dyeing and finishing, fibre production, spinning, weaving and clothing manufacturing.

As for water consumption, the share of the textile industry in the entire manufacturing industries is 5.2% for fresh water and 1.1% for sea water. Considering the fact that most of this water is used for easy-to-recycle temperature control and cooling purposes, the industry's total water consumption cannot necessarily be regarded as high. However, as is widely accepted, the dyeing and finishing division is placed in a special position in that its water consumption is mainly for processing and washing purposes.

THE GLOBAL TEXTILE AND CLOTHING INDUSTRIES

Textile making is a very ancient craft, with a history almost as old as mankind itself. Remembered and recorded in poetry and ancient stories and myths, textiles have always been important to man. As well as providing protection from the elements, the first textiles were used as decoration, providing status for the owner. They were also used as tools; bags for transporting belongings and for holding food as it was gathered. Textiles are produced in almost every country of the world, sometimes for consumption exclusively in the country of manufacture, sometimes mainly for export.

From cottage industry to multi-national corporation, textiles and clothing are truly global industries. In 1782, the invention of the steam engine gave the world a new power source and started the Industrial Revolution. Previous to this the production of textiles had been a domestic system, a cottage industry with textiles spun, knitted and woven in the home. By the middle of the nineteenth century, however, there was a whole range of new machines and inventions that were to take textiles into an era of mass production in factories.

The development of man-made fibres and new dyestuffs in the early part of the twentieth century, and continuing technological developments, have led and continue to lead to new products and applications. The actual processes of textile manufacture, however, are still very much as they have always been, with the vast majority of cloth being woven or knitted from yarn spun from fibre. And, while much production may be very technologically advanced, hand-produced textiles are still made in many countries exactly as they were many, many years ago. Nowadays, many different types of companies are involved in the production of textiles and clothing world-wide; some companies own many huge manufacturing plants in many different countries while others will have only a few employees and some may not actually manufacture at all.

TEXTILE MATERIALS, PROCESSES, AND PRODUCTS

Fibres are manufactured or processed into yarns, and yarns are made into fabrics. Fabrics may be manufactured by a variety of processes including knitting, weaving, lace making, felt-making, knotting, and stitch bonding. These fabrics may be industrial textiles with detailed technical and performance specifications, or they may be sold either to retail or contract as apparel, furnishings or household textiles, where aesthetics may be as, or sometimes even more important than performance.

The fabrics may be coloured by dyeing or printing, or be finished to enhance their appearance or performance. A wide diversity of products are made from textile products or have some textile components; textiles go into car tyres, and geotextiles are used for lining reservoirs, while medical applications include artificial ligaments and replacement arteries.

Design in textiles and Clothing

Every textile product is designed: that is, it is made specifically to some kind of plan. Design decisions are made at every stage in the manufacturing process—what fibres should be used in a yarn, what yarns in a fabric, what weight of fabric should be produced, what colours should the yarn or fabric be produced in, what fabric structures should be used and what finishes applied. These decisions may be made by engineers and technologists in the case of industrial or medical textiles where performance requirements are paramount, or, more often in the case of apparel, furnishings and household textiles, by designers trained in aesthetics, technology and marketing. The designers found in the textile and clothing industries are frequently involved throughout the design process, from initial identification of a need/ requirement, through research, generation of initial design ideas, design development and testing to ultimate product specification.

Designers Found in the textiles and Clothing Industries

The designers found in textiles and clothing include:

- Colourists predicting and forecasting future colour ranges
- Yarn designers
- Knitted fabric designers
- Woven fabric designers
- Carpet designers
- Print designers
- Embroidery designers
- Knitwear designers
- Garment designers
- Accessory designers
- Print producers
- Stylists
- Colourists developing colourways
- Repeat artists

Fibres

Fabric is made from yarn, and yarn is made from fibres. These fibres can be either natural or man-made. Natural fibres include animal fibres (e.g. wool and silk), vegetable fibres (e.g. jute and cotton) and mineral fibres (e.g. asbestos). Man-made fibres are either regenerated or synthetic; viscose rayon, based on regenerated cellulose, is man-made but not synthetic while polyester, polypropylene and nylon are all synthetic fibres. Synthetic fibres are produced by the large chemical companies including Dupont, Bayer, Hoechst and Astra Zeneca. Many of these companies produce no fabric but specialise in the production of certain types of fibre which they sell on as fibres or manufacture into yarns.

Yarns

Yarn producers or spinners buy in natural and/or man-made fibres to make these into yarns of different sizes and characters; regular and fancy yarns. For many years the main spinning systems could be given as woollen, worsted and cotton, and these systems gave rise to the woollen, worsted and cotton industries. Developments in spinning, however, have led to new spinning systems including 'open-end', 'self-twist' and 'jet' spinning.

At its simplest, yarn production is essentially about taking fibres, organising them so that they lie in a lengthways direction and twisting them to create a yarn. By combining fibre types, and using different spinning systems and machinery, yarns can be developed with individual profiles suitable for a vast range of end uses. Regular yarns are those which have a regular straight profile and these can be twisted together, making 'two-fold' or 'three-fold' yarns for example. Fancy yarns can be created by deliberately introducing irregularities or intermittent effects along their length. Yarns can be combined together as components of new yarns with different effects and properties from their component parts. As well as changing the appearance of a fabric, the introduction of a fancy yarn will affect the handle and performance of that fabric.

Woven Fabrics

Strictly speaking, the definition of a textile is 'a woven fabric' but the term textile is now considered to cover any product that uses textile materials or is made by textile processes. Essentially, woven fabrics are structures produced by interlacing two sets of threads; the warp which runs in a lengthways direction and the weft which runs in a widthways direction. Weaving methods include tapestry and jacquard.

Knitted Fabrics

Knitted fabrics are produced by interlacing loops of yarn. In weft knitting, loops are formed one at a time in a weft-ways direction as the fabric is formed. Hand-knitting with a pair of knitting needles is weft knitting. In warp knitting there is a set of warp yarns which are simultaneously formed into loops. To connect these chains of loops the warp threads are moved sideways in such a way as to cause the loops to interlink.

Lace and Non-woven Fabrics

Fabrics may also be produced by methods other than weaving and knitting. Lace is an open-work fabric made by looping, plaiting or twisting threads by means of a needle or a set of bobbins. Fabrics produced by crochet and macramé are often called lace, although strictly speaking they are not. Knotting is another way of making fabrics. Knotting was a popular pastime for women in eighteenth-century Europe and colonial North America, and one method still seen today is macramé.

A knotting process is also used for fishing nets, and some rugs and carpets are knotted — made by tying yarns onto a foundation weave. There is also a group of fabrics called non-wovens which include true felt (where animal fibres are matted together) and fabrics produced by bonding webs of fibres together by stitching or by sticking with adhesive. However, in terms of volume produced, knitted and woven fabrics are by far the most common methods of fabric production.

Fabric Terms

A length of woven or knitted fabric is usually referred to as a 'piece'. Often, fabric woven by a mill will not be coloured and this undyed fabric is called 'grey cloth'. Colour can be added by dyeing the piece, and such fabric is referred to as being 'piecedyed'. Colour can also be added to a fabric by applying pigments or dyes in a printing or other colouring process after weaving or knitting, or by using already dyed yarns in the construction of the fabric. Cloth made from dyed yarns will not normally be dyed again or printed.

'Finishing' is what happens after the fabric has been made. The finishing processes employed will be determined by the type of fabric and its performance requirements. Any excess dye will normally be removed, any applied pigment will normally be set, and any dye will be fixed. Fabrics may be brushed or raised to enhance appearance and handle, or fire-retardant and soil-resist treatments may be applied. Fire retardancy may be a product performance prerequisite; anti-soiling and anti-static finishes, while not necessarily pre-requisites, enhance performance, as do methods of coating fabrics to produce microporous surfaces.

Geography and Fabric Types

Certain countries, and areas within countries, have developed industries around specific fibres/fabric types and there are still parts of the world where craftsmen produce fabrics exclusive to them, such as some hand-crafted batiks and weaves. In the UK, Manchester was nicknamed 'Cottonopolis' as it was built in the main (as was much of Lancashire) from money earned through the cotton trade. Scotland developed a woollen trade through both woven and knitted fabrics, while, again in the UK, Yorkshire was home to the worsted industry and the Midlands became famous for knitting and lace making. India has a history of cotton manufacture and, in the eighteenth century, was famous throughout Europe for its mordanted cottons or chintzes.

RECENT TRENDS IN TEXTILE MANUFACTURE

Throughout the 20th century, the trend in textiles has been toward lighter- weight materials. Better transportation and improved indoor heating have made warmth a less important aspect of clothing for most people than it was in earlier centuries. Since 1900 the weight of average clothing fabric has fallen by more than one-third. When people need extremely warm clothes, they tend to wear special outer garments such as parkas that today are typically made of lightweight synthetic materials.

Synthetic materials, produced from chemical compounds rather than from plant fibres or animal hair, have provided less-expensive substitutes for natural fabrics. Synthetic materials can also be superior to natural fibres in strength and durability.

Rayon was an early synthetic substitute for silk. Nylon, a synthetic fabric introduced in the 1930s, was another early substitute for silk and quickly became the fibre of choice for women's stockings. Polyester, a form of plastic, was introduced in clothing in the early 1950s. Blended with rayon or cotton, polyester found its first use in so-called wash-and-wear fabrics that needed little or no ironing.

Synthetic fibres fell out of favour in the late 1960s but new kinds of polyester that are more durable and have a softer, more natural feel to them have become increasingly popular in the late 20th century. Synthetic fibres such as spandex have revolutionized clothing by making possible the production of extremely flexible, form-fitting garments. Other synthetic fibres, created for special purposes, range from lightweight but extremely warm or water-resistant fabrics, such as polypropylene and the composite polymer Gore-tex, to woven, bullet- proof fabrics such as Kevlar that serve as body armor.

HAT FELT

HAT, a covering for the head worn by both sexes, and distinguished from the cap or bonnet by the possession of a brim. The word in O.E. is hcet, which is cognate with O. Frisian hatt, O.N. hotte, &c., meaning head-covering, hood; it is distantly related to the hood, which is cognate with the German for "hat," Hut. The history of the hat as part of the apparel of both sexes, with the various changes in shape which it has undergone, is treated in the article Costume. Hats were originally made by the process of felting, and as tradition ascribed the discovery of that very ancient operation to St Clement, he was assumed as the patron saint of the craft.

The first and most ancient is concerned with the manufacture of felt hats, and the second has to do with the recent but now most extensive and important manufacture of silk or dress hats. In addition to these there is the important manufacture of straw or plaited hats and hats are occasionally manufactured of materials and by processes not included under any of these heads, but such manufactures do not take a large or permanent position in the industry.

Felt Hats: There is a great range in the quality of felt hats: the finer and more expensive qualities are made entirely of fur; for commoner qualities a mixture of fur and wool is used; and for the cheapest kinds wool alone is employed. The processes and apparatus necessary for making hats of fur differ also from those required in the case of woollen bodies; and in large manufactories machinery is now generally employed for operations which at no distant date were entirely manual. An outline of the operations by which the old beaver hat was made will give an idea of the manual processes in making a fur napped hat, and the apparatus and mechanical processes employed in making ordinary hard and soft felts will afterwards be noticed.

Hatters' fur consists principally of the hair of rabbits (technically called coneys) and hares, with some proportion of nutria, musquash and beavers' hair; and generally any parings and cuttings from furriers are also used. Furs intended for felting are deprived of their long coarse hairs, after which they are treated with a solution of nitrate of mercury, an operation called carroting or secretage, whereby the felting properties of the fur are greatly increased. The fur is then cut by hand or machine from the ski and in this state it is delivered to the hat maker.

The old process of making a beaver hat was as follows. The materials of a proper beaver consisted, for the body or foundation, of rabbits' fur, and for the nap, of beaver fur, although the beaver was often mixed with or supplanted by a more common fur. In preparing the fur plate, the hatter weighed out a sufficient quantity of rabbit fur for a single hat, and spread it out and combined it by the operation of bowing. The bow or stang ABC was about 7 ft. long, and it stretched a single cord of catgut which the workman vibrated by means of a wooden pin E, furnished with a half knob at each end. Holding the bow in his left hand, and the pin in his right, he caused the vibrating string to come in contact with the heap of tangled fur, which did not cover a space greater than that of the hand.

At each vibration some of the filaments started up to the height of a few inches, and fell away from the mass, a little to the right of the bow, their excursions being restrained by a concave frame of wicker work called the basket. One half of the material was first operated on, and by bowing and gathering, or a patting use of the basket, the stuff was loosely matted, about 50 by 36 in., called a bat. In this formation care was taken to work about two- thirds of the fur down towards what was intended for the brim, and this having been effected, greater density was induced by gentle pressure with the basket.

It was then covered with a wettish linen cloth, upon which was laid the hardening skin, a piece of dry half-tanned horse hide. On this the workman pressed until the stuff adhered closely to the damp cloth, in which it was then doubled up, freely pressed with the hand, and laid aside. By this process, called basoning, the bat became compactly felted and thinned toward the sides and point.

The other half of the fur was next subjected to precisely the same processes, after which a cone-shaped slip of stiff paper was laid on its surface, and the sides of the bat were folded over its edges to its form and size. It was then laid paper-side downward upon the first bat, which was now replaced on the hurdle, and its edges were transversely doubled over the introverted side- lays of the second bat, thus giving equal thickness to the whole body. In this condition it was reintroduced between folds of damp linen cloth, and again hardened, so as to unite the two halves, the knitting together of which was quickly effected. The paper was then withdrawn, and the body in the form of a large cone removed to the plank or battery room.

The battery consisted of an open iron boiler or kettle A filled with scalding hot water, with shelves, B, C, partly of mahogany and partly of lead, slop ing down to it. Here the body was first dipped in the water, and then withdrawn to the plank to cool and drain, when it was unfolded, rolled gently with a pin tapering towards the ends, turned, and worked in every direction, to toughen and shrink it, and at the same time prevent adhesion of its sides.

Stopping or thickening any thin spots seen on looking through the body, was carefully performed by dabbing on additional stuff in succes sive supplies from the hot liquor with a brush frequently dipped into the kettle, until the body was shrunk sufficiently (about one-half) and thoroughly equalized. When quite dried, stiffening was effected with a brush dipped into a thin varnish of shellac, and rubbed into the body, the surface intended for the inside having much more laid on it than the outer, while the brim was made to absorb many times the quantity applied to any other part.

On being again dried, the body was ready to be covered with a nap of beaver hair. For this, in inferior qualities, the hair of the otter, nutria or other fine fur was sometimes substituted. The requisite quantity of one or other of these was taken and mixed with a proportion of cotton, and the whole was bowed up into a thin uniform lap. The cotton merely served to give sufficient body to the material to enable the workman to handle the lap.

Being damped, the workman spread over it a covering of this lap, and by moistening and gentle patting with a brush the cut ends of the hair penetrated and fixed themselves in the felt body. The hat was then put into a coarse hair cloth, dipped and rolled in the hot liquor until the fur was quite worked in, the cotton being left on the surface loose and ready for removal.

The blocking, dyeing and finishing processes in the case of beaver hats were similar to those employed for ordinary felts, except that greater care and dexterity were required on the part of the workmen, and further that the coarse hairs or kemps which might be in the fur were cut off by shaving the surface with a razor. The nap also had to be laid in one direction, smoothed and rendered glossy by repeated wettings, ironings and brushings. A hat so finished was very durable and much more light, cool and easy-fitting to the head than the silk hat which has now so largely superseded it.

The first efficient machinery for making felt hats was devised from the United States the machine-making processes were introduced into England about the year 1858; and now in all large establishments machinery such as that alluded to below is employed. For the forming of hat bodies two kinds of machine are used, according as the material employed is fur or wool. In the case of fur, the essential portion of the apparatus is a "former," consisting of a metal cone of the size and form of the body or bat to be made, perforated all over with small holes. The cone is made to revolve on its axis slowly over an orifice under which there is a powerful fan, which maintains a strong inward draught of air through the holes in the cone. At the side of the cone, and with an opening towards it, is a trunk or box from which the fur to be made into a hat is thrown out by the rapid revolution of a brushlike cylinder, and as the cloud of separate hairs is expelled from the trunk, the current of air being sucked through the cone carries the fibres to it and causes them to cling closely to its surface. Thus a coating of loose fibres is accumulated on the copper cone, and these are kept in position only by the exhaust at work under it.

When sufficient for a hat body has been deposited, it is damped and a cloth is wrapped round it; then an outer cone is slipped over it and the whole is removed for felting, while another copper cone is placed in position for continuing the work. The fur is next felted by being rolled and pressed, these operations being performed partly by hand and partly by machine.

In the case of wool hats the hat or body is prepared by first carding in a modified form of carding machine. The wool is divided into two separate slivers as delivered from the cards, and these are wound simultaneously on a double conical block of wood mounted and geared to revolve slowly with a reciprocating horizontal motion, so that there is a continual crossing and recrossing of the wool as the sliver is wound around the cone.

This diagonal arrangement of the sliver is an essential feature in the apparatus, as thereby the strength of the finished felt is made equal in every direction; and when strained in the blocking the texture yields in a uniform manner without rupture. The wool wound on the double block forms the material of two hats, which are separated by cutting around the median or base line, and slipping each half off at its own end. Into each cone of wool or bat an "inlayer" is now placed to prevent the inside from matting, after which they are folded in cloths, and placed over a perforated iron plate through which steam is blown.

When well moistened and heated, they are placed between boards, and subjected to a rubbing action sufficient to harden them for bearing the subsequent strong planking or felting operations. The planking of wool hats is generally done by machine, in some cases a form of fulling mill being used; but in all forms the agencies are heat, moisture, pressure, rubbing and turning.

When by thorough felting the hat bodies of any kind have been reduced to dense leathery cones about one-half the size of the original bat, they are dried, and, if hard felts are to be made, the bodies are at this stage hardened or stiffened with a varnish of shellac. Next follows the operations of blocking, in which the felt for the first time assumes approximately the form it is ultimately to possess.

For this purpose the conical body is softened in boiling water, and forcibly drawn over and over a hat-shaped wooden block. The operation of dyeing next follows, and the finishing processes include shaping on a block, over which crown and brim receive ultimately their accurate form, and pouncing or pumicing, which consists of smoothing the surface with fine emery paper, the hat being for this purpose mounted on a rapidly revolving block. The trimmer finally binds the outer brim and inserts the lining, after which the brim may be given more or less of a curl or turn over according to prevailing fashion.

❐

Index

A

Absorption 7, 87, 88, 109, 111, 131
Acrylic 82, 83, 84, 96, 99, 109, 126
Adding of Feeds 78
Amino Acids 125
Amorphous 102, 113, 117

B

Bale Storage 65, 66
Basket Weave 24,
Biconstituent 146, 185, 188, 189
Blending 66, 139

C

Carding 75, 149, 181, 184, 198
Coagulation 69, 70, 71, 116, 140
Condensation 114, 126, 141
Consumption 78, 79, 80, 82, 132, 133
Cross Dyeing 98, 136

D

Degradation 59, 69, 71, 100, 121, 126
Digital Printing 24, 25, 26
Digital Textile Printing 52, 53
Dyeing 42, 55, 56, 57, 65, 66, 71
Dyeing Machines 102, 172, 211
Dyeing Techniques 47, 82, 185

E

Elastomeric 83, 109, 126
Elongation 113, 116, 138
Environment 5, 8, 16, 19, 20, 22, 26, 29, 30
Extremely 82, 83, 88, 89, 119, 124, 133, 180, 182, 194

F

Fabric Computing 105, 106
Fashion Design 32, 33, 175
Flammability 78, 82
Flexibility 77, 78, 79
Formaldehyde 84, 85

G

Garment industry 1, 3, 11, 12, 13, 36

H

Hydrocarbon 84, 97, 165
Hypothesis 143, 162

I

Implementation 78
Industrial Revolution 36
Industry Segments 52, 53, 54, 56, 57
Information Technology 36, 61

J

Jacquard Loom Weaveing 208
Jute Diversification 12, 13

O

Orientation 183, 185, 186, 188, 189
Oriented Nature 45, 46

P

Plain Weave Fabrics 163, 164
Polyester Fibres 94, 175
Polymerization 138, 139, 140, 141, 152
Production Control 74, 122

R

Raw Stock-dyeing 135
Rayon 5, 6, 106, 136, 140, 165, 192, 194,
Reactive Dyes 81, 82, 84, 86, 91, 94

L

Linen 108, 123, 125, 130, 132, 135, 136, 171
Location Analysis 143, 144, 145

M

Machine Printing 61, 137,
Morphology 101, 112, 113, 117
Multimedia Design 11

N

Natural Fibres 5, 9, 106, 108, 110
Novelty Nature 133
Nylon Salt 138

O

Online Quality Control 209, 211

S

Synthetic Polymers 114, 128
Synthetic Textiles 13, 53
Synthetic-Fiber Production 145

T

Technical Advisory Committee 80
Textile Design 6, 11, 17, 18, 19, 160
Textile Materials 6, 175, 191, 211
Textile Printing 27, 52, 57, 58, 65, 66, 171

U

Ultraviolet 63, 87, 88, 91, 122, 128
Untwisting 119

V

Variation of Plain Weave 130
Vertical Integration 11, 15, 19
Viscose Rayon 6, 127, 136, 140, 165, 192

W

Waste water Treatment 66, 68, 70, 72
Weaving Machines 171
Weberian Framework 142

❒❒❒